CHINESE UNDER GLOBALIZATION

Emerging Trends in
Language Use in China

CHINESE UNDER GLOBALIZATION
Emerging Trends in Language Use in China

Edited by

Jin Liu
Georgia Institute of Technology, USA

Hongyin Tao
University of California, Los Angeles, USA

NEW JERSEY · LONDON · SINGAPORE · BEIJING · SHANGHAI · HONG KONG · TAIPEI · CHENNAI

Published by

World Scientific Publishing Co. Pte. Ltd.
5 Toh Tuck Link, Singapore 596224
USA office: 27 Warren Street, Suite 401-402, Hackensack, NJ 07601
UK office: 57 Shelton Street, Covent Garden, London WC2H 9HE

British Library Cataloguing-in-Publication Data
A catalogue record for this book is available from the British Library.

CHINESE UNDER GLOBALIZATION
Emerging Trends in Language Use in China

Copyright © 2012 by World Scientific Publishing Co. Pte. Ltd.

All rights reserved. This book, or parts thereof, may not be reproduced in any form or by any means, electronic or mechanical, including photocopying, recording or any information storage and retrieval system now known or to be invented, without written permission from the Publisher.

For photocopying of material in this volume, please pay a copying fee through the Copyright Clearance Center, Inc., 222 Rosewood Drive, Danvers, MA 01923, USA. In this case permission to photocopy is not required from the publisher.

ISBN-13 978-981-4350-69-3
ISBN-10 981-4350-69-9

In-house Editor: Dan Jun

Typeset by Stallion Press
Email: enquiries@stallionpress.com

Printed in Singapore.

CONTENTS

Introduction		1
Chapter 1	Synchronic Variation or Diachronic Change: A Sociolinguistic Study of Chinese Internet Language *Liwei Gao*	7
Chapter 2	The Metaphorical World of Chinese Online Entertainment News *Chong Han*	29
Chapter 3	The Use of Chinese Dialects on the Internet: Youth Language and Local Youth Identity in Urban China *Jin Liu*	59
Chapter 4	"My Turf, I Decide": Linguistic Circulation in the Emergence of a Chinese Youth Culture *Qing Zhang and Chen-Chun E*	79
Chapter 5	Chinese Via English: A Case Study of "Lettered-Words" As a Way of Integration into Global Communication *Ksenia Kozha*	105
Chapter 6	Learning English to Promote Chinese — A Study of Li Yang's Crazy English *Amber R Woodward*	127

Chapter 7	More than Errors and Embarrassment: New Approaches to Chinglish *Oliver Radtke*	145
Chapter 8	Writing Cantonese as Everyday Lifestyle in Guangzhou (Canton City) *Jing Yan*	171
Chapter 9	Negotiating Linguistic Identities Under Globalization: Language Use in Contemporary China *Jin Liu and Hongyin Tao*	203
About the Contributors (in order of appearance)		213
Index		217

INTRODUCTION*

In the history of the Chinese language, there have been numerous instances where rapid changes took place in the forms of expansion of vocabulary, development of new grammatical markers and syntactic structures, appearance of new phonological features, and emergence of new writing styles. Typically, these rapid and sometimes radical changes correlate with the heightened interaction between indigenous and non-Chinese cultural elements. Thus, during the late Han period (2nd century AD) through the Tang Dynasty (10th century AD), the introduction of Hindu Buddhism brought to China not only Buddhist doctrines and practices but also an expanded vocabulary (such as loanwords from Persian, Sogdian, Sanskrit, Mongolian, Manchu, and other Asian Languages) (see Gao and Liu, 1958, esp. Chap. 2) and novel syntactic features (as exemplified by the disposal construction, see Cao and Yu (2000)). The best known example, however, belongs to the period from the late 19th century to the early 20th century, leading to the May Fourth New Culture Movement. During this period, severance of ties with traditional Chinese culture (as represented by the Confucian tradition) along with major influxes of Western ideas and thoughts resulted in a near total reconfiguration of the landscape of the Chinese language. Not only were writing styles changed, literary forms invented, and syntaxes increasingly Europeanized but even some basic vocabulary forms and a large number of neologisms were

---

* The editors wish to acknowledge Jeoffrey Spinoza and Thomas Hazzard for providing proofreading assistance.

added (especially Sino–Japanese–European loanwords) (Gunn, 1991; Liu, 1995). In the Mao's era, partly following the former Soviet Union's model in symbolic and ideological control, the Chinese Communist Party (CCP), after it won power in 1949, launched a massive revolutionary program of linguistic engineering, formalization, and orthodoxization, which culminated in the Cultural Revolution (Schoenhals, 1992; Wagner, 1999; Ji, 2004; and Wang, 2011). This seems an especially apt piece of evidence for Bourdieu's prediction: political crises are conducive to verbal explosion (Bourdieu, 1977, p. 663).

Fast-forwarding to the 21st century, we are now at the start of yet another period of historical significance. As China experiences an unprecedented level of economic and social transformation since its reform and opening policy in the early 1980s, and as the world becomes increasingly globalized and interconnected through the use of technology, freer flows of trade and information, and the spread of cultural artifacts, language use in China has also undergone dazzling changes in the past two decades: a global level clash between the ubiquitous global English and the Chinese native language. Within China proper, the struggles between the national language and local regional dialects and ethnic minority languages at multiple levels play out partly as a matter of nationalization versus the preservation of local heritages. There is also the emergence of the Internet language, which has become a creative source for the Chinese youth to construct their distinct youth identity. Moreover, the Internet language transcends locality and redefines key theoretical notions in sociocultural linguistics such as the speech community (Gumperz, 1968) and Linguistic Landscape (Landry and Bourhis, 1997).

We are certainly not the first to notice such dramatic linguistic changes in China, as evidenced by book-length studies on why the Chinese language is "in crisis" (e.g., Pan, 2008), by widespread media coverage on the need to preserve local dialects and the associated regional cultural heritages in places like Shanghai, Hangzhou, and Guangzhou, by officially and unofficially sanctioned annual selection of Internet/media buzzwords of the year over the past few years, as well as by government legislation to regulate the use of speech and orthographic forms.

However, we believe that much needs to be done in terms of documenting the emerging trends in China at this important juncture. To begin with, changes in language use are taking place literally on a daily basis, and there is need for a consistent effort in tracking these changes over time. Second, although individual studies are beginning to appear, very few systematic studies are available. Last but not least, we need theoretically informed analysis and not just formal descriptions. How does globalization impact the Chinese language exactly? What do emerging uses say about Chinese cultures, societies, and identity construction? What do these emerging uses suggest about style, genres, and the future of the Chinese language? This volume can be viewed as one of the initial efforts to address these questions.

The chapters in this volume examine the recent trends in language use in Mainland China and the associated social, economic, political, and cultural manifestations. Drawing on their backgrounds in sociolinguistics, linguistic anthropology, and cultural studies, the authors offer interdisciplinary and critical analysis of linguistic struggles and linguistic politics in China.

Liwei Gao, building on his long-term work in this area, describes one of the most prolific areas of language change: computer-mediated communication (CMC) in Chinese. He provides comprehensive analyses from lexical, syntactic, and discourse perspectives. Applying the construct of apparent time change in sociolinguistics, he predicts that some of the online usages may further evolve into the core of the Chinese language and signify diachronic linguistic change in progress. His work shows how profound a role CMC has played in sociolinguistic lives in China.

Chong Han examines metaphors used in entertainment news. After identifying both the common source domains of metaphors (war, martial arts, fire, wind, food, etc.) and target domains (conflict, celebrity, etc.), she moves on to discuss the functions of metaphors in media language, highlighting the fact that metaphors serve multiple purposes: they can not only embody abstract concepts but also serve as an ideological tool for describing and evaluating people and situations in discourse and influence the viewers' perception of the world. Metaphors in use can thus serve as a window into the changing media ecology in contemporary China.

Jin Liu's work is on the increasing use of local dialects on the Internet among the Chinese urban educated youth. While nationalization often comes as a concomitant phenomenon of globalization, and while local features, including local dialect use, tend to be viewed as substratum and low on the prestige continuum, the increasingly popular association of urban youth culture with local dialects caught many people off guard. Liu's close analysis of dialect texts, dialect proficiency tests, dialect rap songs, and websites shows how these linguistic manifestations can be seen as challenging the dominant national standard Mandarin and global English languages, in a quest to forge a distinct local identity.

Perhaps an even clearer case of identity formation and shift can be found in Qing Zhang and Chen-chun E's analysis of the slogan "My turf, I decide," originally a commercial slogan for mobile phone services, and its spread to a wide spectrum of social life. They demonstrate that this slogan and the associated, productive syntactic structure, "My NP, I decide," have become a salient semiotic resource for stance taking among Chinese youth. An emerging identity revealed here is a craving for individuality and independence from authorities.

Three chapters in this volume deal with the role of English in contemporary China, a testimony to the deep impact of the one and only current global language. In "Chinese via English," Ksenia Kozha describes the graphic and orthographic borrowing in Chinese *Zimuci* (lettered-words), mainly from English sources. Amber Woodward focuses on a particular brand of English teaching and on a social phenomenon known as Crazy English as initiated and made famous by Li Yang. Oliver Radtke discusses the use of English of an equally bizarre variety: Chinglish, where unintended non-standard use of English is found. All three chapters provide fascinating specimens of English use that are deeply rooted in commercialism, nationalism, as well as a host of sociological and psychological factors during China's quest for modernization and its engagement in globalization.

The final two chapters deal with, once again, identity issues from different perspectives. Jing Yan finds a case study in written Cantonese in southern China. She investigates the Cantonese–Mandarin bilingual speakers in Guangzhou who are biliterates in Standard Written Chinese (SWC) and Vernacular Written Cantonese (VWC), showing that the latter is positively viewed as an indicator of Guangzhou regional identity and how mass media and Hong Kong culture play powerful roles in promoting the use of VWC in Guangzhou area. Jin Liu and Hongyin Tao, on the other hand, provide a panoramic overview of the issues confronting China today in terms of globalization, identity, multiculturalism, and multilingualism. That paper plants the seeds for the initiation of the current project.

As one of the first concerted efforts to present a scholarly view of the emerging trends in language use in China, we hope that this volume can serve as a stepping stone for more comprehensive and large-scale studies in the near future.

References

Bourdieu, P (1977). The economics of linguistic exchanges. *Social Science Information*, 26, 645–668.

Cao, GS and HJ Yu (2000). The influence of translated later Han Buddhist Sutras on the development of the Chinese disposal construction. *Cahiers de Linguistique Asie Orientale*, 29(2), 151–177.

Gao, MK 高名凯 and ZT Liu 刘正埮 (1958). *Xiandai Hanyu Wailaici Yanjiu* 现代汉语外来词研究 (*Studies of Loanwords in Modern Chinese*). Beijing: Wenzi gaige chubanshe.

Gumperz, J (1968). The speech community. *International Encyclopedia of the Social Sciences*. New York: Macmillan.

Gunn, E (1991). *Rewriting Chinese: Style and Innovation in Twentieth-Century Chinese Prose*. Stanford: Stanford University Press.

Ji, FY (2004). *Linguistic Engineering: Language and Politics in Mao's China*. Honolulu: University of Hawai'i Press.

Landry, R and R Bourhis (1997). Linguistic landscape and ethnolinguistic vitality: An empirical study. *Journal of Language and Social Psychology*, 16, 23–49.

Liu, LH (1995). *Translingual Practice: Literature, National Culture, and Translated Modernity — China, 1900–1937*. Stanford: Stanford University Press.

Pan, WG 潘文国 (2008). *Weijixia de Zhongwen* 危机下的中文 (*Chinese under Crisis*). Shenyang: Liaoning Renmin Chubanshe.

Schoenhals, M (1992). *Doing Things with Words in Chinese Politics*. Berkeley: Center for Chinese Studies Research Monographs 41.

Wagner, R 瓦格纳. 鲁多夫 (1999). Zhonggong 1940–1953 nian jianli zhengyu zhengwen de zhengce dalüe, 中共1940–1953年建立正语、正文的政策大略 (An overview of the CCP policies in eastablishing an orthodoxical language and discourse in 1940–1953). In *Wenyi lilun Yu Tongsu Wenhua* 文藝理論與通俗文化 (*Literary Theory and Popular Culture*), XY Peng 彭小妍 (ed.), pp. 11–38. Taipei: Zhongyang yanjiuyuan Zhongguo wen zhe yanjiusuo zhoubeichu.

Wang, B (ed.) (2011). *Words and Their Stories: Essays on the Language of the Chinese Revolution*. Leiden; Boston: Brill.

CHAPTER 1

SYNCHRONIC VARIATION OR DIACHRONIC CHANGE: A SOCIOLINGUISTIC STUDY OF CHINESE INTERNET LANGUAGE

LIWEI GAO

Defense Language Institute, Monterey, USA

With its ever increasing popularization, computer-mediated communication (CMC) has become a progressively well-documented research area (e.g., Baron, 1984, 1998a, 1998b, 2000; Crystal, 2006; Danet and Herring, 2007; Herring, 1996). The linguistic aspects of CMC in the Chinese context have also been examined (e.g., Gao, 2006, 2007; Liu, 2010, 2011; Yu, *et al.*, 2001a, 2001b). In this chapter, an analysis of emergent language usages in CMC in Chinese, which covers the lexical, syntactic, as well as the discourse dimension is presented. Applying the construct of apparent time change (Labov, 1963, 1966), it is argued that some of the online usages may stay as part of the Chinese language. In other words, the use of Internet expressions in the Chinese CMC may signify diachronic linguistic change in progress.

1. Introduction

Since the Internet became available, particularly since the worldwide Internet service was officially launched in the United States, computer-mediated communication (CMC) has become increasingly widespread throughout the world, thanks partly to the rapid development of the computer technology, especially the networking know-how (Yu *et al.*, 2001a). In Mainland China, the Internet service has been developing very rapidly since 1994. According to the first state-sponsored study dated October 1997 by China Internet Network Information Center (CNNIC), there were around 620,000 Chinese netizens.[1] And approximately 30,000 computers were connected to the Internet. According to the latest CNNIC report in January 2011, there were approximately 457 million netizens in Mainland China, which had 278 IPv4 addresses. And there were about 1,910,000 websites in China. It is apparent from these statistics that there has been a tremendous growth of the Internet network in China over recent years.

In addition, the Internet has penetrated the various spheres of the daily lives of Chinese people. When online, Chinese netizens often do such things as listening to and downloading music, chatting, watching and downloading movies, reading news, searching for information, playing online games, and emailing. And entertainment is the most important purpose for most online activities. The Internet has been so pervasive in China that the sentence *Shangwang le meiyou?* 上网了没有? "Have you been online [recently]?" has currently become one of the most commonly uttered greetings when Chinese people, especially city dwellers, meet on the streets (Lü, 2002).

The rapid development of Internet communication in Mainland China has created a huge impact on the Chinese language. Researchers have documented that CMC has helped give rise to a new variety of Chinese language, which generally terms as Chinese Internet language (CIL) (Yu *et al.*, 2001a). According to Yates (1996), a new medium of communication such as the Internet not only draws upon existing linguistic practices but also generates new forms of practice. This partly explains why there has emerged CIL in China's Internet communication. CIL is represented not only by different lexical usages but also by unique syntactic and even discursive features (Gao, 2006; Yu *et al.*, 2001b; Zhang, 2007). As for the demographics of the netizens in Mainland China, approximately 60% were aged below 30 years, mostly studying either in junior high schools (32.8%), senior high schools (35.7%), or colleges (23.2%) (CNNIC January 2011 report). In other words, Chinese netizens can be roughly categorized as young people.

---

[1] In mainland China, a "netizen" was defined as a person aged six or older who surfed the web for at least one hour per week (http://tech.sina.com.cn/i/2007-07-18/14161623503.shtml).

This chapter discusses the impact of the emergence and use of CIL in CMC on the Chinese language. Applying the construct of apparent time change (Labov, 1963, 1966) and based on a variety of other considerations, it argues that some of the CIL usages employed by young Chinese netizens in CMC may start to be used by people belonging to other age groups and also outside of the electronic media. In other words, the appearance and use of the CIL may represent a case of diachronic linguistic change in progress. In so doing, this chapter demonstrates that electronic communication indeed provides rich data for linguistic analysis, which therefore warrants serious attention from linguists.

The chapter first provides the theoretical framework that guides the argument for the possible change of the Chinese language prompted by the use of CIL online. It then presents objective linguistic data, viz., online words, sentences, and paragraphs. In the following sections, the chapter discusses what type of CIL usages are likely to be incorporated into the Chinese language. The chapter concludes with a highlight of the need for a real time study to corroborate its argument.

2. The Theoretical Framework

This study is primarily guided by the apparent time construct (Labov, 1963, 1966). It also takes into consideration other theoretical as well as practical assumptions.

2.1. *The apparent time construct*

In the study of language variation and change, Labov (1963, 1966) distinguished between apparent time and real time changes. The underlying idea of the apparent time change is that age stratification of linguistic variables can reflect not only the change in the individual as he or she moves through life (age grading) but also the historical change in the speech community with passage of time. In other words, some of the variables used by one age group, usually young people, may spread through the entire population and consequently slowly change the language. Using the apparent time construct, Labov (1963, 1966) demonstrated in his study of the social stratification of English in New York City that it is quite possible to analyze language change in progress by comparing the speech of older and younger speakers from the same community. Within this theoretical framework, this study considers the CIL as variables of standard Mandarin Chinese, which are used primarily by young and educated Chinese, as is aforementioned.

Meanwhile, it is worth noting that the disambiguation of age-stratified data (change in apparent time) in linguistic change versus age-grading is a complicated matter. To get an apparent time reflection of language change in progress, the individual's linguistic behavior would have to remain stable throughout his or her life, or at least changes during his or her life course would have to be systematic and regular. In other words, caution should be taken that without real time evidence. It is virtually impossible to determine whether age-stratified patterns of change reflect language change in progress or are simply a matter of age-grading.

2.2. *Other considerations*

In the following section, other theoretical as well as practical assumptions, which also help to support the argument that the emergence and use of CIL in Chinese CMC indicates language change in progress are discussed.

2.2.1. *The prestige of CIL*

Given that CIL is used mostly by educated young Chinese and that it is associated with many desirable personal identities such as being modern and being able to keep abreast with social and technological developments, it is generally considered as prestigious linguistic variety, especially among young people (Gao, 2007). The emergence of such a distinctive language variety has significant sociolinguistic implications for the change in Chinese.

As Chambers (1995, p. 185) puts it, "variability in language often indicates instability" and hence linguistic change. Moreover, according to variationist sociolinguists (e.g., Labov, 1972, 2000), the language variety with high social prestige, be it overt or covert prestige, is likely to show its impact upon people's language use and to be emulated by people who seek prestige. If this is true, CIL may exert its influence upon the linguistic behavior of those who do not have access to CMC and/or those who do not belong to the young and educated group but wish to.

2.2.2. *The likelihood of cross-modality influence*

As is noted in Baron (1984), cross-modality linguistic influence is quite possible. Take English as an example, many instances of usage clearly show that speech and writing, two different modalities of communication, have been influencing each other. In terms of speech affecting writing, there is, for example, written use of contractions like "haven't." Concerning writing influencing speech, there is, for example, professorial talk like: "But it is now widely recognized that we must make a distinction between the formal objects licensed by a grammar and feature descriptions used to impose constraints on these structures." Likewise, CIL, the language employed in online communication, may also gradually spread to the domain of non-electronic communication, both spoken and written, and consequently lead to the change of the Chinese language.

2.2.3. *The role of youths in linguistic change*

As Wardhaugh observes, "the young are usually in the vanguard of most [language] changes" (1998, p. 202). This observation, which is underpinned by his experience, constitutes another piece of support for the potential impact of CIL on the Chinese language and hence its change. As is mentioned earlier, users of CIL are predominately young people in their late teens or early twenties up until this stage (http://tech.sina.com.cn/focus/cnnic_12/index.shtml). One more piece of supporting evidence is that the electronic language used by young Chinese netizens is usually more dynamic, vivid, and rich in creativity than non-electronic language. Generally speaking, such a vibrant variety of language is contagious; people are not very resistant to the use of such an innovative variety of language.

3. The Data

The data for this study consist of Chinese Internet lexical items, sentential expressions characteristic of Chinese Internet discourse, and paragraphs from the Internet, which feature the use of CIL terms, sentences typical of Chinese Internet discourse, and/or discursive practices typical of China's Internet communication.

The data were collected primarily from five Internet situations — online bulletin board systems (BBSs), chat rooms, Internet literature, personal emails, and other posts at public websites, such as news and advertisements. BBSs and Internet relay chat rooms were the major sources among all. To ensure that the data collected and examined are representatives of CIL, the author has gathered them from posts on a variety of topics, including recreation, sports, school life, education, career, politics, marriage life, and economics. In addition, from October 2002 through December 2009, samples of CIL from the five Internet situations on a weekly basis were collected.

3.1. *The lexical usages*

Based on the source code, the Chinese Internet lexicon may be divided into three main categories. They are (1) words solely composed of Chinese characters, (2) words that only consist of pinyin alphabets, English letters, Arabic numbers, or paralinguistic symbols, and (3) words of mixed sources. Each type may then be further subcategorized. For words that only contain Chinese characters, they can be further divided into those coined in the following different ways[2]:

(1) *Jiajie* 假借 ("borrowing"), e.g., *mao* 猫 cat "modem," *guanshui* 灌水 irrigate-water "posting low-quality articles on BBS's," *lei* 雷 thunder "accidentally seeing something unpleasant, feeling intensive discomfort," *shanzhai* 山寨 mountain village "counterfeit"

(2) *Hecheng* 合成 ("compounding"), e.g., *dianduidian* 点对点 point-face-point "computer to computer," *xiezai* 卸载 unload-carry "download," *geili* 给力 give-power "cool, awesome, exciting"[3]

---

[2] As has been documented by researchers (e.g., Liu, 2010, 2011; Zhang, 2007; Zhu, 2008), Chinese netizens frequently use local varieties of Chinese in online communication. Since neither the written form nor the meaning of these expressions has changed in CMC, the use of dialects is not treated as a way in which online words are coined. Moreover, some of these classifications below may not be mutually exclusive.

[3] The Internet word *geili* 给力 give-power "cool, awesome, exciting," which started to grab broader public attention after it appeared in an episode of a Chinese-dubbed Japanese comic animation 《西游记：旅程的终点》 (*Xiyouji: Lücheng de zhongdian, Journey to the West: End of a Journey*) and gained real popularity online during the 2010 World Cup,

(3) *Fangni* 仿拟 ("analogy"), e.g., *diaoxia* 钓虾 angle-shrimp "females chasing males" (cf. *diaoyu* 钓鱼 angle-fish "males chasing females"), *hantuo* 汉托 Chinese-TOEFL "Chinese TOEFL–HSK" (cf. *tuofu* 托福 hold-happiness "TOEFL")
(4) *Yijie* 译借 ("calquing"), e.g., *qiate* 恰特 exactly-special "chat," *ku* 酷 cruel "cool," *bensan* 笨三 stupid-three "Pentium III," *fensi* 粉丝 flour-string "fans"
(5) *Bini* 比拟 ("metaphor and personification"), e.g., *daxia* 大虾 big-shrimp "Internet expert," *konglong* 恐龙 scary-dragon "unattractive but extremely active female"
(6) *Yinbian* 音变 ("phonological fusion"), e.g., *jiangzi* 酱紫 sauce-purple "this way" (from *zheyangzi* 这样子 this-form-Suffix "like this"), *biao* 表 watch "don't" (from *buyao* 不要 no-want "don't"), *niangzi* 酿紫 brew-purple "that way" (from *nayangzi* 那样子 that-form-Particle "like that")
(7) *Shuoming* 说明 ("explanation"), e.g., *wangchong* 网虫 net-insect "people very fond of visiting the Internet," *wangba* 网吧 net-bar "computer site open to the public," *zhainü* 宅女 residence-woman "Otaku girl," 房奴 house-slave "mortgage slave"
(8) *Cisuchongdie* 词素重迭 ("morpheme repetition"), e.g., *piaopiao* 漂漂 beautiful-beautiful "beautiful," *huaihuai* 坏坏 bad-bad "bad"
(9) *Yinjingaizao* 音近改造 ("near homophonization"), e.g., *banzhu* 斑竹 speckle-bamboo "person in charge of a BBS topic," *junnan* 菌男 germ-male "unattractive guy"
(10) *Jiucixinjie* 旧词新解 ("semantic shift"), e.g., *ouxiang* 偶像 idol-picture "a disgusting person," *tiancai* 天才 sky-material "a born dumb person," *danbaizhi* 蛋白质 egg-white-quality "an idiot and neurotic," *ding* 顶 hold something on one's head "support," *fubai* 腐败 decay-failure "eating out or participating in recreational activities," *beiju* 杯具 glass-tools "tragedy," *canju* 餐具 tableware "tragedy"
(11) *Xizi* 析字 ("word decomposition"), *lanjie* 蓝介 blue-introduce "awkward" (from *ganga* 尴尬 "awkward"), *zouzhao* 走召 walk-summon "super" (from *chao* 超 "super")

---

is currently the No. 1 buzzword. It was used quite a few times during the 2011 CCTV Spring Festival Eve Gala by both performers and hosts. It has even been translated into other languages such as English and French (http://www.china.org.cn/china/2010-11/12/content_21327924.htm).

(12) Examples of words that only consist of pinyin alphabets, English letters, Arabic numbers, or paralinguistic symbols are given in (12). In (12), *JS* consists of pinyin alphabets, E, ICQ, cookies, banner, and …ing are in English, 668 and 886 are in Arabic numbers, and the components of :-) and ^0^ are only paralinguistic symbols.

JS ("shrewd businessmen," from *jianshang* in pinyin), E ("electronic"), ICQ ("I seek you."), cookies ("small file saved on a computer hard disk"), banner ("advertisement that props up across the width of a computer screen"), …ing (indicating present continous tense), 668 ("Let's chat."), 886 ("Bye-bye."), :-) ("smile"), ^0^ ("laugh out loud")

Examples of words of mixed sources are given in (13). In (13), ^B and ^K both consist of a paralinguistic symbol and an English letter, b2b, b2c, f2f, and MP3 are each composed of English letters and an Arabic number, and BIG5码 is a mixture of English letters, an Arabic number, and a Chinese character.

(13) ^B ("to say good bye with tears"), ^K ("to kiss stealthily"), b2b ("business to business"), b2c ("business to customer"), f2f ("face-to-face"), and BIG5码 ("the big 5 code")

3.2. *The sentential features*

One of the most conspicuous features of web sentences is that they are usually relatively short and are used to express meanings in a concise and straightforward manner. It is particularly so in regard to language used in chat rooms and on BBSs. An excerpt from an online chat in (14) below exemplifies this characteristic. Among the 10 sentences in this sample, there is only one complex sentence, 如果有机会我一定送花给你 ("If I have a chance, I'll surely send you flowers."). In addition, eight out of these ten sentences consist of six or fewer words.

(14) 欢迎进入中华网聊天室!:) ("Welcome to the chatroom at www.China.com.")
    A: I think so.
    B: 上网明天能休息。("If I go online, I can take a rest tomorrow.")

C: 叹了口气，不知道哪里不对了。("Sigh. [I] don't know what's wrong.")
D: 混古起？("Excuse me?")
E: 你哪的？("Where are you from?")
F: 在？("Preposition, indicating time, place, etc.")
G: 如果有机会我一定送花给你。("If I have a chance, I'll surely send you flowers.")
H: 你在吗？("Are you there?")
I: oh.
G: 最好有伊妹儿。("[You'd] better have an email.")

Web sentences also involve novel usages, which are usually represented by (1) a change in sentence word order, (2) the use of sentence-final redundant words, (3) a change in word category, (4) the use of an unusual sense of a word, and (5) the use of bound morphemes as free morphemes. Some examples are given in (15)–(23) below. The sentences in (15) and (16) involve a change in sentence word order. The sentences in (17) and (18) feature the use of semantically superfluous expressions. The sentences in (19) and (20) represent a change in word category. The sentence in (21) exemplifies the use of a very uncommon sense of a word. And the sentences in (22) and (23) are characterized with the use of usually bound morphemes as free morphemes.

In (15), the adverbial prepositional phrase *zaitushuguan* 在图书馆 Preposition-picture–book–place "in the library" was moved from before the verb phrase *kanshu* 看书 look-book "to read books" to after it. In (16), the adverbial time phrase *mingnian* 明年 following-year "the following year" was moved from before the verb phrase *qumeiguo* 去美国 go-U.S. "to go to the U.S." to after it.

(15) 我　看书　　在　　图书馆。
　　　I,　look–book, Preposition, library
　　　"I was reading books in the library."
(16) 我　去　美国　明　年。
　　　I,　go,　U.S., next, year
　　　"I am going to the U.S. the next year."

In (17), the expression *deshuo* 的说[4] Auxiliary-talk "say" is semantically redundant. Similarly, in (18) *diao* 掉 fall "result" is redundant, although it is true that *sidiaole* 死掉了 die-fall-Aspect "die" by itself is a perfectly grammatical usage in Mandarin Chinese.

(17) 去 哪儿?
   go, where
   "Where are you going?"
   回 家 的 说。
   return, home, Auxiliary, talk
   "Going home."

(18) 我 要 高兴 死 掉 了。
   I, will, happy, die, fall, Particle
   "I am extremely happy."

In (19), the noun *dian* 电 electricity "call" was used as a verb, meaning "to call." And in (20), the proper noun CNN was used as an adjective, meaning "behaving like CNN."

(19) 有 事 电 我。
   have, thing, call, I
   "Call me if you need anything."

(20) 做 人 不 能 太 CNN。
   do, people, not, Auxiliary, too, CNN
   "A person cannot be too much like CNN."

In (21), an atypical usage of the expression *feichang* 非常 not-ordinary "very; unusual" in the sense of "unusual" was used. In other words, 非常 is usually used as an adverb in Chinese, but here it is used as an adjective.

(21) 她 是 非常 宝贝。
   she, be, unusual, treasure
   "She is an extremely lovely girl."

---

[4] The usage *deshuo* 的说 Auxiliary-talk "say" is a translation of the Japanese sentence-final expression: Object marker + say.

Finally, in sentence (22), the bound morpheme *ju* 巨 big "extremely" was used as a free morpheme. Analogously, in (23) the bound morpheme *chao* 超 exceed "super" was used as a free morpheme as well.

(22) 小　王　巨　怕　辣。
　　 Little, Wang, gigantic, afraid, spicy
　　 "Little Wang is extremely afraid of spicy food."

(23) 这　场　球　赛　超　没　意思。
　　 This, Classifier, ball, game, super, not, meaning
　　 "This ball game was extremely boring."

3.3. *The discursive level*

In many cases, China's Internet discourse is marked by (1) Chinese–English codes-witching, (2) a written spoken style, and (3) a joking style, which is represented by the use of, among other things, overly concise and straightforward language.

3.3.1. *A bilingual code*[5]

Guo (1999) points out that bilingualism or multilingualism is an inevitable occurrence in the modern society, where people speaking different languages frequently interact with each other. It is particularly so with CMC, which is in itself a product of modern technology that expedites the process of globalization. According to Danet and Herring (2007) and Melchers and Shaw (2003), Internet communication is recurrently characterized by the mixing of two or more languages.

The excerpt in (24) below is from the web novel, *Zuiaishini* 《最爱是你》 "My most beloved is you" by *Meiguitianshi* 玫瑰天使 "Rose Angel" (http://

---

[5] Mixing not only occurs on the discourse but also, much more frequently, on the sentential level. For example, the sentence 你 out 了! ("You're left behind the times!"), one of the top 10 Internet expressions used most frequently in China in 2009, features Chinese–English code-switching.

gzg.16167.com/wenxue/sanwen/03.htm). In this excerpt, English items include the expression "bbs" and the greeting "hi."

(24) 布谷很少主动给别人打招呼，没人理的时候，她就到bbs上看帖子。那天晚上，布谷心情实在有些压抑，所以见谁给谁打招呼，深夜了，聊天室也没几个人，布谷就遇见了阿民。

布谷：hi!
阿民：你好！
布谷：还没睡？
阿民：你也是啊。

("*Bugu* seldom communicates with others actively. When people ignore her, she will read posts on BBS. That night *Bugu* felt depressed indeed, so she said hello to whomever she met. It was late in the night and only a few people were still chatting. At this time, *Bugu* met *Amin*.

Bugu: Hi.
Amin: Hi.
Bugu: Still awake?
Amin: You too.")

The excerpt in (25) below is quoted from the web novel, *Huodexianggerenyang* 《活得像个人样》 "To live like a human being" by *Niepan* 涅磐 "Nirvana" (www.21gbook.com/yx.htm), in which the English word "kiss" was employed.

(25) 很长的一封信，看得我累的不行，大概意思就是她芳心甚悦，情意绵绵，仍想见我一面。最后居然写了个kiss。我觉得很滑稽。琢磨一下她肯定是鼓起全身勇气写了个这么脸红心跳的字句。

("A very long letter. I was exhausted reading it. Her main idea is that she was happy and had affection for me too. Also, she would still like to see me one more time. She even ended her mail with the word "kiss." I felt very funny. I figured that she must have gathered up all her courage to have used this bold expression.")

3.3.2. *A written spoken style*

Much CIL discourse features a written spoken style (Crystal, 2006; Danet and Herring, 2007; Frehner, 2008). On the one hand, CIL maintains the characteristic of a written mode. On the other hand, it is marked by an oral style on most informal occasions.

The fact that CIL is partly marked by a written style has at least four reasons: (1) most people still have to use a keyboard to communicate online, (2) the Internet is a public arena, (3) most Chinese netizens are educated, and (4) *Putonghua* is the most commonly used language on China's Internet.

Generally speaking, communicating via the Internet is not as fast as people desire. Meanwhile, Internet service in China is still relatively expensive at present. Customers are usually charged based on the amount of time that they spend online. In order to offset these limitations, when engaged in electronic communication, people frequently utilize abbreviated words, subjectless sentences, and single-word sentences. Such practices provide CIL with features of a spoken style. Moreover, cyberspace is essentially a communication arena in which there is few, if any, formal censorship. As a result, when interacting via the Internet, people are likely to use a spoken style, which tends to be more vivid than a written style, to voice their opinions about hot sociocultural and political issues in China, among other things.

The following dialogues in (26) below, which were gathered from an Internet relay chat room, clearly demonstrate the spoken style of much CIL discourse. More significantly, these expressions are even more concise than the oral language found in daily interaction.

(26) A: 哪? ("Where are you from?")
    B: 深圳, u? ("Shenzhen. And you?")
    A: 扬州。认识你很高兴! ("Yangzhou. Good to know you!")
    B: me2! ^o^ ("Me too!")
    A: 家? ("Are you at home now?")
    B: 单位。("No. At my working unit.")
    A: M or F? ("Are you a male or a female?")
    B: M! 我有事, 走先! 886! ("Male. I need to take care of something. I'm leaving now. Bye-bye!")

The passage in (27) below, which is from the web novel *Yingxiongshidai* 《英雄时代》 "The age of heroes" by Mikko, is also characterized by an oral style. In this excerpt, the expressions *tamadi* 他妈的 he-mother-Auxiliary "goddamn" and *zhunaozi* 猪脑子 pig-brain-Suffix "stupid person," which are used to swear and to describe a foolish person, respectively, are primarily used in spoken discourse, but they were used in this passage. Moreover, the expressions *sa* 仨 three "three" and *dawanbanshangr* 大晚半晌儿 big-evening-half-period-Rhotacization "in the dead of the night" are almost used exclusively in spoken discourse, but they also appeared in this excerpt.

(27) "真他妈的都是猪脑子!" 我苦于说不出话, 气得一个眼珠乱 转。"我又不是有病! 大晚半晌儿的, 一个人找人家仨持刀的见义勇为? 我脑子又没进水! 没常识!!" 这时去现场的警察走了进来, 几个人低声地交谈了一会儿, 证实了现场情况和小小的陈述基本一致。(Mikko, 2000)

("'Stupid!' I was too upset to be able to talk but just moved one of my eyeballs frantically. 'Was I insane? I was alone fighting against three hooligans with knives in the dead of the night? I'm not that stupid! I don't lack common sense!' At this moment, several policemen walked over, who had been to the crime scene. They whispered for a while and confirmed among themselves that what they found out at the scene was basically consonant with *Xiaoxiao*'s statement.")

3.3.3. *A joking style*

A large proportion of China's Internet discourse features a joking style, which is usually achieved through using overly terse and straightforward language, unusual homophones, enigmatic folk similes, and other metaphorical devices. The following passage from the "Holy Writ of Love" in (28), which originated in the movie series *A Chinese Odyssey* (quoted from Klinkner (2003)) and is now an integral part of CIL, illustrates this joking style. In this case, the joking effect lies in the straightforwardness of language use. In the traditionally reserved Chinese culture, such a direct discursive style is striking and even hilarious.

(28) 曾经有一份真诚的爱情放在我面前
我没有珍惜

等我失去的时候我才后悔莫及
人间最痛苦的是莫过于此
如果上天能够给我一个再来一次的机会
我会对那个女孩子说三个字
我爱你
如果非要在这份爱上加上一个期限
我希望是一万年

("Once somebody sincerely loved me, but I didn't take that love preciously. I started to regret only when it was gone. This is the most miserable thing in life. If God gave me another chance, I'd say three words to that girl, 'I LOVE YOU!' If I must place a deadline to this love, I hope it is TEN THOUSAND YEARS.")

4. Possible Types of Linguistic Changes[6]

Language is constantly in the process of evolution. The change is either caused by language-internal factors (e.g., Anttila, 1989), which is exemplified by the first Germanic consonant shift known as Grimm's Law, a consequence of the language-internal pressure, or various language-external or social forces (e.g., Bright, 1997; Labov, 2000), exemplified by the simplification of the Chinese writing system in Mainland China (Cheng, 1979). According to Weinreich *et al.* (1968), language, especially the vocabularies of a language, is closely entwined with diverse sociocultural dimensions of the society. When the society changes, language as a sign that mirrors the reality of society will also undergo transformation. It is then no wonder that the arrival of the digital age in China, one of the representations of which is the beginning of CMC, and recent dramatic social, economic, and political changes that have taken place in China should lead to a change in the Chinese language.

4.1. *Lexicon*

Vocabulary is usually the most active component of a language, which constantly changes to accommodate the needs of the speakers. The question

---

[6] Gao (2006) specifically examines the impact of English on the Chinese language.

then arises: what types of CIL lexicon[7] are likely to stay as an integral component of the Chinese language? Generally speaking, in addition to the words that must be used to refer to new Internet technologies, those that conform to the convention of the Chinese language have the highest possibility of survival, which would include new coinages that follow the rules of Chinese word formation. This would probably cover at least two groups of CIL words: (1) some of those borrowed from foreign languages, such as *zaixian* 在线 at-line "online," and *ku* 酷 cruel "cool," and (2) some of those formed by phonological fusion, e.g., *biao* 表 (from 不要) watch "don't," for borrowing and phonological reduction are two active word formation processes for the Chinese language.

The fact is that some of the CIL usages have already been used by the general public and beyond the modality of CMC. Two examples (underlined) are given in (29) and (30) below, which are quoted from Jiao (2003). In (29), the CIL expression *tiezi* 帖子 paste-Suffix "online post" is used, and in (30) *dongdong* 东东 east–east "stuff" is used.

(29) 昨天　还　整理　了　网　友们　的　<u>帖子</u>。
(陆幼青:《生命的留言》)
Yesterday, still, sort, Aspect, web, friends, Auxiliary, Post
"Yesterday I too sorted out the posts by (my) Internet friends."

(30) 生活　中, 我　为　自己　的　很多　<u>东东</u>　而　无比　惊喜 (《大众电影》2002:18)
Life, in, I, for, self, Auxiliary, many, east–east, Conjunction extremely, happy
"In my life, I am extremely pleasantly surprised by so many things I have."

According to Li (2002), the following passage in (31) appeared in a composition by an elementary school student, which also featured the use of many CIL expressions (underlined). In this case, although the use of CIL vocabulary is still confined to adolescents, it has gone beyond the CMC modality.[8]

---

[7] Elsewhere, Ma (2002) also discusses the spread of the CIL vocabulary to the non-CMC context, particularly people's daily life.
[8] It is also recognized that the public controversy usually evoked by this kind of composition illustrates the struggles that the CIL has to undergo in its institutionalization and legitimization as an officially accepted language form.

(31) 昨天晚上，我的GG带着他的恐龙GF到我家来吃饭，饭桌上，*GG 的GF*一个劲的向我妈妈*PMP,* 那酱紫真是好*PT, 7456,* 我只吃了几口饭，就到*QQ*上打铁去了。
("Yesterday evening, my brother brought his unpleasant-looking girlfriend home for dinner. At the dinner table, this girl kept flattering my mother. Her behavior was so abnormal. I was really fed up with her. I only ate a few mouthfuls before I left to post messages via the caller machine.")

Furthermore, at least the three CIL expressions given in (32) below have been collected by the *Xiandai hanyu cidian* 《现代汉语词典》 "A modern Chinese dictionary" (Chao and Han *et al.*, 2005), one of the most authoritative dictionaries on the modern Chinese language, which marks the official completion of the lexical change prompted by CMC.

(32) *yimeier* 伊妹儿 her-sister-Rhotacization "email," *ku* 酷 cruel "cool," *heike* 黑客 black-guest "hacker"

4.2. *Grammar*

Compared with lexical items, grammatical categories of a language, including its sentence structures, are more stable and hence less easily subject to change even though such changes do occur. In the following section, the author discusses two possible types of grammatical changes regarding sentence word order and word category, respectively. It should be noted that the discussion here is rather speculative in nature. The discussion is also intended to be illustrative rather than exhaustive.

4.2.1. *Word order*

The issue of the Chinese sentence word order has been broadly discussed. According to Greenberg's Word-order Correlation (1963), the order of all types of modifies in relation to their heads follows the same order as that of the verb and its direct object. In other words, if the direct object follows the verb, then modifiers of the verb tend to follow the verb. If this is the case, then examples in (15) and (16), which are given below in (33) and (34) again for convenience, apparently help to support the argument that Chinese is moving more toward an SVO language, which is different from the suggestion in Li and Thompson (1981) that the Chinese language may be experiencing a transformation from an SVO to an SOV sentence word order.

(33) 我 看 书 在 图书馆。
    I, look, book, Preposition, library
    "I was reading books in the library."

(34) 我 去 美国 明 年。
    I, go, U.S., tomorrow, year
    "I am going to the U.S. the next year."

4.2.2. *Change in word category*

As a result of the influence from the use of CIL in CMC, the part of speech of some Chinese words may undergo changes. A potential candidate is the use of nouns as adjectives, as illustrated by the usage of *cai* 菜 vegetable "weak; incapable" in (35) below. For one thing, the use of nouns as adjectives has already been documented in the *Xiandai hanyu cidian* 《现代汉语词典》 "A modern Chinese dictionary" (Chao and Han *et al.*, 2005), as is shown in (36) below, where the noun *yangguang* 阳光 sun "healthy and optimistic" is used as an adjective.

(35) 这 个 人 太 菜。
    This, Classifier, person, too, vegetable
    "This person is too incapable."

(36) 她 是 一 个 阳光 女孩。
    She, be, one, Classifier, sun, girl
    "She's a very healthy and sanguine girl."

Another potential change is the use of adjectives as adverbs, as illustrated by the currently very popular use of the adjective 严重 *yanzhong* "serious" as an adverb. Example is given in (37) below.

(37) 我 严重 同意。
    I, serious, agree
    "I seriously agree."

4.3. *Discourse*

The discourse structure of a language is even more unlikely to change, which is tightly intertwined with the way of thinking of the people who speak that language. Nevertheless, as is documented in Baron (2000), the styles of English writing have continuously evolved along with the invention of new media of communication. If this is the case with English, then it is not completely out of the question that the Chinese language may also undergo discourse transformation as a result of the new electronic and the word-processing medium that produce new language.[9]

5. Concluding Remarks

In light of the apparent-time construct, this chapter argues that some current CIL used by young netizens in CMC may spread to other age groups and beyond the CMC modality and consequently lead to changes in the Chinese language. In this sense, some of the CIL usages may represent language change in progress, rather than merely synchronic variation, which is prompted primarily by the use of computers as a media of communication and young Internet users' creativity. This being said, as is noted earlier, not all age-related variation is indicative of change in progress. Instead, it may simply be an age-graded variation. That is to say, the applicability of the apparent-time hypothesis should be confirmed by real-time evidence, which may be gathered from a longitudinal study of a population over an extended period of time.

References

Anttila, R (1989). *Historical and Comparative Linguistics*. Philadelphia: John Benjamins.

Baron, N (1984). Computer mediated communication as a force in language change. *Visible Language*, 18(2), 118–141.

---

[9] The distinctive features of Chinese CMC discourse have been documented (e.g., Jin, 2000). If these features persist, they may influence the non-CMC discourse structures of Chinese, just as they do with the Chinese lexicon and syntax.

Baron, N (1998a). Letters by phone or speech by other means: The linguistics of email. *Language and Communication*, 18(2), 133–170.

Baron, N (1998b). Writing in the age of email: The impact of ideology versus technology. *Visible Language*, 32(1), 35–53.

Baron, N (2000). *Alphabet to Email: How Written English Evolved and Where It's Heading*. London: Routledge.

Bright, W (1997). Social factors in language change. In *The Handbook of Sociolinguistics*, F Coulmas (ed.), pp. 81–91. Cambridge, MA: Blackwell.

Chambers, J (1995). *Sociolinguistic Theory*. Oxford, UK: Blackwell Publishers.

Chao, JZ(晁继周), JT Han (韩敬体) *et al.* (2005). Xiandai Hanyu Cidian <<现代汉语词典>> (A Modern Chinese Dictionary) (5th edition). Beijing: Shangwu Yishu Guan.

Cheng, CC (1979). Language reform in China in the seventies. *Word*, 30(1/2), 45–57.

Crystal, D (2006). *Language and the Internet*. Cambridge, UK: Cambridge University Press.

Danet, B and S Herring (2007). *The Multilingual Internet: Language, Culture, and Communication Online*. Oxford, UK: Oxford University Press.

Frehner, C (2008). *Email — SMS — MMS: The Linguistic Creativity of Asynchronous Discourse in the New Media Age*. Frankfurt: Peter Lang.

Gao, LW (2006). Language contact and convergence in computer-mediated communication. *World Englishes*, 25(2), 299–308.

Gao, LW (2007). *Chinese Internet Language: A Study of Identity Constructions*. Munich: Lincom Europa.

Greenberg, J (1963). Some universals of grammar with particular reference to the order of meaningful elements. In *Universals of Language*, J Greenberg (ed.), pp. 73–113. Cambridge, MA: MIT Press.

Guo, X (郭熙) (1999). *Zhongguo Shehui Yuyanxue* 中国社会语言学 (*Chinese Sociolinguistics*). Nanjing: Nanjing University Press.

Herring, S (ed.) (1996). *Computer-Mediated Communication: Linguistic, Social and Cross-Cultural Perspectives*. Amsterdam: John Benjamins.

Jiao, XX (焦晓晓) 2003. Jinnian lai zhongguo jingnei chuxian de xinciyu jiqi dui haiwaihanyu jiaoxue de tiaozhan. 近年来中国境内出现的新词语及其对海外汉语教学的挑战 (The new lexis that has emerged in China and its challenge to Chinese teaching overseas). *Journal of Chinese Language Teachers Association*, 38(1), 197–216.

Jin, S (劲松) (2000). Mantan yangweir hanyu 漫谈洋味儿汉语 (A discursive discussion of foreign-flavored Chinese language). *Yuwen Jianshe*, 137, 4–5.

Klinkner, K (2003). *Joker's Mirror: Reflected Images of Urban Chinese Youths*. Urbana-Champaign: University of Illinois.

Labov, W (1963). The social motivation of a sound change. *Word*, 19, 273–309.

Labov, W (1966). *The Social Stratification of English in New York City*. Washington: Center for Applied Linguistics.

Labov, W (1972). *Sociolinguistic Patterns*. Philadelphia: University of Pennsylvania Press.

Labov, W (2000). Principles of linguistic change, Vol. 2, *Social Factors*. Oxford, UK: Blackwell.

Li, CN and S Thompson (1981). *Mandarin Chinese: A Functional Reference Grammar*. Berkeley, CA: University of California Press.

Li, J (李军) (2002). Qiantan wangluo yuyan dui xiandai hanyu de yingxiang 浅谈网络语言对现代汉语的影响 (A brief discussion of the impact of the Internet languageon modern Chinese). *Social Science Front*, 6, 265–266.

Liu, J (2010). The use of Chinese dialects on the Internet: Youth language and local youth identity in urban China. In *Vallah, Gurkensalat 4U & me! Current Perspectives in the Study of Youth Language*, JN Jørgensen (ed.), pp. 99–112. Frankfurt: Peter Lang. The revised version was included in this volume.

Liu, J (2011). Deviant writing and youth identity: Representation of dialects with Chinese characters on the Internet. *Chinese Language and Discourse*, 2(1), 58–79.

Lü, XP (闾小波) (2002). *Bainian Chuanmei Bianqian* 百年传媒变迁 (*The Evolution of the Mass Media over the Last Hundred Years*). Nanjing: Jiangsu Fine Arts Publishing House.

Ma, J (马静) (2002). Wangluo yongci xiang richang yuyan de shentou 网络用词向日常语言的渗透 (The spread of Internet lexicon to everyday usage). Journal of Northwest Industrial University, 22(3), 53–57.

Melchers, G and P Shaw (2003). *World Englishes: An Introduction*. London: Arnold.

Mikko(王少雄) (2000). Yingxiong Shidai (The Age of Heroes). www.rongshuxia.com/book/23999.html <http://www.rongshuxia.com/book/23999.html>.

Wardhaugh, R (1998). *An Introduction to Sociolinguistics*. Oxford, UK: Blackwell.

Weinreich, U, W Labov and M Herzog (1968). Empirical foundations for a theory of language change. In *Directions for Historical Linguistics*, W Lehmann and Y Malkiel (eds.), pp. 95–188. Austin, TX: University of Texas Press.

Yates, S (1996). Computer-mediated English: Sociolinguistic aspects of computer-mediated communication. In *Using English: From Conversation to Canon*, J Maybin and N Mercer (eds.), pp. 76–83. London: Routledge.

Yu, GY (于根元), ZY Xiong (熊征宇), HY Liu (刘海燕), SX Sun (孙述学) and L Zhang (张莉) (2001a). *Wangluo Yuyan Gaishuo* 网络语言概说 (*Survey of the Internet language*). Beijing: China Economy Publishing House.

Yu, GY (于根元), ZY Xiong (熊征宇), HY Liu (刘海燕), SX Sun (孙述学) and L Zhang (张莉) (ed.) (2001b). *Zhongguo Wangluo Yuyan Cidian* 中国网络语言词典 (*A Dictionary of China's Internet language*). Beijing: China Economy Publishing House.

Zhang, YH (张云辉) (2007). Wangluo yuyan de cihui yufa tezheng 网络语言的词汇语法特征 (The lexical and grammatical features of the Internet language). *Zhongguo Yuwen*, 321, 531–535.

Zhu, B (2008). A sociolinguistic analysis of dialect use in Chinese weblogs. Paper presented at the 20th North American Conference on Chinese Linguistics, Columbus.

CHAPTER 2

THE METAPHORICAL WORLD OF CHINESE ONLINE ENTERTAINMENT NEWS

CHONG HAN

University of Western Sydney, Australia

Entertainment news is one of the most popular forms of online news in contemporary China (cf. Yu, 2007). It serves not only to convey information about the entertainment industry and its products but also to entertain readers. Metaphor, a salient linguistic feature of this news genre, is the object of investigation in this study. The findings are based on the exploration of a general corpus of Chinese online entertainment news: 1,016 full-length news items, totalling 856,374 Chinese characters, collected during May to June in 2007 from online news sources in China. Popular source domains of metaphors (war, martial arts, fire, wind, food, etc.) and target domains (conflict, celebrity, etc.) are identified, as well as the patterns of interaction and the functions of metaphors in Chinese entertainment news. These findings demonstrate that metaphors are powerful linguistic means of explaining and embellishing abstract concepts, an ideological tool for describing and evaluating people and situations in discourse, and a conceptual force that both reflects and potentially influences people's perception of their world. The findings also show that China's changing media ecology has affected the way that metaphors emerge into discourse, are communicated, and interact with each other.

1. Entertainment News in China

A popular cliché about news media in China claims that the media is tightly controlled by the Chinese government and serve as the mouthpiece of Chinese Communist Party, playing an essential role in ideological propaganda and blocking the Chinese audience from accessing important information from the outside world. This cliché ignores the fact that the cumulative effect of China's social and economic reforms in the late 1980s. Fuelled by its rapid economic and technological development, and the trend toward globalization, as well as numerous other factors have managed to change the ecology of Chinese news media dramatically and fundamentally. The news media in present-day China consists of two sectors, traditional Party-controlled and commercialized, though they are not completely separated as the commercial news outlets are under the "supervision" of the Central Publicity Department or the State Administration of Radio, Film and Television (SARFT). The commercial news outlets, including entertainment news as many researchers have observed (e.g. Li, 2002; Luo, 2003; Zhang, 2005), have been heavily influenced by the global trend of market-oriented "infotainment" and the tabloidization of news, which prioritizes entertainment over information, sensationalism over rationalism, and trivia and gossip over the weighty and the serious. Indeed, "entertainment news" as an independent genre has flooded TV, print media, and the Internet, and has gradually become an integral part of Chinese people's life (Li, 2002). Chinese in the post-Mao era can now enjoy watching TV, going to cinemas, listening to music, surfing online, or participating in many other forms of entertainment at anytime of the day. The growing demand for entertainment has caused the expansion of China's culture industry, and entertainment service is an essential part of the expansion. According to the *Report on Development of China's Culture Industry* (Zhang et al., 2005), the culture industry has a dramatic increase in revenues, which accounted for 3.1% of GDP in 2003. In the same year, urban residential expenditure on cultural and entertainment services increased by 52%.

Consequently, since the late 1980s, people in the print news media industry have spotted the market opportunity for turning news into entertainment for ordinary urban readers. Reader-oriented newspapers heavily laden with soft news and infotainment became fierce market competitors of the propaganda-oriented Party newspapers (Huang, 2001). From the late

1990s, online news media began to take a share of the market (Li, 2002), making entertainment news one of their major drawing cards. Entertainment news provides readers with information on daily entertainment, projecting entertainment circles as glamorous, mysterious, or even chaotic, worlds apart from the everyday life of most citizens, and gossiping about entertainers' private affairs, scandals, and other dark issues. Although in 2009, it attracted attention from "the authorities," who control or at least "supervise" media outlets, this controversial news genre in China still plays an active role in Chinese people's daily lives. According to the "Survey Report on the Utilization and Influence of the Internet in Five Urban Cities in China in 2005," entertainment news was the most frequently read online news (65.5%), followed by domestic news (55%), and society news (48.4%) in contemporary China.

2. Metaphorical Tricks

How does the news manage to attract the attention of so many readers? Certainly, people have curiosity about the lives of celebrity entertainers, newly released films, and the latest pop songs. However, readers are deluged with news every day, and there are literally thousands of entertainment news websites in China. This motivates journalists to write in ways that will stand out in order to attract, and entertain as many readers as possible, thus maximizing the profits to be gained through selling advertising space. One of the ways they manage this is by framing news materials as much as possible in language which the readers of a community are familiar with and enjoy. The example (1) may serve to make this point clearer. On April 23, 2009, the ent.people.com.cn reported[1]:

(1) 孙红雷,段奕宏,张译"戏"斗四月荧屏
"Sun Honglei, Duan Yihong, Zhang Yi engage in a **combat** for TV screens in April"
三月荧屏,《团长》强势登陆四大卫视,风头无人能及。随着《团长》首轮的完美落幕,四月荧屏则出现"三足鼎立"的势头。孙红雷,段奕宏,张译三位实力演员各携作品开始了新一轮的荧屏鏖战。

---

[1] The link is <http://ent.people.com.cn/GB/42075/81374/9174180.html>, accessed on April 23, 2009.

"In March, the TV drama *Regimental Commander* **made a massed landing** on four satellite TV stations, gaining overwhelming popularity. With the conclusion of this series, the screen will be the stage for **a tripartite confrontation**. Three actors, Sun Honglei, Duan Yihong, and Zhang Yi, each appearing in a new drama, will engage in **a fresh round of battle for your TV screen**…"

The report describes the broadcast of three TV dramas, each featuring a celebrity actor, with the ability to attract a large audience. But, interestingly, it transforms the reported issue via metaphor into a war scenario, using the phrase *sānzúdǐnglì* (literally, "three leg tripod stands" referring to a three-part confrontation among equals), thus enhancing the entertainment value of the news report through exaggeration and highly conventional sensationalism.

Hyperbolic expressions are intended to catch readers' attention and entertain them; however, the appeal of war metaphors in Chinese entertainment news seems different from that discussed in the literature. War metaphors, as many researchers suggest (Lakoff and Johnson, 1980; Beer and De Landtscheer, 2004; Charteris-Black, 2005; Steuter and Wills, 2008; Semino, 2008), construct binary oppositions of winners and losers, invaders and defenders, aggressors and victims, warriors and civilians. They appeal to people's emotions, calling for feelings of national pride, solidarity, and righteousness, as well as rage and hatred toward enemies. Thus, the use of war metaphors can be an ideologically laden and persuasive propaganda tool, especially in political communication. This interpretation can also apply to war metaphors used in Chinese political news and current affairs as well.

The example given above is not an individual case. Rather, entertainment news is laden with metaphors. What, then, motivates the recurrent use of metaphors in entertainment news? It is necessary to consider the impact on Chinese news media of the "economy of attention" (Yu, 2004, 2005) and the development of technology. According to Yu Guoming, "economy of attention" means the ability of contemporary media outlets to engage people's attention. This ability determines their chance of success in the fierce competition for market shares. Although newsgathering and writing have always been the task of in-house journalists, in the last few years, news sources have expanded to include publicists and ordinary readers equipped with modern technology (e.g., bloggers). Publicists aim to promote entertainers and events. They feed the news media with descriptions of the glamour of those they promote so as to ensure a high degree of public exposure. By turning advertisements into news, the people promoted may gain greater attention and credibility, arouse more public interest, and thus become even more marketable.

Another source of metaphors is ordinary readers, some of whom have become active information providers. Being largely free from political, economic, and cultural restraints, bloggers, for instance, may create metaphors and ways of talking that are readily adopted by and popularized in the online community.

The selection and presentation of news information is an essential part of the wider process of news content management within newsrooms. One role of news editors is to develop strategies that both reinforce the spectacle aspect of the entertainment world and also "direct" readers' attention to specific issues highlighting entertainers or entertainment events. Careful choice of language, then, is required to ensure effectiveness in both the delivery of information and the entertainment value of the news. Metaphor has the potential to help writers and commentators meet this demand and China's changing media ecology, which has largely been influenced by globalization, has affected the way that metaphors are adopted into discourse, are communicated, and interact with each other.

3. Defining Metaphor

What is metaphor? Since the time of Aristotle, metaphor has been viewed as an implicit comparison or an elliptical simile in which the linguistic comparison cues "like" and "as" are omitted (cf. Mooij, 1976). It has also been seen as a rhetorical device that embellishes "plain language" and makes the style of expression lofty, lifting it "above the commonplace" (Aristotle, see Baxter and Atherton (1997, p. 152)), and its occurrence in literary works has long been discussed.

In more recent years, cognitive linguists have argued that metaphor is constitutive of everyday language. From the perspective of Conceptual Metaphor Theory (CMT), which is a widely accepted metaphor theory, metaphor can be defined as (A) understanding one thing in terms of another, or (B) "a cross-domain conceptual mapping" (Lakoff and Johnson, 1980). For example, "popularity" is an abstract notion. Chinese speakers convey an understanding of it by comparing it to something more familiar and more concrete, such as "fire." This understanding, as Lakoff and Johnson argue, is grounded in people's physical experience of the world. The "popularity is fire" is a metaphor that is based on people's bodily experience of fire as something that produces a large amount of heat and light while burning. Here, the abstract notion "popularity" is termed the *target domain*, while the concrete notion "fire" is the *source domain*. Then, the metaphor is a cross-domain conceptual mapping in which inferential structures of the source domain "fire" are imposed on the target domain "popularity." Building upon this, the expression "Wang Baoqiang *set* the whole nation *on fire*" involves the use of the metaphor, and thus may be interpreted as "Wang Baoqiang has gained nation-wide popularity."[2]

Recent critiques and expansion of CMT by researchers, including Charteris-Black (2004, 2005), Cameron (2003, 2007a), and Deignan (2005), have criticized Lakoff and Johnson for building their theory on invented or de-contextualized data, and have issued a call for research on metaphor as it occurs in authentic discourse such as news, business and economic magazines, political speeches, and so on. For instance, Charteris-Black (2005) investigates the use of metaphor in speeches delivered by leading politicians in Britain and US (e.g., Winston Churchill, Martin Luther King, Bill Clinton, etc.). He argues that metaphor is a key rhetorical strategy to make these speeches persuasive since it influences our beliefs, activates our emotions, and impacts on our moral view of life. Some scholars also bring the dimension of genre into their discussion and argue for the rhetorical implications of metaphors in a given genre. Caballero (2003), for instance, examines the use of metaphor in building reviews in architectural magazines. She lays out the structure of the review, showing how reviews typically fall into several parts, including framing parts. She then demonstrates that different metaphors function to fulfil rhetorical purposes of different parts of the textual structure.

A number of metaphor studies also argue for the cultural dimension of metaphor. Zinken (2003), for instance, questions physical experience being the only key motivation for metaphor. He argues that such metaphorical

---

[2] Here, the meaning of the expression "set the nation on fire" in Chinese is slightly different from English, which involves excitement and interest among a large group of people. Unlike the English expression which highlights the emotional intensity of people, the Chinese expression emphasizes the large quantity of people involved.

expressions as "scientific progress leads to Frankensteins" (which he terms as "intertextual metaphors") originate in cultural products (e.g., novels, films, and art). Metaphors of this kind are based on our culturally grounded experience rather than bodily experience.

Two more interesting studies deserve attention. Cameron and Deignan (2006), Cameron (2007a, 2007b), Larsen-Freeman and Cameron (2008) and Cameron *et al.* (2009) propose to view metaphor as emerging, evolving, changing, and interacting in a real-world discourse that itself is a dynamic flow of language use. In this process, metaphor tends to stabilize its linguistic form. Eventually, some of these emergent metaphors may spread across sociocultural groups and may even become part of the linguistic and cognitive repertoire of these groups.

Ritchie and Dyhouse (2008) propose the concept of "metaphor play" or "empty metaphor," which involves playful qualities at both formal and semantic levels: these play with sounds, but are empty in semantic content. One of his examples is "fine as frog's hair." But "frog's hair" has no real-world referent since frogs are hairless amphibians, and so it evokes an absurd image. The "Love as garbage disposal" in Johnny Cash's "Flushed from the bathroom of your heart" is another playful metaphor creation. The metaphor in the song is humorous partially because of its depiction of a counter-normative image of romantic love and partially by its counter-conventional writing of love songs.

These two studies have particular relevance to the understanding of the use of metaphor in Chinese entertainment news presented on the Internet. In the age of the Internet, news writing is no longer the preserve of professional journalists; rather outsiders, bloggers, online commentators, and others are now participating in news production. Meanwhile, online news and comment facilities allow rapid online exchange of information between journalists and the masses. In short, the impact of the Internet on the use of language in news writing has been profound. It provides great potential for the emergence and stabilization of metaphors in people's linguistic and cognitive repertoires recently. Wang's (2006) research on the evolution of Chinese language in Mainland China newspapers, reveals that an increasing number of new terms have entered Chinese news discourse since the introduction of the Internet, and metaphor is an important word-creation mechanism. The main impulse for this phenomenon, as Wang argues, is the trend of "information entertainment" (资讯娱乐化) in Chinese media.

This chapter combines the main insights and tenets of CMT and the recent studies of metaphor in discourse to examine the use of metaphor in Chinese online entertainment news in this era of globalization.

4. Description of the Data

The data illustrating the metaphorical world of Chinese online entertainment news was obtained from the *Entertainment Channel* (娱乐频道) of the online news portal people.com.cn (人民网). There are four reasons for choosing people.com.cn. First, it is one of the largest online news portals in Mainland China. Second, its entertainment news receives high click-through rates (Li and Li, 2007). Third, it collaborates with more than 1,000 media outlets, and thus has a great diversity of information sources. Fourth and most importantly, it has a very powerful search engine in its *Search Channel* (人民网搜索频道). This search engine has filters that not only allow keyword search in the news archives of people.com.cn but also allow users to specify time period, news categories, original source of news, the frequency and place of occurrence of the keyword in news items, and so on by box-ticking, thereby making the search and download of news items easier. Such filters are not available in other large and popular Chinese news portals such as xinhuanet.com (新华网) and sina.com.cn (新浪).

The examples are drawn from 1,016 full-length news items, totalling 856,374 Chinese characters. Only online written news reports from 1 May to 31 June in 2007 in the People's Republic of China are drawn on. Other genres available on the webpage of the *Entertainment Channel*, such as commentaries, editorials, blogs, online posts, and video news, are excluded.

The identification of metaphors in this corpus took place in three steps. First, a keyword[3] list of the corpus was generated by using the

---

[3] The key words are those words that are most unusually frequent in the corpus of Chinese online entertainment news compared with their occurrence in the reference corpus Lancaster Corpus of Mandarin Chinese (LCMC) (McEnergy and Xiao, 2004). LCMC covers a diverse range of written genres, from reportage to adventure and martial arts fiction, over the period of ±2 years of 1991. About 500 texts are involved, generating 1,000,000 words (around 1,600,000 characters) in total.

keyword function of *WordSmith Tools 4.0* (Scott, 2004). This software program is designed for examining the way that words behave in texts. Likely metaphorical expressions such as *pàohōng* (炮轰, bombing) and *zhànzhēng* (战争, war) were jotted down during the reading of the list. Second, these retrieved metaphor candidates were grouped semantically into various lexical domains, such as war and fire, either by intuition or with the assistance of dictionaries and thesauri. The occurrence of each candidate in the news text was examined in order to determine their metaphorical sense. This was achieved by the *concordance* function of *WordSmith*. Once the candidates' metaphorical senses were determined, conceptual metaphors were then proposed to account for them. Third, the salience of a particular conceptual metaphor in the corpus was determined by their frequency of occurrences in the corpus.

5. The Identified Metaphors

5.1. *War*

The first and most salient group of metaphors is those associated with the domain of WAR. It accounts for 39% of the total resonance[4] in the corpus.

Three main types of war metaphorical projections were identified in the corpus, namely "Competition is War," "Business is War," and "Interaction is War."

5.1.1. *Competition is War*

The time that the data were collected for this study was when TV talent shows were attracting great media attention, so a number of examples concern these shows. War is a potent source domain for these talent contests because it provides a clear schema that includes required elements for a competition — such as personnel, physical contest behavior, and outcomes. The war metaphors are highly entrenched in the news concerning these shows, with

---

[4] Resonance is a statistical method proposed by Charteris-Black (2004, p. 89) to calculate and compare the productivity of metaphor source domains. That is, the sum of the token is multiplied by the sum of the types of metaphorical expressions in the same source domain.

numerous war expressions appearing at several levels of news texts, forming a "Competition is War" metaphor. In these war scenes, one can see that contestants engage in a *battle* for continuing to the next round of the competition (e.g., *zhōngjí* PK, "final PK"[5]); judges fill the roles of *military leaders* (e.g., *jiàng*, "general"); the competition is conducted in accordance with the prototypical stages of a military combat, such as *joining a battle* (*shàngzhèn*), *defending and allying* (e.g., "safeguard", *bǎowèi*; "to assist in array", *zhùzhèn*), *winning or losing a battle* (e.g., "to defeat", *jībài*; "to lose the battle", *luòbài*). Two examples are presented below:

(2) "快乐男声"9进7 硝烟今再起
 "7 out of 9 candidates will go into the next round of Happy Boy. Today, **the smoke of gunpowder** is rising again."

(3) "快乐男声"比赛进入第二轮组合大战。
 "Happy Boy now enters the second round of **a large-scale war** of pairs."

The conceptualization of a TV talent contest as a war is a deliberate exaggeration of the scale and intensity of conflict: contestants are pitted against each other, and so are their supporters. This can cultivate in-group intimacy. Conflict also creates a win-lose binary opposition, which has the power to arouse passions. Thus, the hyperbolic construction of TV talent contests in the frame of a war functions to grab the viewers' attention, invite their emotional involvement in the event, and convey the impression that these TV talent shows have mass appeal.

Entertainment products are also presented as engaged in war-like competition:

(4) "陕西味"电影《盲山》出征 打动戛纳评委
 "Blind Mountain, the film with the Shanxi flavor, **goes out to battle**; it touches the heartstrings of the jury at the Cannes Film Festival."

Many award-winning occasions like film festivals are great opportunities for filmmakers to sell their works to distributors from all over the world. In this

---

[5] PK is an abbreviation for "personal killing" or "player killing."

sense, entertainers and entertainment products are commodities being consumed rather than pieces of art appreciated by a mass audience. In other words, the value of an entertainer or an entertainment product is not only recognized by winning an award but also associated with market appeal. Thus, the "War for Peer Recognition" metaphor has a tight link with another popular metaphor "Business is War."

5.1.2. *Business is War*

Present-day entertainment is a highly commercialized operation run as a business in which producers, agents, promoters, publicists, and marketing personnel are engaged in establishing chains of attraction between entertainers or entertainment products and consumers for profit rather than for mere pleasure. Thus, one major contest in contemporary entertainment circles is competition over making money: the more popular the entertainers, the more profit they accrue for themselves, their associates, and other businesses relying on their names.

Just like war, business belongs to the realm of conflict and aggressive interaction. Consequently, it is common to see celebrity entertainers being reported as "equipped" with famous brand dresses, "weapons" they use to fight for media attention at red carpet events, as shown below.

(5) 红地毯历来是女明星们寸土必争之地，昨日，记者从颁奖现场了解到，今年各大国际名牌纷纷赞助女星出战金像奖，没个百八十万打造的战袍，女星们简直羞于见人。以角逐最佳新人奖的霍思燕一身"装备"为例，整套造价高达3000万人民币，其中，包括价值11万的华 伦天奴晚装，和价值不菲的"七彩云南"翡翠钻饰，风头十足。此外，大S、梁洛施也穿上华伦天奴出战。

"The red carpet has always been **the place at which female celebrities fight for every inch of ground**. Yesterday, the reporter was informed at the awarding ceremony that various internationally famous brands financed the female celebrities to **go to war** for the Golden Elephant Award. Without a **war robe** worth millions of dollars, female celebrities would feel embarrassed to turn up at the ceremony. Take, for example, the "**equipment**" of Huo Siyan, who **competed** for the Award for Best Newcomer. The whole outfit was worth 30 million RMB, including a

110,000 RMB Valentino evening dress and a set of jade-diamond accessories named "Seven Color Yunnan." This equipment made her extremely glamorous. In addition, Elder S and Luisa Isabella Nolasco da Silva **went out to battle** wearing Valentino as well."

The war metaphorical expressions clustering in this news excerpt construct not only intense competition for media attention between female entertainers but also competition for market potential between the commodities that such entertainers represent. Here, entertainers are used as an advertising strategy to endorse products and to increase their strength of competition for market shares.

5.1.3. *Interaction is War*

The business of entertainment also involves clashes of ideas, wills, control of publicity via verbal conflict and turbulent relationships between participants in the world of entertainment. An example is given as follows:

(6) 昨日下午, 冯导演被复旦大学视觉艺术学院聘为客座教授。
在随后的"冯小刚纵论华语电影演讲会"上, 冯教授却毫不客气, 在大力宣传自己的新片同时, 火力十足频频开炮。
第一炮 目标——电影人…
第二炮 目标——某些媒体…
第三炮 目标——贾樟柯…
"Yesterday afternoon, Director Feng was offered a guest professorship at the School of Visual Art, Fudan University. In the following 'Speech on Chinese Films by Feng Xiaogang,' Professor Feng showed no trace of reservation, and **concentrated his firepower, ejecting a cluster of bomblets**, while promoting his new film….

The first bomblet Target — Filmmakers…
The second bomblet Target — some media outlets…
The third bomblet Target — Jia Zhangke…"

In this extract, the news writer creatively elaborates a conventional metaphor "Argument is War" in Chinese, constructing a film director's public condemnation as the ejection of cluster bomblets. Here, war metaphors are used to emphasize the aggressiveness and strong tone of the denunciation. The list of targets of the bombing presents the arguments made by the director in a clear and organized manner, and dramatizes the opposition between the director and his different rivals.

To sum up, war metaphors in entertainment news are largely used as hyperbole, which represents as well as amplifies the conflicting aspects of entertainment circles. Goatly (1997, pp. 164–165) points out that hyperbolic metaphors have two functions. First, they can express emotion. Readers are expected to transfer to the target domain the sense of wonder associated with the source domain. Second, such metaphors can grab viewer attention by their deliberate exaggeration. War metaphors are one typical example of this type of metaphor.

War metaphors in entertainment news do not indicate to readers what should be valued and what should be rejected. Rather, they function to represent the entertainment world as a place full of bloodless but intense spectator activity. It is of note that the famous 20th century scholar Qian Zhongshu (2001, pp. 372–377) has demonstrated that warfare and show or spectator activities have long been seen as closely related in the Chinese literary tradition. He (*ibid.*, p. 373) argues, "*Weiyan songting, xiyizhanye; qingmiaodanxie, zhanyixiye*" 危言耸听, 戏亦战也; 轻描淡写, 战亦戏也 (In a battle of verbal wit, a show becomes war; treated with the lightest of touches, war becomes a show). Clearly, talking of entertainment events in terms of war in news reports is to dramatize them, hyping the news content.

Moreover, Lakoff and Johnson (1980) contend that metaphors have an ideological function. The metaphorical construction of reality in discourse is done through a selection of features such as source domains or entailments, as a means of maintaining or challenging power relations in society. In entertainment news, the metaphorical construction of entertainment issues as intense wars corresponds with news value: conflict sells! Thus, war metaphors may assist in enhancing online news circulation. But they can also "have pernicious and misleading effects if their presence and operation are not recognized and, if appropriate, challenged" (Semino and Masci, 1996, p. 267). War metaphors in entertainment news may highlight the struggles that entertainers face in order to achieve fame; however, they downplay the fact that entertainers become very attractive and wealthy via their personal efforts and as such, they are always regarded as role models for individual success and wealth.

5.2. *Martial arts*

Similar to "War," the domain of the "Martial Arts" is metaphorically applied to much online infotainment.

The martial arts domain involves a culture-specific model of opposition and conflict, which is largely structured in Chinese martial arts fictions. This is an aspect of Chinese civilization dramatically different from the stereotypical image of Chinese society in which everyone conforms to the Confucian code of behavior (Liu, 1967). The realm of martial arts represents a psychological inclination for personal freedom and nonconformity in conventions, and expresses a desire for heroes, who can save people from difficulty, evil, and misery. Martial arts novels represent a unique kind of popular literature in Chinese culture with more than 1,000 years of history and they are still being written today. In fact, with the adaptations of this literature into films, television dramas, comic books, electronic games, and other media, they still constitute an important part of Chinese popular culture.

The metaphorical use of martial arts expressions in Chinese news writing, especially in Chinese sports news, is a result of market-oriented socioeconomic reforms and, reflecting the industrialization of sport since 1990s, creates or enhances narrative tension in a sports story. Plain sports events are transformed into martial scenarios, and these metaphors also make news more digestible. As Ni (2003) argues, such use of the "Martial Arts" metaphor plays a significant role in reducing the presence of overt Marxist and communist ideology in Chinese sports news, and thus renders it more entertaining.

The following example of an "Entertainment World is a Martial Arts Contest" metaphor is taken from a news report on a popular TV talent show *Super Girl*.

(7) 拳打南山猛虎, 脚踢北海蛟龙
"Fists punching the fierce tiger on the South Mountain;
Feet kicking the writhing dragon in the North Sea"

"超级女声"总决赛开始, 各路一流好手走向最终擂台"
"The *Super Girl* Final Competition starts; All first-class practitioners walk toward the final platform of contest"

各派高手一览
"[section title]
An overview of practitioners from different clans"
广州赛区 ｛咏春拳｝
"[body]
Guangzhou Competition venue {Yongchun Quan}"
掌门人: 周笔畅
绝密私人资料: 星海音乐学院社会音乐系大三
参赛必杀技: 《爱我还是他》《氧气》
修行: R&B
假想敌手: 自己
修炼过程: 平和
修炼级别: (自我评定, 菜鸟级为100级, 得道成仙级为1000级, 下同。) 500级
拉票口号: 我会用心唱自己的歌
"Clan leader: Zhou Bichang
Top-secret private information: Year 3, Department of Popular Music, Xinghai Institute of Music
Fatal killings skills in competition: 'Love me or him,' 'Oxygen'
Mastery: R&B
Imagined enemy: Herself
Process of practicing skills: mild
Level of skills: 500 (Self-evaluation criteria: the level of freshman: 100; the level of becoming an immortal: 1000. The criteria are adopted in the following)
Slogan: I will sing my songs with my heart."

大师姐: 易慧
绝密私人资料: 星海音乐学院社会音乐系大三
参赛必杀技: 《蓝色》
修行: R&B
假想敌手: 每一个
"Senior Apprentice under the same master: Yi Hui
Top-secret private information: Year 3, Department of Popular Music, Xinghai Institute of Music
Fatal killings skills in competition: 'Blue'

Mastery: R & B
Imagined enemy: everyone"

小师妹: 李娜
绝密私人资料: 星海音乐学院社会音乐系大三
参赛必杀技: 原创歌曲
假想敌手: 所有人
"Junior Female Apprentice under the same master: Li Na
Top-secret private information: Year 3, Department of Popular Music, Xinghai Institute of Music
Fatal killings skills in competition: original musical works
Imagined enemy: everyone"

In the news text, the *Super Girl* competition is portrayed as an upcoming "platform contest" (*lèitái sài* 擂台赛 a fight taking place on a stage in front of an audience) between different martial arts clans. Such conceptualization involves knowledge beyond the domains of the *Super Girl* competition and platform contest; it invokes blends of Chinese traditional platform contests and the cultural model of the martial arts world.

In the headline, a popular couplet (*duìlián*, 对联) is cited: "Fists punching the fierce tiger on the South Mountain; Feet kicking the writhing dragon in the North Sea." This couplet, which originated in the Chinese vernacular novel *Outlaws of the Marsh* (*Shuǐhǔzhuàn*, 水浒传), has been widely used in Chinese martial arts literature that involves a platform contest scene, thus setting the whole news story as a Chinese platform contest.

The news text is divided into five parts in terms of the competition venues, each of which is portrayed as a martial arts clan. The excerpt here reproduces the first part in which the clan is termed *Yongchun Quan*. The news text involves three *Super Girl* candidates, who have been given different ranking titles. Interpretation of these titles is determined by the extent of the reader's background cultural knowledge of Chinese martial arts: practitioners in each clan are ranked in terms of age and skills. Five martial arts clans are involved in this musical "combat." They are: Yongchun Quan (咏春拳), Emei Clan (峨嵋派), Hengshan Clan (衡山派), Shaolin Temple (少林派), and Peach Blossom Island (桃花岛), but among them, only Yongchun Quan and Shaolin Temple are real, the rest are fictional. Readers with a good knowledge of martial arts literature will agree that it is hard to rank these five martial arts clans. Thus, it can be assumed that these clans are equally competent, and that the *Super Girl* candidates from these clans, in general, are equally competent.

The news text here involves a complex metaphorical blend in which the *Super Girl* candidates will soon engage in a head-to-head competition: it is intense, and the outcome is totally unpredictable.

5.3. *Fire*

Typically, fire metaphors in Chinese entertainment news are based on three conceptual metaphors: *Success in Market is Fire (or Heat or Explosion)*, *Enthusiasm is Fire (or Explosion)*, and *Sexual Appeal is Fire (or Explosion)*.

5.3.1. *Success in market is fire (or heat or explosion)*

Metaphors of fire are used to exploit their potential for exaggeration in intensity. The common metaphorical patterns include *huǒ* (火, fire), *huǒbào* (火爆, fire-explode), and *huǒrè* (火热, fire-heat). Although it is a nominal term, the lexeme *huǒ* is used either as an adjective or as a verb in entertainment news, describing the abstract notion "success" as fire. As a free morpheme, *huǒ* is also in compound with *bào* (explosion) and *rè* (heat), constructing the metaphor "Success is Fire/Heat/Explosion." Since an explosion is a process that emits a large amount of heat and produces extremely high temperatures, the metaphorical use of *huǒbào* (fire-explosion) implies a higher degree of intensity than the metaphorical use of *huǒrè* (fire-heat).

Typically, fire metaphors in Chinese entertainment news are based on the conceptual metaphor "Success in Market is Fire (or Heat or Explosion)." For the entertainment industry, popularity is the indicator of fame and success, gauged in terms of market achievement, and measured by audience ratings, box office, sale of musical albums, and so on. An example is given below.

(8) 《越狱》堪称目前在中国内地最火的美剧, 火爆程度远远超过了早前的《绝望主妇》,《六人行》等"前辈"。
"At present *Prison Break* can be termed **the most popular** American TV drama in Mainland China. Its **skyrocketing** audience rating has far exceeded than its "predecessors" as *Desperate Housewives* and *Friends*."

5.3.2. *Enthusiam is fire (or explosion)*

The appearance of a well-liked entertainer tends to excite the fans' emotions. This concept is commonly expressed in the metaphor "Enthusiasm is Fire (or Explosion)" as the following examples show.

(9) 陈炜、贺刚二人在杭州新华书店为根据该剧改编的同名小说进行签售, 活动场面十分火爆。

"In the Hangzhou Xinhua Book Store, Alice Chan and He Gang signed and sold books whose story was adapted from the drama in which they performed. There was **great enthusiasm** at the event."

(10) 马天宇在天津和大连举办了签售活动, 两地现场均是人山人海、场场爆棚。

"Ma Tianyu held two sign-and-sell events in Tianjin and Dalian. Both events were packed with people whose enthusiasm was **explosive**."

As the examples show, fans' enthusiasm is constructed as fire as well as explosion. Since an explosion is accompanied by a loud noise, its metaphorical reading depicts a highly exciting and noisy scene in an entertainment event.

5.3.3. *Sexual appeal is fire (or explosion)*

For entertainers, being attractive is essential for success. All efforts are made to ensure a glamorous appearance in the public. Beauty is always the first thing to catch attention. Magazines, newspapers, websites, and advertisements decorate their covers or front pages and fill their space with photos of good-looking entertainers, and many are obsessed with these images.

Physical attractiveness is often evaluated in terms of sexual appeal. In Chinese, the literal equivalent of the word "sexy" is *xìnggǎn* (性感). In Chinese entertainment news, however, this concept is usually found to be expressed in a metaphorical way, that is, "Sexual Appeal is Fire/Heat/Explosion." Consider the following:

(11) 应采儿和天心扮演性感冷酷的杀手, 以自身火爆的身材为诱饵, 迷惑男人进行猎杀。

"Cherrie Ying and Tian Xin played the roles of sexy and cold-blooded killers. They used their **sexy** bodies as baits to seduce and kill men."

(12) 韩彩英一向以身材骄人、性感火辣著称，被赞为"芭比娃娃"和"最适合穿比基尼"的韩国女星。

"Han Chae Young has always been famous for her **hot, sexy** body, which she is proud of. She has been praised as having a figure like 'Barbie' and as being 'the Korean female star who is most suited to wearing a Bikini.'"

In example (11), the metaphor is based on the physiological reactions provoked by the perception of an entertainer's appearance such as an increase in body heat. In example (12), "fire" compounds with "spicy." Spicy food produces a pleasantly pungent taste and causes an increase in body temperature as well. Such metaphorical readings are consonant with a conventional "synthetic metaphor" (Yu, 2003) "Physical Attractiveness is Food" in Chinese, which is typically evidenced in the four-character set phrase *xiùsèkěcān* (秀色可餐, be a feast for the eyes) (Lan, 1994).

5.4. *Wind*

Like spreading fire, blowing wind is another hyperbolic metaphor used to construct popularity, as exemplified in the following:

(13) 《常回家看看》在北京地区刮起了一阵亲情剧旋风，上周一上档就取得了收视第二。

"The TV drama *Go Back Home More Frequently* stirred up quite a **whirlwind** of family drama in Beijing. Since its release last Monday, it has gained the second highest rating."

(14) 《七剑》像飓风一样席卷了威尼斯，冲击力非常大。

"The movie *Seven Swords* swept across Venice like a **hurricane**, exerting great impact."

In these two examples, entertainment news writers represent phenomena of pervasiveness and powerfulness in terms of devastating winds and utilize the metaphor "Popular Trend is Wind." As violent powerful winds have enormous impact on people's lives, the metaphorical use of these terms constructs an overwhelmingly pervasive image.

In addition, wind is also used to conceptualize tendency in the entertainment world.

Consider the following example.

(15) 影视交易市场转"风向"　新题材压倒古装风
"The market in movies and TV programs has changed its **trend**.
Those movies and TV programs featuring new topics **have** blown historical drama off the screen."

Here, the word "wind direction" has an idiomatic association with "trend" in Chinese — and trends, like winds, can change direction. As the following example shows, trends in entertainment news are constructed as a wind that is subject to change. In the compound *gǔzhuāng fēng* (ancient-costume-wind, "wind of historical drama"), *gǔzhuāng* is the modifier of *fēng*, labeling the prevailing trend in the entertainment world.

Besides the noun–noun compounding form shown above, the morpheme *fēng* can also co-occur with verbal morphemes as in the compound *gēnfēng* (跟风, "follow-wind" — to follow a trend).

(16) 周杰伦的中国风歌曲十分流行, 对此有人质疑黄征有跟风的嫌疑。
"Since Jay Chou's Chinese-style songs are very popular, people suspect Huangzheng of being **a trend follower**."

Here, the compound *gēnfēng* is a verb–object compound in which "wind" is combined with an action verb, "follow." The literal image is that one goes behind a wind which motivates the metaphorical shift to the meaning "to follow trend." Moreover, since "follow" is passive, this wind compound word implies a negative evaluation, that is, lack of creativity or want of intellectual judgment.

Generally speaking, the use of "Popular Trend as Wind" metaphor in entertainment news discourse suggests that the media always keeps an eye on popular trends in the world of entertainment and inform their readers with the updated information.

5.5. Food

Food metaphors are a distinctive group of metaphors in Chinese online entertainment news. Considering the following examples:

(17) "玉米"、"盒饭"、"维生素"、"荔枝"等粉丝团都纷纷走上街头，为偶像们拉人气。
"'**Corn**,' '**box lunch**,' '**vitamin**,' '**lychee**,' and other fan groups could all be found in the streets, promoting their idols."

(18) 李宇春现场演唱了《中国娃》，玉米们的尖叫声不绝于耳。
"Li Yuchun sang the song China Doll. This made the '**corn**' scream wildly nonstop."

The food terms in the examples above became popular in 2005 when the TV talent show *Super Girl* was broadcast (Xu, 2006, p. 18). They represent a linguistic phenomenon that is both unique and productive in present-day Chinese daily discourse. Of them, *yùmǐ*, *liángfěn*, and *héfàn* were evaluated as "the key words of Chinese popular culture in 2005" in the Chinese media.[6]

The creation of these terms may have been largely influenced by the transliteration of the English term "fans" as *fěnsī*, which literally denotes "dry noodles." Because of the huge success of *Super Girl* in 2005, *fěnsī* became a popular word in Chinese daily discourse. It also gave rise to a number of food terms. "Fans are Food Items" was elaborated by association with the given names of the stars who inspired the groups of fans. The term *yùmǐ* was created by fans of Li Yuchun, the *Super Girl* champion in 2005, as a label for themselves in Baidu's online chat room. It was chosen to keep the food convention initiated by *fěnsī*: *yùmǐ*, which means "corn" in Chinese, is a combination of the pronunciations of *yǔ* in the name of *Lǐ Yǔchūn*, and "x-*mí*" (迷, fans of x). Therefore, *yùmǐ* ("corn") is a pun on *yǔmí* (fans of *Yǔ*(chūn) — fans of *Lǐ Yǔchūn*).

---

[6] People (2005). "流行语05秋季榜公布 文化类榜首：傅彪". (*The ranking list of the popular words in the autumn of 2005 has been released; the word "Fubiao" tops the list of culture words*) <http://life.people.com.cn/GB/1089/3758399.html>, accessed on September 8, 2008.

Soon a variety of food terms appeared, such as *liángfěn* (凉粉, cold noodles) and *héfàn* (盒饭, box lunch) found in my corpus. *Liángfěn* refers to fans of Zhang Liangying, who won the third place in *Super Girl* in 2005. Here, *liáng* is homonymous with "*liàng*" in the name of *Zhāng Liàngyǐng*. Since the syllable *liàng* is not part of any food term in Chinese, and in order to keep the convention of "Fans are Food," Zhang's fans chose *fěn* as in *fěnsī* (dry noodles) to form the food term *liángfěn* (cold noodles). The term, "box lunch" (*héfàn*), refers to fans of He Jie. As is obvious, *hé* is homonymous with *hé* in the name of *Hé Jié*, and *fàn* may also bear some relation to "fan." Moreover, as Li Yuchun, Zhang Liangying, and He Jie all came from Sichuan Province, their fans invented the term "*Chéngdū xiǎochī tuán*" (成都小吃团, Chengdu snack team) as their collective name.

As the above analysis shows, this naming strategy involves a combination of puns and metaphor, as summarized below.

"Fans are Dry Noodles"
Noodles are food
From the above, a metaphorical formula is formed:
"Fans are Food" + Pun on one character of the given name of the person in question
Therefore, we have:

Fans of AX	A food
Fans of BY	B food
Fans of CZ	C food

It is found that many food metaphors are directly adopted by entertainment news writers in their writing. Some terms are even creatively incorporated into news discourse. Two examples from entertainment news appear below:

(19) 李宇春亮相遭围堵　上海机场变"玉米地"[7]
   "Li Yuchun was besieged by fans when she appeared in Shanghai Airport, turning it into a '**corn field**.'"

---

[7] Sohu (2005). "李宇春亮相遭围堵　上海机场变'玉米地'" (*Li Yuchun was besieged by fans when she appeared in Shanghai Airport, turning it into a "corn field"*). <http://yule.sohu.com/20051006/n227136337.shtml>, accessed on September 8, 2008.

(20) 李宇春个唱出错幽默救场　玉米兴奋成"爆米花"[8]
"Li Yuchun covered up her mistake in singing by telling a joke; the '**corn**' were so excited that they became '**popcorn**.'"

Here in example (19), the airport packed with fans of Li Yuchun is depicted as a "cornfield." In example (20), the excited fans of Li Yuchun are described as "popcorn." Both terms are creative derivatives from the metaphor "Fans of Li Yuchun are Corn." The creative use of "popcorn" to describe Li Yuchun's fans is particularly interesting in that it cleverly associates the corn metaphor with the Chinese conceptual metaphor "Excitement is Explosion." The Chinese equivalent of "popcorn" is "爆米花" (explode-rice-flower), and the visible link of the character "爆" with the concept "explosion" in this compound word evokes an image of people suddenly bursting emotionally.

Xu (2006) argues that fans originally created those metaphorical names as a means of expressing their affection toward their idols. Beer and De Landtsheer (2004, p. 25) mention that metaphorical naming is also a common strategy of persuasion in political discourse.

As the above examples show, the use of food metaphors in news discourse is attention-grabbing. They help to establish connections between news writers and readers, who are fans of a particular person, and engage them in news reading by creating a sense of group intimacy. In other words, the use of "dry noodles," "corn," and "popcorn" in entertainment news tends to invite readers into meaning creation, which is like solving puzzles and cultivates in-group intimacy.

Cameron and Deignan (2006, p. 674) suggest using "an emergentist perspective to bring together the linguistic, conceptual and sociocultural aspects of metaphor in use." The origin and gradual formation of a food metaphorical system in Chinese discourse show that certain metaphorical ways of talking and thinking emerge from and are promoted by instances of use in a specific discourse context. They then spread across sociocultural groups and become a form of linguistic as well as cognitive resource for members of those groups, and even for members of a speech community. They also show that pragmatic factors (e.g., playfulness) and emotions (shared affection) play a central role

---

[8] Sina (2006). "李宇春个唱出错幽默救场　玉米兴奋成"爆米花" (*Li Yuchun covered up her mistake in singing by telling a joke; the "corn" were so excited that they became "popcorn"*). <http://ent.sina.com.cn/x/2006-05-24/14581091696.html>, accessed on September 8, 2008.

in the emergence and spread of particular forms of language play based on metaphor.

The creation of new metaphors, and the prevalence of these metaphors in Chinese media and even daily discourse, may be attributed to the fact that

> [w]e experience today a new media "ecology" (Cottle, 2006), or media "surround," that scholars and analysts increasingly characterize using terms such as connectivity, saturation, and immediacy. Many have hypothesised that people, events and news media have become increasingly connected and interpreted, thanks to developing technologies, all part of "time-space compression," the collapse of distance, and the availability of information immediately. (Hoskins and O'Loughlin, 2007, pp. 2–3)

In other words, the changing ecology of media potentially affects the emergence and exponential spread of metaphors, such as "Fans are Food Items."

6. Conclusion

In this chapter, it has been shown that the discourse of online entertainment news in China today is saturated with metaphor. The entertainment world is depicted as a world of public prominence by using metaphors of "War, Martial Arts, Fire, Wind, and Food." These metaphors take "Popularity, Publicity, and Physical Appeal" as their major target focus, constructing the world of entertainment as a spectacle: "War" and "Martial Arts" portray the entertainment world in terms of fierce competition; "Fire" and "Wind" highlight extreme popularity; "Food" suggests the attractiveness of entertainers and involvement of large audiences.

What is the reason for creating and recycling such a metaphorical world in entertainment news? The Chinese scholar Yu Guoming (2004, 2005, citing Goldhaber and McLuhan) argues that the ability of contemporary media outlets to engage people's attention determines their chance of success in the fierce competition for market shares. In other words, the more attention the media outlets can engage and the more favor they gain from the advertisers, then the higher the profit they can make in the market. He also points out that what engages attention is likely to be information catering to people's needs and desires. With the rising culture and entertainment industry in China, the public has an increased desire to know more about entertainers. This desire makes the entertainers highly eye-catching characters. The portrayal of celebrities as prominent using metaphors in the entertainment news as illustrated in the examples in the preceding sections, then, gives them excessive visibility and makes their images even more notable and then more marketable.

Moreover, the choice of metaphors of war and martial arts may serve to echo Chinese people's daily experience of 21st century popular entertainment. Chinese popular culture is steeped in spectacles of war, martial arts, and talent competitions, as evidenced by the vast number of films and TV programs about war and martial arts. As well, there are the booming TV talent shows, with their box office success and their high audience ratings. The anti-Japanese war, the War of Liberation, as well as the ancient military romance of the Three Kingdoms are recurring themes in these high-grossing war films and TV dramas. Cinematic and TV adaptations of Jin Yong's martial arts novels have also been produced nonstop since the 1970s.

The prevalence of food metaphors in Chinese entertainment news is attributed to the huge success of *Super Girl* and other TV talent shows in China. This group of metaphors represents and reinforces a particular Chinese style of entertainment reporting, forming an important part of understanding the popular entertainment style of contemporary China.

Since the late 1980s, economic reform and the trend of globalization has prompted the Chinese media to be more market-oriented, paralleling the propagandist and instructional model of news reportage with a "soft," apolitical, and de-ideological model, which is perceived to be particularly appealing to a mass audience. On the other hand, before the prevalence of the TV talent shows in 2005, entertainment circles had long been perceived as places largely for well-trained professional elite. In addition, the huge rapid success and fame of some entertainers has made the entertainment industry seem even more glamorous and mysterious to most people. This situation may have been the driving force behind the adoption of play metaphors in news writing. By interpreting complex situations in terms of more familiar experience and in a more amusing manner, news writers can help to unveil the entertainment world from a specific perspective.

Then again, the use of metaphors in Chinese online entertainment news may be associated with the rise of the "economy of attention" in China as they have the potential to promote or even hype the news content. In a *Sina* online interview, Zeng Zihang and Zhang Man, two "insiders" of the Chinese entertainment circle, discussed *chǎozuò*, an important promotional strategy that has been widely adopted by the contemporary Chinese entertainment industry.[9] Literally, *chǎozuò* refers to the Chinese cookery method of "stir-frying." Metaphorically, it means dissemination of information with themes, images, or content meant to shock, elicit emotional responses and grab attention in a short period of time. According to Zeng and Zhang, "stir-frying" is a strategy that uses unreliable or fabricated information to promote the reputations of the people or sales of products in question. In their opinion, there are two reasons underlying the prevalence of "stir-frying" promotion (or "hype") in China.

First, the generation of sensational news is an important way of enhancing the profiles of entertainers and entertainment products and increasing their exposure in the interests of more profit-gaining opportunities. It is common to find that entertainers busily engage in *bó chūwèi* (博出位, fight-out-of-space — compete for publicity): media are hungry for audience ratings and ticket sales; agents and publicists strive to build profiles for their products and entertainers. Second, as Zeng and Zhang claim, there has also been an increase in the demand for sensational news, given that there is an assumption that "it is human nature to be *bāguà* (八卦, Eight-Diagrams — gossipy)",[10] and that "people love reading *bāguà* (tabloid) news" (*rénmín ài bāguà*). This demand has created a huge market potential for consuming "stir-fried" information. Thus, the metaphorical construction of the entertainment world as war, martial arts contests, fire, wind, and food in entertainment news reports, which function to exaggerate the superficial triviality of the personal actions of people, resonates strongly with the "stir-frying" characteristics of the discourse of entertainment in contemporary China.

References

Baxter, J and P Atherton (eds.) (1997). *Aristotle's Poetics Translated and with a Commentary by George Whalley.* Montreal and Kingston: McGill-Queen's University Press.

---

[9] "明星的另类宣传手法, 八卦炒作全解析" (*A comprehensive analysis of celebrities's unusual hype-creating tricks*), online video created by *Sina*, available at <http://video.sina.com.cn/ent/s/2007-12-25/02557402.shtml>, accessed on November 22, 2008.

[10] *Bāguà* is a Cantonese term. Originally it referred to the Eight Diagrams used in Taoist cosmology to represent a set of interrelated concepts. In contemporary Chinese, it means "gossipy," perhaps through association with "superstitious (old woman)."

Beer, FA and CL De Landtsheer (eds.) (2004). *Metaphorical World Politics (Rhetoric and Public Affair)*. Michigan: Michigan University Press.
Caballero, R (2003). Metaphor and genre: The presence and role of metaphor in the building review. *Applied Linguistics*, 24(2), 145–167.
Cameron, L (2003). *Metaphor in Educational Discourse*. London and New York: Continuum.
Cameron, L (2007a). Confrontation or complementarity? Metaphor in language use and cognitive metaphor theory. *Annual Review of Cognitive Linguistics,* (5), 107–135.
Cameron, L (2007b). Patterns of metaphor use in reconciliation talk. *Discourse & Society*, 18(2), 197–222.
Cameron, L and A Deignan (2006). The emergence of metaphor in discourse. *Applied Linguistics*, 27(4), 671–690.
Cameron, L, R Maslen, Z Todd, J Maule, P Stratton and N Stanley (2009). The discourse dynamics approach to metaphor and metaphor-led discourse analysis. *Metaphor and Symbol*, 24(2), 63–89.
Charteris-Black, J (2004). *Corpus Approaches to Critical Metaphor Analysis*. Basingstoke and New York: Palgrave-MacMillan.
Charteris-Black, J (2005). *Politicians and Rhetoric: The Persuasive Power of Metaphor*. New York: Palgrave Macmillan.
Chinese Academy of Social Science (2005). *Zhongguo Wu Chengshi Hulianwang Shiyong Xianzhuang Ji Yingxiang Diaocha Baogao* 2005年中国5城市互联网使用现状及影响调查报告 (*Survey Report on the Utilization and Influence of the Internet in Five Urban Cities in China in 2005*) <http://tech.sina.com.cn/other/2005-07-06/2014656115.shtml>, accessed on September 29, 2008.
Deignan, A (2005). *Metaphor and Corpus Linguistics*. Amsterdam and Philadelphia: John Benjamins Publishing Company.
Goatly, A (1997). *The Language of Metaphors*. London: Routledge.
Hoskins, A and B O'Loughlin (2007). *Television and Terror: Conflicting Times and Crisis of News Discourse*. New York: Palgrave Macmillan.
Huang, CJ (2001). China's state-run tabloids: The rise of "city newspapers." *Gazette: International Journal for Mass Communication Studies*, 63(5), 435–450.
Lakoff, G and M Johnson (1980). *Metaphors We Live By*. Chicago: University of Chicago Press.
Lan, HR (1994). Her beauty is EATable — A culturo-linguistic study. *Journal of Chinese Language Theachers Association*, 29(3), 79–98.

Larsen-Freeman, D and L Cameron (2008). *Complex Systems and Applied Linguistics*. Oxford: Oxford University Press.

Li, L (李蕾) and S Li (李松) (2007). Zhuanfang renminwang zongcai He Jiazheng (专访人民网总裁何加正) (An interview with People's CEO, He Jiazheng). <http://media.people.com.cn/GB/22114/76466/77471/5313182.html>, accessed on September 20, 2008.

Li, X (李幸) (2002). Wenhua Yule Xinwen de Caifang yu Xiezuo 文化娱乐新闻的采访 与写作 (Interviews and Writing on Culture Entertainment News). Beijing: China's Broadcast and TV Press.

Liu, JY (1967). *The Chinese Knight-Errant*. London: Routledge and Kegan Paul.

Luo, YC (罗映纯) (2003). *Dangqian Woguo Dazhong Meijie Xinwen Yulehua Xianxiang Poxi* 当前我国大众媒介新闻娱乐化现象剖析 (*On the News Entertainment of China's Present Mass Media*). MA thesis, Jinan University, Guangzhou.

McEnery, A and Z Xiao (2004). The Lancaster corpus of Mandarin Chinese: A corpus for monolingual and contrastive language study. *Proc. of the 4th* Int. Conf. on Language Resources and Evaluation (LREC) 2004, Lisbon.

Mooij, JJA (1976). *A Study of Metaphor: On the Nature of Metaphorical Expressions, with Special Reference to Their Reference*. Amsterdam, New York and Oxford: North-Holland Publishing Company.

Ni, M (倪沫) (2003). Tiyu xinwen de jianghu gushishi xushu 体育新闻的江湖故事式 叙述 (The rivers and lakes narration in sports news reports). *Xinwen Daxue,* Spring, 62–64.

Qian, ZS (钱钟书) (2001). *Guan Zhui Bian* 管锥编 (Limited Views: Essays on Ideas and Letters), Vol. 1. Beijing: SDX joint Publishing Company.

Ritchie, LD and V Dyhouse (2008). Hair of the frog and other empty metaphors: The play element in figurative language. *Metaphor and Symbol*, 23, 85–107.

Scott, M (2004). *WordSmith Tools* (Version 4.0). Oxford: Oxford University Press.

Semino, E (2008). *Metaphor in Discourse*. Cambridge: Cambridge University Press.

Semino, E and M Masci (1996). Politics is football: Metaphor in the discourse of Silvio Berlusconi in Italy. *Discourse & Society*, 7(2), 243–269.

Steuter, E and D Wills (2008). *At War with Metaphor: Media Propaganda and Racism in the War on Terror*. Lanham: Lexington Books.

Wang, JH (王建华) (ed.) (2006). *Xinxi Shidai Baokan Yuyan Genzong Yanjiu* 信息时代 报刊语言跟踪研究 (*Research on Newspaper Language in the Information Age*). Hangzhou: Zhejiang University Press.

Xu, SH (徐盛桓) (2006). "Chengduxiaochituan" de renzhi jiedu "成都小吃团" 的认知解读 (A cognitive study of metaphorical expressions about "Chengdu Food Club"). *Waiguoyu,* 2, 18–24.

Yu, GM (喻国明) (2004). "*Shilun Shouzhong Zhuyili Ziyuan De Huode Yu Weixi: Guanyu Chuanbo Yingxiao De Celue Fenxi*" 试论受众注意力资源的获得与维系: 关于传播营销的策略分析 (*A Tentative Discussion of the Audience's Attention Resources: A Strategic Analysis of Marketing Communication*). <http://www.people.com.cn/GB/14677/22100/26521/26522/2699192.html>, accessed on September 23, 2008.

Yu, GM (喻国明) (2005). *Biange Chuanmei: Jiexi Zhongguo Chuanmeixing Wenti* 变革传媒: 解析中国传媒转型问题 (*Media Revolution: An Analysis of the Transformation of the Chinese Media*). Beijing: Huaxia Press.

Yu, N (2003). Synesthetic metaphor: A cognitive perspective. *Journal of Literary Semantics,* 32(1), 19–34.

Yu, N (2007). Cultural identity and globalization: Multimodal metaphors in a Chinese educational advertisement. *China Media Research,* 3(2), 25–32.

Zhang, MZ (张名章) (2005). *Xinwen Yulehua Xianxiang Tanlun* 新闻娱乐化现象探论 (An discussion on the entertainmentalisation of news), MA thesis, Guangxi University, Guilin.

Zhang, XM (张晓明), HL Hu (胡惠林) and JG Zhang (章建刚) (2005). *2005 Nian: Zhongguo Wenhua Chanye Fazhan Baogao* 2005年: 中国文化产业发展报告 (*2005: Report on Culture Industries in China*). Beijing: Social Sciences Academic Press (China).

Zinken, J (2003). Ideological imagination: Intertextual and correlational metaphors in political discourse. *Discourse & Society,* 14(4), 507–523.

CHAPTER 3

THE USE OF CHINESE DIALECTS ON THE INTERNET: YOUTH LANGUAGE AND LOCAL YOUTH IDENTITY IN URBAN CHINA[1]

JIN LIU

Georgia Institute of Technology, Georgia, USA

This chapter examines recent proliferation of the use of Chinese local dialects on the Internet among the Chinese urban educated youth. With a close analysis of dialect texts parodying the standard Mandarin and the Chinese writing system, so-called standard tests on dialect competence that mimic the formats of the official English exams, and Internet-mediated rap songs rendered in dialects and their hosting websites. This study explores how the Chinese educated youth promote dialect on the Internet to challenge the hegemonic languages, either the standard Mandarin or English, how the conventionally stigmatized dialects have been explored as a fashionable, edgy youth language in China, and how Internet-savvy Chinese youth employ local dialect to articulate a distinct local identity in their negotiation with a dramatically globalizing culture.

---

[1] This chapter is based on a paper originally published in the volume *Vallah, Gurkensalat 4U & me! Youth Language in the Study of Youth Language*, JN Jørgensen (ed.), pp. 99–112. Frankfurt: Peter Lang (2010). Here is the revised and updated version.

1. Introduction

Generally speaking, there are seven major local-language or dialect (*fangyan* 方言, regional speech)[2] groups in China: Mandarin, Wu, Min, Cantonese, Gan, Xiang, and Hakka. These dialects have been a fundamental feature for the Chinese people's daily life and popular culture. But for years, the central government in Mainland China has been promoting the standard Chinese (*Putonghua* 普通话, common speech), as the official national language, the principal language for mass media and school education. The subnational, non-standard local dialects have been thus subordinated and suppressed in this project of building a modern national culture, but they have never disappeared. Particularly in recent years, there is a resurgence of the use of dialects in mass media. Among others, the Internet plays an increasingly prominent role in promoting and disseminating the use of dialects among the Chinese urban educated youth.

Ever since its introduction to China in the early 1990s, the Internet has been passionately embraced by Chinese youth. According to a recent state-sponsored study dated in January 2010 by China Internet Network Information Center (CNNIC), more than 70% of the Internet users (384 million) are young people under 35 years, and the age group between 18 and 24 years old has consistently accounted for a much higher portion (usually 35%–42% between 2000 and 2009) than any other age groups. Regarding their level of education, approximately half of the users had a college or associate degree by 2007, and those who only have high school diplomas have increased rapidly in the past two years (39.4% in 2008 and 40.2% in 2009). Roughly one-third of China's netizens are currently students, and the incidence of Internet use in urban areas is 6.5 times greater than in rural areas. Therefore, Internet users compose a distinct urban youth culture in China.

This chapter first traces back the arguably first Chinese Internet-mediated song, Xue Cun's "The Northeasterners are All Living Lei Fengs" (2001) rendered in Northeastern Mandarin. The university-educated youth's appreciation and promotion of local languages and noninstitutional knowledge in

---

[2] The controversy over the relationship between dialect and language is a global and often politicized problem. This chapter mainly uses the term of "dialect" for the Chinese *fangyan*. For a historical study of standard languages and dialects in the context of nation building, see Hobsbawm (1992, pp. 51–63). For the terminological dilemma faced in the Chinese linguistic situation, see DeFrancis (1984, pp. 55–57).

the context of globalization is examined. As both the global English and the national standard Mandarin are more identified with homogenization and centralization, local-dialect texts celebrate the value of pluralism and diversity. This is further demonstrated in the various dialect renditions of a single Mandarin text and the deviant written representation of dialect with the Chinese characters. The so-called standard tests on dialect competence that mimic the formats of the official English exams are further examined. Rather than dismissing these tests as meaningless entertainment, it is argued that in fashioning a test that appears official, the young, educated authors of these exams seem to esteem the colloquial, oral dialects as conduits of knowledge that have been neglected by and excluded from the formal education yet deserves equal value as the standard Mandarin and English. Finally with the emergence of the Chinese dialect rap songs, which was made possible by the Internet, I explore how the conventionally stigmatized dialects have been transvalued as a fashionable, edgy youth language in China. Taking Shanghai Rap and the hosting SHN website as a case study, I discuss how the Shanghai youth employ Shanghai Wu and sometimes switch codes to Mandarin and/or English to construct a distinct, priviledged Shanghainese identity. The bilingual or multilingual competence that mediates the inadequacies of either language is earning them a distinct identity from those who define themselves either through one language/dialect or through a multilingual ability with combination of other languages. In the context of the global/local dialectical dynamic, on one hand, the urban youth draw on locally embedded knowledge and resources to construct a distinct local youth identity. On the other hand, this local identity is articulated by making paradoxical use of globally synchronized music resources and the Internet technology; hence, localities so constructed are simultaneously associated with a global, cosmopolitan subjectivity.

2. The Educated Youth's Promotion of Dialects on the Internet

2.1. *Xue Cun's internet song in Northeastern Mandarin*

The Chinese urban educated youth's promotion of dialects on the Internet can be traced to Xue Cun's (雪村's) Internet song (*wangluo gequ* 网络歌曲), "The Northeasterners are All Living Lei Fengs" 东北人都是活雷锋 (*Dongbeiren doushi huo Lei Feng*)[3] in 2001. This song, with a distinctive Northeastern spin, aided by Flash-animation cyber-technology, arguably became the first widely circulated Chinese online song. The song eulogizes the good deeds of the Northeasterners through a synecdochic substitution of an ordinary working-class or peasant Northeasterner for their entire population. In a basic, mostly repetitive diatonic melody, the 75 second song tells a simple story: Mr Zhang drives to the Northeast and gets injured in a car accident. The driver who causes the accident flees the scene. Fortunately a Northeasterner helps out by sending Mr Zhang to the hospital. After recovering, Mr Zhang invites the Northeasterner for an appreciation dinner, and the Northeasterner "says":

俺们那旮都是东北人/俺们那旮特产高丽参/俺们那旮猪肉炖粉条/俺们那旮都是活雷锋/俺们那旮没有这种人/撞了车哪能不救人/俺们那旮山上有真蘑/这个人他不是东北人!
Anmen neiga dou si dongbeiyin/anmen neiga tecan gaolicen/anmen neiga zuyou dun fentiao/anmen neiga dou si huo leifen'r/anmen neiga meiyou zeizong yin/zuang le ce naneng bu jiuyin/anmen neiga sansang you zengmo/zeigeyin ta busi dongbeiyin!
"We are all Northeasterners. The regional specialty in our place is the Korean ginseng, and pork stewed with bean noodle. We are all living Lei Fengs. In our place, we do not have such a person. How can someone not help the injured after causing the accident? Fungus mushrooms grow in our place on the hills. That man is not a Northeasterner!"

In the song, typical Northeast Mandarin pronunciations, such as *ren* (person) as *yin* and *zhurou* (pork) as *zuyou*, are integrated with the use of characteristic Northeast Mandarin words such as *anmen neiga* (our place), words for well-known regional specialties such as *gaolisen* (Korean ginseng), and words for the local cuisine *zuyou dun fentiao* (pork stewed with bean noodle).

The Internet played a key role in making the song a national hit. The singer-songwriter Xue Cun, a dropout from Peking University (PKU), wrote

---

[3] In this chapter, the Pinyin Romanization system is used to transcribe standard Mandarin and northern Mandarin dialects vocabulary. For southern dialects such as Shanghai Wu, Hangzhou Wu, and Zhangjiagang Wu, the romanization appearing in this chapter are mainly based on the corresponding dialect dictionaries, which usually adopt the International Phonetic Alphabet (IPA) system.

the song as early as 1995, but it was easily dismissed by the record companies at the time. In 2001, a PKU alumnus Liu Lifeng, 刘立丰, among others, made a quirky Flash animation and uploaded it to a PKU-hosted website, http://newyouth.beida-online.com, which soon became the major source for the song's dissemination among PKU alumni and peer college students, including overseas diasporic students. In 2002, Ying Da, 英达, also a PKU alumnus, adopted the song as the theme for his popular Northeast Mandarin sitcom *Dongbei yijiaren* 东北一家人 (*A family in the Northeast*, 2002), which revolves around a working-class family's everyday life in the Northeast. Thus in 2003, the song's final soliloquy "Cuihua, get me pickles" 翠花, 上酸菜 (*Chuihua'r, shang shuaichai*) ranked among the top three catchiest expressions among Chinese youth in a survey (Chen and Yang, 2003).

As this chronology of the song's success clearly shows, the song, although written by a college dropout, was first appreciated and promoted by university-educated youth, particularly those cultural elites from the most prestigious universities, such as PKU. These cultural elites already have a good command of the standard Mandarin and, most of the time, of English. Their (re-)appreciation of noninstitutional knowledge that lies beyond the scope of their formal education, for example, knowledge of local language, and indigenous regional culture, cannot be understood without the context of globalization.

2.2. *A reaction to the global English and the national Mandarin*

In his article "Dialect in the age of the Internet" 网络时代的方言 (Wangluo shidai de fangyan), the writer, Li Rui 李锐, expresses great consternation that the Internet would encourage the global dominance of hegemonic English to the point that all other languages, including standard Chinese, would be marginalized as local dialects and face the fate of elimination. He cites Han Shaogong's (韩少功's) critically acclaimed novel *Maqiao Cidian* 马桥词典 (*Dictionary of Maqiao*) as an admirable effort to demonstrate the complexity, richness, and liveliness of Chinese local dialects and cultures, "which are hardly substituted for by the standard *Putonghua* Mandarin, nor can they be expressed by the English formatted computer" (Li, 2000, p. 47). In spite of Li's self-admitted reservations about new technology, as a member of the cultural elite, he acutely senses the contemporary significance of dialects. As he voices out, "In such an age of the Internet, under such circumstances, resisting formatting, resisting the hegemonic control of the language of the centre, insisting on the independence of local dialect, and re-examining the value and significance of local dialect, and appealing for and establishing the equality of languages are issues unavoidable not only for literature but also for every person" (*ibid.*, p. 44).

Tacitly implementing Li's insights, the younger techno-savvy cultural elite challenge the hegemonic, homogenizing languages, either standard Mandarin or English, on the Internet. In an entertaining way that Li could not have anticipated, the young people draw on the dialects as unexpected, unpredictable, refreshing sources of popular youth culture. The laughter generated by local language texts helps, on the one hand, to undermine the institution of formal education, where standard Mandarin as well as English is generally acquired, and, on the other hand, to celebrate the distinct local identity of the urban youth — in both ways serving to undercut the globalization the Internet paradoxically functions at the same time.

2.3. *Signifying pluralism and diversity in dialect-rendered texts*

In 2001, the most memorable line of the Hong Kong comedian Zhou Xingchi 周星驰 (Steven Chow)'s hit film *Dahua Xiyou* 大话西游 (A Chinese Odyssey, 1995), beginning with "there used to be a genuine love in front of me," was rendered into more than 20 Chinese dialects on the Internet.[4] The various dialect renditions of a single Mandarin text signify the value of pluralism and diversity. Take the word "(the) girl" as an example, "nü haizi" 女孩子 in the standard Mandarin becomes "nü wa" 女娃 in the Shaanxi Mandarin version, "nü xionin" 女小宁 in the Shanghai Wu version, "gui nü" 闺女 in the Tianjin Mandarin version, "mei'r" 妹儿 in the Chongqing Mandarin version, "lü wazi" 驴娃子 in one Sichuan Mandarin version, and "nü zai" 女仔 in the Cantonese version. In a similar vein, a short text "A mouse gets drunk" 一个老鼠醉了 (*yige laoshu zuile*) written in the standard Mandarin was reworked in more than 50 local dialects in 2005. The drunken mouse dares to challenge a cat in the various local distinct gang argots and street slang denoting hooliganism or chivalry. This is the original text and a Sichuan Mandarin-dubbed version.

---

[4] The original text can be found in Gao's paper in this volume.

今天我就站这儿了，你动动我试试看。别看你个子大，逼急了我直接拿块砖头拍你头上！

"Original text: A mouse drank too much and challenged the cat: I will stand right here today and see what you will do about it. It does not matter how big you are. Mess with me and I will smash a brick on your head if I have to!"

四川话 (A Sichuan Mandarin version): 今天老子就站到这个塌塌了，你热老子搞哈看，莫看你娃娃个头zuai, 把老子热毛老捞起砖头han到你娃娃脑ko镐头！

2.4. *Writing of dialect with Chinese characters on the Internet*[5]

The Internet has proven to be a vehicle to encourage the writings of formerly spoken-only varieties, as studied for vernacular Singapore English (Singlish), colloquial Arabic, and Swiss-German dialects (cf. Warschauer, 2002; Warschauer *et al.*, 2002; and Siebenhaar, 2006). The "lack of institutional constraints" and the "triumph of informality" (Androutsopoulos, 2006, p. 429) that characterize Internet communication also encourage the online experimental attempts at the characterization of the Chinese dialect varieties that were traditionally confined to spoken forms. As colloquial in form, largely spoken languages, most Chinese dialect varieties have no corresponding written forms. Since the Chinese writing system is traditionally based on northern Mandarin, those whose native dialects are other than Mandarin, have to type in Chinese characters that denote the same or similar phonetic sounds as those of a particular dialect to transcribe that dialect. Take, for example, the lyrics of the Jiangsu Zhangjiagang Wu dialect song "Living Leifeng in the city of Zhangjiagang" (Gangcheng huo Leifeng 港城活雷锋, 2006), a dubbed version of Xue Cun's "Northeasterners are all living Leifengs":

偶里几朗都是港城人/偶里几朗特产拖炉饼/偶里几朗韭菜裹馄饨/偶里几朗都是活雷锋/偶里几朗恩驳里种人/撞了车他哪能不救人/偶里几朗身朗有良心/个只棺材佛是里郎人

---

[5] The author has developed a paper on this topic, "Deviant Writing and Youth Identity: Representation of Dialects with Chinese Characters on the Internet," which appeared in the journal *Chinese Language and Discourse*, 2(1) (2011), pp. 58–79.

"We are all Zhangjiagangers. The regional specialty is the Toulou Pie baked in a double furnace, and wonton stuffed with Chinese chives. We are all living Lei Fengs. We do not have such a person in our place. How can someone not help the injured after causing an accident? Our people have consciences. That man is not a native here."

In this redubbed version, the singer Ye Zhenhong borrowed the *Putonghua* characters 偶里几朗 *oulijilang* for Zhangjiagang words *houlitjilah* (we here), 恩驳 *enbo* for *mbeq* (have no), 里 *li* (mile) for *li* (this), 棺材 *guancai* (coffin) for *kutsai* (that fellow), and 佛 *fo* (Budda) for *və* (no, not). The above mentioned method of phonetic transcription in Chinese characters, coupled with alphabetical spellings and additional explanative notes, is widely practiced by the Internet-savvy youth in their e-chat conversations, BBS postings, blog writing, and other typographical online activities.

Sometimes, young people entertain themselves by playing with the Chinese characters in transcribing the largely oral dialect varieties into written forms. For example, a Shaanxi Mandarin version of Zhou Xingchi's famous monologue is as follows:

曾经右倚份真诚地干情拜灾饿面浅, 饿莫气拯西, 挡饿史气塔地时候, 饿干倒后会. 人师间贼搭地通酷摸锅愚呲. 入过, 伤舔给饿挤灰让饿从来椅回地花, 饿灰对那个女娃奢: 饿哀馁, 入过, 匪要吧这端干情假伤歌椅接先地花, 饿希枉是 …… 椅弯撑!

"There was once an instance of true love set before my eyes, but I did not treasure it. It was not until after this love was gone that I felt regret. The human world contains no greater pain than this. If the heavens were to give me one more chance, I would tell that girl: I love you. And if this love was required a limit, then let it be … 10,000 years!"

In this rendition, the Chinese character is no longer a totality which conventionally integrates both meaning and sound. Rather, the character is deprived of its semantic reference function, and disintegrated only as a phonetic symbol. For example, the characters 椅弯撑 have nothing to do with "chair, bent, or to drive away," but just function as a similar pronunciation notation *yǐwānnián* for the Shaanxi Mandarin pronunciation of "10,000 years." The intentional avoidance of the use of the original characters — 万

年 *yíwànnián* subverts the conventional association of the Chinese characters and their standard Mandarin pronunciations. The aggregation of such superficially nonsensical characters makes sense only when the characters are decoded as a transcription of the phonetics of one identifiable oral dialect or another. When the nonsensical gradually emerges as sensical, pleasure arises.

2.5. *The "standard" tests on dialect competence*

If the playful transcription of dialect somewhat challenges and undermines Chinese writing tradition based on the standard language, the widely circulated online written tests on dialect competence endow the local languages so transmitted with the status and value traditionally reserved for the official language. Mimicking the formats of the authoritative, official English exams CET (College English Test), TOEFL, and GRE, the so-called standard tests on dialects are entitled, for instance, "Quanguo tongyi Tianjinhua dankexing biaozhunhua ceshi kaoshi: siliuji" 全国统一天津话单科性标准化测试考试: 四六级 (The national standard subject test on the Tianjin Mandarin: CET-4 and CET-6) and "Tuofu Changshahua ban kaojuan" 托福长沙话版考卷 (TOEFL test on the Hunan Changsha Xiang).

Obviously demonstrating an excellent grasp of the standard Mandarin, the anonymous college-educated examiners show their professional expertise in the local languages and local knowledge. The examinations test local slang, argot, idioms, and expressions, which demand an essential familiarity with local history, local culture, and local everyday experience. For example, a Shanghai Wu CET-8 test on the old Shanghai Wu words such as 包脚布 (*baojiaobu*, it literally means the stinky cloth wrapped in a woman's bound feet in the pre-modern China, but actually refers to a local pancake for breakfast in Shanghai Wu) and 四马路的女人 (*Simalu de nüren*, it literally means the women in the No. 4 Road, which is actually a nickname for the Fuzhou Road, where the prostitutes were most famous in the old Shanghai), and a Beijing Mandarin CET-4 test on the appropriate setting for the phrase "how much for a beng'r (a game-room token)?" 多少钱一个蹦儿? (*Duoshaoqian yige beng'r?*)

Moreover, some examiners demonstrate their expertise in Chinese linguistics. For example, some questions in a Beijing Mandarin test are related to the rules of the "[er]-suffixed rhymes" (*er hua yun*), a distinct phonetic feature of the Beijing Mandarin. In fashioning a test that appears official, the young, educated authors of these exams seem to esteem the colloquial, oral dialects as conduits of knowledge that have been neglected by and excluded from the formal education yet deserve equal value as the standard Mandarin and English. Furthermore, it is likely that one's competence in the latter two languages is interpreted by this population as an ability inferior to that in the former in at least one way: mastering a dialect often implies a sort of experiential or existential privilege, as it can be rarely acquired in a classroom — as mastery of the standard Mandarin or English quite commonly can.

3. Dialect Rap Songs and Local Youth Identity

In addition to the respect and value the Internet activity confers on Chinese dialects through the symbolic official tests, it also enables avenues of approach between local dialects and the perceived cosmopolitan and fashionable Western-imported musical genre of Rap music or Hip-hop music. The Hip-hop culture, largely consisting of four major elements (rapping, DJing, break-dancing, and graffiti art), allegedly emerged as an ethnic African–American street culture in the South Bronx area of New York in the late 1970s. In the past three decades, rap music, originally annunciated in a strong African–American accent, has gained an international currency, and has been continually re-localized by a global youth culture speaking many different languages.

Although Chinese rap in standard Mandarin predates the Internet, as epitomized in a 1993 album "*Daoban: guoyu RAP zhuanji*" 盗版：国语 RAP 专辑 (Pirated Copy: An Album of Rap in Standard Chinese), the emergence of rap songs performed in the rhythmic patois of Chinese dialects was clearly made possible by the Internet. Since 2001, there have been rap songs blending English and standard Mandarin words with Shanghai Wu, Hangzhou Wu, Suzhou Wu, Wenzhou Wu, Yixing Wu, Jinyun Wu, Changsha Xiang, Hakka, Nanjing Mandarin, Wuhan Mandarin, Beijing Mandarin, Northeastern Mandarin, Sichuan Mandarin, Qingdao Mandarin, Guangzhou Cantonese, and so on.

Most of the rappers are college-educated youth, who are at the same time addicted web surfers. They make songs on home computers with downloaded music software that enables digital sampling. Upon completion of these mostly raw, homemade pieces, they upload them into virtual space. Some major rap-hosting websites or BBS forums are www.hiphop.cn, the "xiha didai" 嘻哈地带 (Hip-hop territory) forum in www.xici.net, www.ent365.com,

The Use of Chinese Dialects on the Internet **69**

Figure 1: The cover of the first Shanghai Rap album, *You sha jiang sha/you sa gang sa* (Say what you gotta say), co-produced by Sony-BMG/Xinsuo Records and Shanghaining.com in 2005. *Courtesy*: SHN website.

www. shiftcn.com, as well as www.shanghaining.com (SHN), which will be elaborated later. Often accompanied by Flash versions, the songs are disseminated among the globally diasporic Chinese youth, particularly those who share the same native dialect. Therefore, the Internet is the major venue for the dialect rap songs' production, circulation, and consumption.

3.1. *Distinctive local sensibilities*

The dialect rap songs are infused with distinctive knowledge and sensibilities which originate from the particular place in which they were acquired. Take three songs as examples.

The Hangzhou-based band *Koushuijuntuan* 口水军团 (Saliva Regiment, 2001–2003), one of the earliest dialect rap bands, had a distinctive Hangzhou spin. Their song titles and the lyrics abound with expressions characteristic of Hangzhou Wu. For instance, the song "Jian'erfan/Jie'r ve-" 贱儿饭 (A mooched meal, 2002), about eating in a restaurant with no intention to pay, is peppered with local gang argots and street slang: *Jie'r ve-* 贱儿饭 (a mooched meal), *bahuangce-* 霸王餐 (a despot's meal [unpaid by force]), *made* 麻袋 (no money in one's pocket), *gaoqinie-se-* 搞七捻三 (mess around), *pie-se-ve-* 鞭

三饭 (to beat someone), and *sesekue-kue-* 色色宽宽 (more than enough). Once Dong Lei 董磊, the lead singer, sent the song over to a local music website (www.livehouse.cn) and in 2002, several networked campus websites based in Hangzhou and the local young fans overwhelmingly raved about it (Zhang, 2005). The song, augmented by these distinctive local expressions, evokes a gangster-like experience grounded in the specific locality, Hangzhou.

By comparison, D-Evil band's "Ji gongjiao" 挤公交 (Squeeze in the packed bus, 2007) in Nanjing Mandarin depicts the more mundane street-life experience of taking the always-packed bus in Nanjing. Besides the use of distinctive Nanjing Mandarin words, the lyrics integrate a range of locally embedded images and sounds; for instance, the recorded voice from the machine for the monthly bus-pass swipe card "shuaka taikuai qing chongshua" 刷卡太快请重刷 (you swiped your card too quickly. Please swipe again); the bus drivers' pet phrase to keep order, "shang yi bu, wang li zou, dai kuai dian biao du menkou" 上一步, 往里走, 带快点别堵门口 (one step up, keep moving, come up faster and do not block the entrance); comments on the local media celebrities who do not have to take the bus, such as Meng Fei 孟飞, the host of the local hit human-interest news show *Nanjing Ling Juli* 南京零距离 (Nanjing at Zero Distance).

In a similar vein, Qingdao MC Sha Zhou's (沙洲's) "Guang Zhanqiao" 逛栈桥 (Hang out in the Zhanqiao port, 2004) narrates in the authentic Qingdao Mandarin his one-day experience of hanging out in the local place of interest, *Zhanqiao* (the loading dock). The lyrics draw on the everyday knowledge gained through living in Qingdao, for example, taking the No. 5 bus to Zhanqiao and spoofing a 2008 Olympics propaganda song "Welcome to Qingdao," the MV of which was shown daily on the local buses. Coupled with the Qingdao Mandarin words *siaomer* 小妹儿 (form of address for a young girl), *siaoge* 小哥 (form of address for a young fellow), and *zhenjingla* 真惊啦 (dame that's surprising), the rap evokes familiarity with everyday life in the local community and offers the local citizens the pleasure of recognition.

3.2. *Strong local identity and the construction of locality in dialect rap*

As much as the rappers construct different urban narratives, they draw on the same essential local knowledge of place. And a fundamental common theme of the dialect raps is the young urbanities' pride in their home cities.

Such pride is conspicuous from the song titles such as Saliva Regiment's "Hangzhou shige hao difang" 杭州是个好地方 (Hangzhou is a good place, 2002/2003), Xiong Jie's "Zai Wuhan" 在武汉 (In Wuhan, 2004), He Wei's "Wenzhou shige hao defang" 温州是个好地方 (Wenzhou is a good place, 2006), and "Jiushijiu ci lian'ai aishang Shanghai" 九十九次恋爱爱上上海 (Love Shanghai 99 times, 2006) sung by a group of Shanghai rappers. In "Hangzhou is a good place," the band proudly enumerates in Hangzhou Wu the local places of interest (West Lake, *Huqingyutang* pharmacy), local cuisine (West Lake Sour Fish), a local specialty (Meijiawu Longjing tea), and local street names (Wulin road).

Furthermore, as *Stokes (1994, p. 3)* points out, "the 'places' constructed through music involve notions of difference and social boundary." In his controversial song "Qingdao bumpkins" 青岛老巴子 (Qingdao Laobazi, 2004), Sha Zhou unabashedly expresses his strong dislike of the peasant workers migrating to Qingdao, using the derogative local words such as *laobazi* 老巴子 (country bumpkins) and *bae biaola* 别彪了 (stop to be a sucker or an idiot). Outspoken on what is going on around him and what he thinks about it, Sha Zhou complains about the urban chaos and moral decline brought by the migrant workers, such as the "salon prostitutes" from the rural Jimo. His offensive personal opinions were expected to arouse heated discussion among local netizens (Qingdao morning news, August 26, 2004). Nevertheless, by setting up social and moral boundaries between the urban and the rural, the rapper constructs his superior identity as a Qingdaonese. Just as he rhymes in the beginning "born in Qingdao, raised in Qingdao, I will contribute something to Qingdao when I grow up."

As much as the locality of Qingdao is constructed by making a distinction between the urban and the rural, a privileged identity as a Shanghainese is articulated through an implicit comparison between Shanghai and the rest larger national community in PZ-FRAN's "Ala Shanghai" 阿拉上海 (Our Shanghai, 2004). Asserting a unique relationship of Shanghai with China, the rapper intones "阿拉是中国的上只角" (We are the upper corner of China). The local expression, *za-tsako/shangzhijiao* 上只角 (upper corner), refers to the fashionable, expensive neighborhoods in the former French Concession in western Shanghai, as contrasted to the "lower corner" that means the lower- or working-class neighborhoods in the vast northern, eastern, and southern districts of the city (Luo and Wu, 1997).

In addition, to defend the good reputation of one's hometown can be a strong motivation for making a rap. For instance, Chen Xu's "Dongbei techan bushi hei shehui" 东北特产不是黑社会 (The Northeast specialty is not underworld) was written in 2004 when he indignantly read a story about a number of non-Northeastern bandits imitating the Northeast Mandarin accent to carry out robbery (Zhao, 2005). The song is therefore identified as being a Northeasterner refuting the stereotype conceived by the non-Northeasterners with a dense use of Northeast Mandarin words, slang, and idioms pronounced in the unique Northeast intonation, such as *laotie* 老铁 (buddy), *kejing'er* 可劲儿 (exert all one's strength), *shuadadao* 耍大刀 (play tricks), *baxia* 扒瞎 (talk nonsense), *xiaoyang'r* 小样儿 (derogatory idiom about a person), *dang shanpao* 当山炮 (treated as a bumpkin), *huzhoubache* 胡诌八扯 (talk nonsense), *yansi huishui de/dasi jiangzui de* 淹死会水的 打死犟嘴的 (drown to death those who can swim. Beat to death those are stubborn), *xiaoshu buxiu bu zhiliu'r/ren bu xiuli genjiujiu'r* 小树不修不直溜 人不修理艮赳赳 (a tree would not be straight without pruning. A person would be arrogant without fixing).

4. The SHN Website and the Shanghai Youth Identity

Chen Leiqing, a Shanghainese who immigrated to the United States when he was 11 years old, founded the SHN website (www.shanghaining.com) in California in July 2003. It soon proved to be very popular among the Shanghai youth all over the world. It had 63,000 registered members by April 2005, and the number increased to 189,000 by April 2007, and to 280,000 by April 2008. Most of the members are self-identified Shanghainese now in Shanghai or in other countries, such as the US, UK, Canada, Germany, Japan, Australia, and Austria.

The motivation to construct a distinct Shanghai identity can be seen to underpin the website's dedicated promotion of Shanghai Rap and Shanghai Wu. As the website introduces itself, "we are the new generation of Shanghai. We represent the new culture of Shanghai. Come chat in our own language [Shanghai Wu], sing with our own music [Rap], and dance to our own rhythm [Hip-hop]." The website's domain name is spelled as *Shanghaining* (Shanghainese), with *ning* from the Shanghai Wu pronunciation (*nin*) rather than that of the Mandarin (*ren*). Engaged in cyber-chatting in Shanghai Wu, the SHN members follow some tacit rules regarding the most frequently used

The Use of Chinese Dialects on the Internet

Figure 2: An example of Shanghaining.com's homepage.
Courtesy: SHN website.

Shanghai Wu words typed with Chinese characters. For example, to replace 我(们) "women" with 阿拉 "ala" for "I" or "we," 什么 "shenme" with 撒额 "sa'e" for "what," 谢谢 "xiexie" with 下下 "xiaxia" for "thanks," 好 "hao" with 灵 "ling" for "good," (上海)人 "(Shanghai) ren" with (上海)宁 "(Shanghai) nin" for "Shanghainese," and 在 "zai" with 了了 "liaoliao" for "be in/at." Moreover, a part of the homepage, 上海闲话 (Shanghai Wu), is devoted to daily exhibition of a Shanghai Wu word with the English and Mandarin translation. According to the founder and CEO Chen Leiqing, each day the website received more than 200 words or expressions from members. They had accumulated a large online base of Shanghai Wu vocabulary in about two years (Xu, 2005).

In sociolinguistics, the standard language, such as the standard Mandarin, is usually perceived as a prestigious variant, which is endowed with certain cultural and symbolic capital; by contrast, the non-standard dialect is often regarded as a stigmatized variant and associated with lack of education. However, critics of the association of prestige with standard language (e.g., Milroy, 1980) argue that prestige is a matter of point of view and may be differentially assigned in diverse speech communities. Here, the notion "covert prestige" is relevant. Trudgill (1972) employs the term to denote the hidden values associated with non-standard working-class speech that has desirable connotations of signaling group solidarity for urban male speakers in Norwich. Coulmas (1997, p. 122) also illustrates, "A youth who adopts vernacular forms in order to maintain solidarity with a group of friends clearly indicates the covert prestige of these features on a local level, even if the same features stigmatize the speaker in a wider, mainstream context such as school."

This certainly holds true for the SHN members who use Shanghai Wu to foster a sense of solidarity and community. Yet, the function of the Internet in enhancing the "covert prestige" the Shanghai Wu and other Chinese dialects would carry is emphasized. As this research suggests, the dialects' compatibility with the advanced Internet technology, such as the Flash animation, and the Western-imported musical genre seems to provide local dialects an opportunity for aesthetic transvaluation — from sounding rustic, vulgar, uncultured, and obsolete to being modern and stylish. No longer facilely associated with the old-fashioned local opera such as *huju* 沪剧 or *huajixi* 滑稽戏 (Shanghai opera), Shanghai Wu is now linked with the most edgy entertainment and cyber culture. As many SHN members and rappers put it, Shanghai Wu sounds "cool" or "in." The local words and expressions have been explored to mark a distinct visual style for the website and its members. For example, on the SHN homepage, the local expression 谈谈山海经 (to chat) indicates its general forum section (which is usually rendered as 论坛 in the standard Mandarin). Regarding the subforum titles, the website adopts 阿拉卖相好伐 (how about your appearance?) rather than 会员照片 (members' photos); 翻翻行头 (to change clothes/dress) rather than 服装时尚 (fashion); 白相自编书 rather than 博客/播客 (members' blogs). Moreover, the monthly beauty competition (选美) is called 嗲囡囡评选, as 囡囡 *noe noe* means "girls" in Shanghai Wu. A street-snapshot competition in 2007 that has been a trend among the Japanese youth since the late 1990s was called 拗潮型, as 拗 *ao* means "make up or strike a pose" in Shanghai Wu. The local dialect has been re-invented as a fashionable youth language to mark a unique youth identity.

This distinct local identity, defined by local dialect, is achieved to a large extent by replacing Mandarin words with Shanghai Wu words. As the prerogatives of the nation-state seem more and more identified with globalization and its concomitant homogenization and uniformity, the standard Mandarin as the national language has become too common, general, and amorphous, and therefore insufficient for the purpose of articulating a distinct identity for young people. The young SHN members keep a deliberate distance from standard Mandarin, thus the Chinese characters on display are defamiliarized and reoriented. Such a website with a strong local flavor sets up a linguistic and cultural boundary that excludes those Chinese who cannot understand Shanghai Wu, but at the same time the website certainly functions as a virtual community for its qualified members all over the world. The SHN members of globally dispersed diasporas celebrate the imagined collective local identity — Shanghaining in their physically confined places.

Nevertheless, however much Shanghai Wu has become a dominant marker of a distinct youth identity for the young Shanghainese, their inadequate and non-standard Shanghai Wu is often a target of criticism from the perspective of formal linguistics.

First, as some linguists illustrate in their online postings (such as www.pkucn.com and www.sinolect.org), the rappers' pronunciations of Shanghai Wu have been heavily influenced by the standard Mandarin. The young Shanghainese can hardly distinguish between the voiceless sound (*qing yin* 清音, like /f/) and the voiced sound (*zhuo yin* 浊音, like /v/), and between the sharp sound (*jian yin* 尖音, like /tsi, ts'i, si/) and the rounded sound (*tuan yin* 团音, like /tɕi, tɕ'i, ɕi/). Many phrase constructions pronounced in Shanghai Wu are actually based on the standard *Putonghua* Mandarin grammar. For instance, "if, suppose" should be rendered as 假使讲 *tɕia sɿka-* rather than 如果 *zɿku*, which is a typical word from the standard Mandarin.

Second, some linguists complain that the young Shanghainese do not know the original characters for some Shanghai Wu words. For example, the standard, original characters for "Shanghai Wu," one of the most frequently used phrases, should be 上海言话 rather than 上海闲话. A linguistic scholar even made another version of the lyrics of a rap based on the supposedly correct characters (www.pkucn.com), while the local press complained that the incorrectly written characters in the rap lyrics posted in the SHN website were just too numerous to list (Wang *et al.*, 2005). As much as the SHN members sometimes intentionally avoid using the original Chinese characters for the local words in order to mark a distinction, the transcription of the dialect is still a big problem for the Shanghai youth and those in other cities alike. Because of the difficulty of transcribing dialect, there are no lyrics printed in the liner notes of the first Shanghai Rap CD (Han, 2005). Those who experiment with writing blogs in local languages confront this problem as well. For instance, the blogger and newspaper writer Lin Yu 林昱 mentioned her struggle to render the colloquial Shanghai Wu with Chinese characters in an article entitled "My thoughts about writing in Shanghai Wu" posted in her blog in 2005 (http://magnovich.spaces.live.com/default.aspx).

Third, Shanghai Wu, like any other local dialects, betrays its limitations and inadequacies as an independent system of communication in the increasingly cosmopolitanized world. From time to time, Mandarin and English expressions have a way of creeping into the rapping, talking, and writing. For example, in a 10-minute clip of the Shanghai Wu talk show "What a World" (Episode 7), you would hear the idioms and vocabulary pronounced in the standard Mandarin such as *shizaibixing* 势在必行 (be imperative under the circumstances), *buchuwosuoliao* 不出我所料 (as I expect), *nüzhonghaojie* 女中豪杰 (a woman of exceptional ability), *baofali* 爆发力 (explosive force), and *ouxiang* 偶像 (idol), as well as the music and Internet terminologies in English such as "rap," "Reggae," "MC," "music," "BBS," "download," and "keep it cool."

Despite all these normative problems, one may argue that the educated youth in Shanghai as well as in other cities in China do not have to completely replace the standard *Putonghua* Mandarin with their native dialects. The local dialects they employ, no matter to what degree impure and nonstandard, exhibit a linguistic edge undeniably possessed by the urban youth. The bilingual or multilingual competence (dialect, standard Mandarin, and maybe English) that mediates the inadequacies of either language is earning them a distinct identity from those who define themselves either through one language/dialect or through a multilingual ability with combination of languages. In the context of the global/local dialectical dynamic, on one hand, the urban youth draw on locally embedded knowledge and resources to construct a distinct local youth identity. On the other hand, this local identity is articulated by making paradoxical use of globally synchronized music resources and the Internet technology; hence, localities so constructed are simultaneously associated with a global, cosmopolitan subjectivity.

References

Androutsopoulos, J (2006). Introduction: Sociolinguistics and computer-mediated communication. *Journal of Sociolinguistics*, 10(4), 419–438.

Chen, S (陈思) and CZ Yang (杨长征) (2003). "*Qingshaonian 'liuxingyu' xianxiang diaocha baogao*" 青少年"流行语"现象调查报告 (Survey report on the youth's catchy expressions). *Zhongguo Qingnian Yanjiu (China Youth Study)*, 2, 55–63.

Coulmas, F (ed.) (1997). *The Handbook of Sociolinguistics*. Oxford, UK and Cambridge, MA: Blackwell.

DeFrancis, J (1984). *The Chinese Language: Fact and Fantasy*, Honolulu: University of Hawaii Press.

Han, L (韩磊) (2005). Huyu shuochang waidazhengzhao jiu fangyan 沪语说唱歪打正着救方言 (Shanghai Rap saves dialect by a fluke). *Xinwen Wanbao (Evening news)*. July 12, 2005.

Han, SG (韩少功) (1996). *Maqiao Cidian* 马桥词典 (*Dictionary of Maqiao*). Shanghai: Shanghai wenyi chubanshe.

Hobsbawm, EJ (1992). *Nations and Nationalism Since 1780: Programme, Myth, Reality*. Cambridge [UK] and New York: Cambridge University Press.

Li, R (李锐) (2000). *Wangluo shidai de fangyan* 网络时代的方言 (Dialect in the age of the Internet). *Dushu (Reading)*, 4, 42–47. Repeated in Li Rui's book (2002) with the same title, *Shenyang: Chunfeng Wenyi*, pp. 30–39.

Luo, XW (罗小未) and J Wu (伍江) (eds.) (1997). *Shanghai Longtang* 上海弄堂. Shanghai: Shanghai renmin meishu chubanshe.

Milroy, L (1980). *Language and Social Networks*. Baltimore: Basil Blackwell.

Siebenhaar, B (2006). Code choice and code-switching in Swiss–German Internet relay chat rooms. *Journal of Sociolinguistics*, 10(4), 481–506.

Stokes, M. (ed.) (1994). *Ethnicity, Identity, and Music: The Musical Construction of Place*. Oxford, UK and Providence, RI: Berg.

Trudgill, P (1972). Sex, covert prestige and linguistic change in the urban British English of Norwich. *Language in Society*, 1, 179–195.

Wang, HJ (王晔菁), L Ma (马磊) and JQ Ren (任佳琦) (2005). Shanghaihua Rap Jiaohao Bu Jiaozuo 上海话 Rap 叫好不叫座 (The Problems in Shanghai Rap). *Shanghai Xingqisan* 上海星期三 (*Shanghai Wednesday*). July 20, 2005.

Warschauer, M (2002). Languages.com: The internet and linguistic pluralism. In *Silicon Literacies: Communication, Innovation and Education in the Electronic Age*, Ilana Snyder (ed.), pp. 62–74. London and New York: Routledge.

Warschauer, M, GR Said and A Zohry (2002). Language choice online: Globalization and identity. *Journal of Computer-Mediated Communication*, 7, 4. <http://jcmc.indiana.edu/vol7/issue4/warschauer.html>, accessed on January 10, 2011.

Xu, JT (2005). Reviving a mother tongue. *Shanghai Star*, March 3, 2005. <http://app1.chinadaily.com.cn/star/2005/0303/cu14-1.html>, accessed on January 10, 2011.

Zhang, L (张磊) (2005). "*Chang Jian'erfan de nageren*" 唱《贱儿饭》的那个人 (with Dong Lei, the person who sang "A mooched meal"). *Hangzhou Daily*, February 26, 2005.

Zhao, YQ (赵宇清) (2005). "Chen Xu: 'Dongbei techan bushi heishehui' wei dongbeiren *zhengming*" 陈旭：《东北特产不是黑社会》为东北人正名. (Chen Xu's "The Northeast specialty is not underground" provides justification for Northeasterners). *Heilongjiang Daily*, March 30, 2005.

CHAPTER 4

"MY TURF, I DECIDE": LINGUISTIC CIRCULATION IN THE EMERGENCE OF A CHINESE YOUTH CULTURE

QING ZHANG and CHEN-CHUN E

University of Arizona, Arizona, USA

This chapter examines the circulation (Spitulnik, 1996) and recontextualization (Bauman and Briggs, 1990) of a Chinese advertisement slogan "*wode dipan, wo zuozhu,*" 我的地盘,我做主 (my turf, I decide), and its variants in the form of "my noun phrase, I decide" in youth online discourse. The slogan was originally created in 2004 by China Mobile to promote its M-Zone mobile phone service, targeting consumers aged between 15 and 25. It has become immensely popular since 2004 along with the hip-hop song "My Turf," created for the advertisement campaign and performed by the Taiwanese pop culture icon Jay Chou. The slogan, the song and Chou's persona project a stance of individuality and rebellion. Over 12,000,000 instances obtained from Google search, including blogs and social-networking websites, demonstrate that the wide circulation of the intertextual series (Hanks, 1986) is facilitated by: (1) the connotations of the word *dipan*, and (2) the productive syntactic structure, i.e., "my noun phrase, I decide." Drawing on Bakhtin's theory of dialogism, we show that the intertextual series index a set of stances that position speakers away from models of traditional Chinese cultural values. The circulation of such stances in youth online discourse mediates the construction of a Chinese youth style that highlights individuality, rebellion, and independence. The intertextual series have become a salient linguistic resource for Chinese youth to take stances in their endeavor to establish their own social space.

1. Introduction

There have been an increasing number of studies on the formation of a new Chinese youth culture within the context of unprecedented social transformations brought about by China's economic reform and globalization (e.g., Chau, 2006; Farrer, 2002; Moore, 2005; Wang, 2005; Yan, 1999). China's youth are found to share behaviors and values that run counter to traditional and pre-reform socialist norms of "well-behaved youth" (Hooper, 1991, p. 267). There has been rising consumerism, materialism, individualism, pursuit of individual rights and independence, and resistance to parents and state authorities. Numerous studies in linguistic anthropology and sociolinguistics have shown that language is an indispensible cultural resource in forging youth identities and styles (e.g., Bailey, 2000; Bucholtz, 1999; Chun, 2009; Mendoza-Denton, 2008; Rampton, 1995; Roth-Gordon, 2007). However, except for Moore's (2005) study on the semantics of the Chinese word for "cool" among college students, little is done on the role of language in the production of Chinese youth culture.

This chapter seeks to contribute to the sociolinguistic study of Chinese youth culture by examining the circulation (Spitulnik, 1996) and recontextualization (Bauman and Briggs, 1990) of a Chinese advertisement slogan "*wode dipan, wo zuozhu*" 我的地盘, 我做主 (my turf, I decide), and its variants in the form of "my noun phrase, I decide" in youth online discourses. As Bucholtz (2002) notes, while popular media can threaten youth cultures as they promote certain ideologies about and to young people, at the same time they provide a source of knowledge and agency for young people. Research has also shown that popular media and consumer culture provide rich resources for youth to construct their own social space (Liechty, 2003; Wang, 2005; Willett, 2008). As shown in our following analysis, Chinese youth online users take up the ad slogan and its variants as a powerful resource for stancetaking. It is argued that the wide circulation of a particular set of stances indexed by the slogan and its variants contribute to the conventionalization and habituation of such stances (Jaffe, 2009) associated with a new Chinese youth style.

2. Theoretical Frameworks

In the following analysis of the ad slogan and its derived variants, we draw on linguistic anthropological and sociolinguistic concepts of dialogism

(Bakhtin, 1981), recontextualization (Bauman and Briggs, 1990), and the linguistic indexing of stances and identities (Ochs, 1992; Jaffe, 2009). Bakhtin's (1981, 1986) theory of dialogism and the related notion of intertextuality, proposed by Julia Kristeva in her poststructuralist work on Bakhtin (Allen, 2000; Bauman, 2005; Tannen, 2007, for more detailed discussion) are drawn on to account for the recurrence and appropriation of the ad slogan in diverse online discourses. Dialogism emphasizes the heteroglossic and dynamic nature of social meaning (or indexicality). According to Bakhtin, language "lives a socially charged life" (Bakhtin, 1981, p. 293). The social meaning of an utterance (written and spoken) is always imbued with other's voices and intentions from its use in the past and anticipates its future uses. Bauman and Briggs (1990) further develop the notion in terms of two linked processes, decontextualization and recontextualization, wherein an existent text is extracted from a prior context and fitted into another. Dialogism emphasizes the socially and historically constituted nature of language and that "society is communicatively constituted through intersubjective discursive practices and the circulation of discourse" (Bauman, 2005, p. 145; see also Spitulnik (1996)). As Coupland notes (2007, p. 114), "speakers often quote or reconstruct the words of other people, and in so doing they can inflect those source voices in various ways, giving them particular identity traits and qualities." In the analysis of the ad slogan, it is demonstrated how it has been recontextualized widely by Chinese youth as a linguistic resource to index a range of stances.

Stance is defined as "a public act by a social actor, achieved dialogically through overt communicative means (language, gesture, and other symbolic forms), through which social actors simultaneously evaluate objects, position subjects (themselves and others), and align with other subjects, with respect to any salient dimension of the sociocultural field" (Du Bois, 2007, p. 163). The analysis shows that the slogan and its variants have been taken up by Chinese youth online users as a powerful resource for stancetaking to align themselves with some and at the same time disassociate themselves with others.

3. The Origin of "My Turf, I Decide" and Its Metapragmatic Typification

The slogan in question, *wo de dipan, wo zuozhu* "my turf, I decide," originates from advertisements created for China Mobile Telecommunication

Corporation's niche marketing to promote its brand *Dong Gan Didai* 动感地带, or M-Zone, with the capital letter M standing for "mobile." The brand was launched in 2003, providing mobile and multimedia services for "fashionable young people" aged between 15 and 25 (China Mobile). The M-Zone website describes the brand as the following (http://10086.cn/mzone/about/):

"动感地带"（M-ZONE）是一种流行文化、一种生活方式；是年轻人的生活自治区！"时尚、好玩、探索"就是M-ZONE人的DNA！… 在我的地盘，只要敢想敢做，有想法，就行动！一切不在话下！没错！我就是M-ZONE人！我讨厌一成不变，痛恨千篇一律。在我这儿没有烦琐的条条框框，只有最新鲜、最炫酷的玩意才入我的法眼！… 我爱探索冒险，爱勇敢尝试。到哪都是我的地盘！

"M-Zone is a type of popular culture, a lifestyle; it is an autonomy zone for young people's lives! 'Trendy, interesting, and exploring' are in the M-Zoner's DNA! … On my turf, as long as I dare to think and act, and if I have an idea, I will take action! Everything will be a cinch! Indeed! I AM an M-Zoner! I hate invariability and repetition. Here where I am, there are no tedious rules and regulations, only those that are the newest and the coolest catch my eyes! … I love to explore and take risks, I love to try audaciously. It is my turf wherever I go!"

It offers its users four privileges: the privilege of low-cost talking and texting fees, the privilege of frequently upgrading cell phones, the privilege of freedom of choice of services, and the privilege of discounts from affiliated businesses and brands (M-Zone). Similar to many products catering to youth consumers in China today, the message of M-Zone's "my turf, I decide" appeals to a general tendency of Chinese youth aspiring toward individual rights, individualism, and independence. Figure 1 from M-Zone's website best illustrates the images of the brand's intended youth consumers. The slogan "my turf, I decide" appears in the upper right corner of the picture.

On April 15, 2003, Zhou Jielun 周杰伦, or Jay Chou, a Taiwanese pop music singer songwriter, became M-Zone's first spokesperson (see Figures 2 and 3). In addition to owning a music company, his entertainment business also expands to act in movies. His first music album *Jay* was released in 2000, which amazed the pop music market with his unique fusion of R&B, rap, classical music, and traditional Chinese musical elements in particular. The

Figure 1: "My turf, I decide."
Source: http://www.m-zone.cn/photo.do?do=Text.findPost&cid=275386&tid=1139800#picdetail

Figure 2: Zhou Jielun.
Source: http://60.28.252.196/cmccls/images/1.0/photo/jay/z-002.jpg

album immediately became a big hit and brought him wide recognition in Chinese-speaking regions, including China, Hong Kong, Malaysia, Taiwan, and Singapore. The term "Chou Style" was created to describe the unique features of his music, blending Chinese and Western styles, cross-genre fusion, and blurry articulation in his singing (Phipps, 2004). His talents, productivity,

Figure 3: Zhou Jielun.
Source: http://60.28.252.196/cmccls/images/1.0/photo/jay/z-006.jpg

unconventional style, and cool look have brought him to an iconic status in pop culture in Southeast Asia (e.g., Drake, 2003). He represents the image of coolness promoted by M-Zone. In 2004, Zhou Jielun produced a hit song Wode Dipan 我的地盘, "My Turf," for M-Zone's advertisement campaign.[1] The very first line of the lyrics, "on my turf, you have to listen to me," immediately asserts an audacious stance that is deviant from the traditional Chinese image of a "*tinghua de haizi*" 听话的孩子, an "obedient kid" who listens to the words of authoritative figures (see more discussion later). The rap song and its music video[2] depict a high school student's desire to pursue happiness, individuality, uniqueness, and his nonchalant and defiant attitude toward conventions and the school authority.[3] Emphasizing "my" and "I," the slogan "my turf, I decide" conspicuously promotes the ideology of individualism as shown in many of M-Zone's advertisements.[4] Such an ideology positions the

---

[1] The song is included in his album *Qi Li Xiang* 七里香, "Seven-mile Fragrance," also translated as "Common Jasmine Orange."

[2] The music video of the song My Turf can be found at http://www.youtube.com.

[3] The lyrics of the song and its English translation are given in the Appendix.

[4] See, for example, M-Zone's television commercial "*Wode* 我的," "My," at http://www.youtube.com/watch?v=yPvgBG1ANn4.

M-Zoners away from a long Chinese tradition of entrenched conformism and collectivism. M-Zone thus promotes a particular set of stances through the commercial images of Zhou Jielun[5] and the ad slogan. Such stances include coolness, individualism, individuality, and defiance and rebellion against authority and conventional norms. They are repeatedly associated with a particular range of youthful "characterological" figures (Agha, 2003) in numerous M-Zone commercials.

As demonstrated in Bucholtz's (2009) study of *güey*, popular media often participate in what Agha (2007) refers to as matepragmatic typification through which linguistic forms are linked to idealized users of specific age, gender, class, and ethnicity. In Bucholtz's study, media representation of the idealized *güey* user is a young, urban, Hispanic, upper-middleclass man. The M-Zone commercials in this case connect the slogan to an idealized "M-Zoner," a cool youth who is urban, hip, cheerful, confident, and individualistic. While the phrase "my turf, I decide" can be potentially uttered by anybody regardless of age to index a general stance of self-determination, the metapragmatic typification regiments its indexical potential to index particular youthful stances that are believed to be cool and attractive. The metapramatic typification achieved through China Mobile's heavy marketing and the popularity of Zhou Jielun has lent tremendous prominence to the ad slogan. Such prominence, according to Spitulnik (1996), creates a detachability or transportability that facilitates the circulation of the media-generated expression.

4. Linguistic Features of the Slogan

In addition to the semiotic prominence imbued in the slogan from the commercial adverting media, two linguistic features of the slogan also facilitate its wide circulation, namely, the word *dipan* 地盘 and the slogan's productive syntactic paradigm. According to Goodwin and Goodwin (1987), the "particularities of wording" plays an essential role in the recurrence of a linguistic unit in the same discourse or across discourses (cited in Tannen, 2007, p. 58). The word *dipan* contributes to the slogan's semiotic saliency and consequently

---

[5] In 2006, four more Taiwanese pop culture celebrities became M-Zone's spokespersons: the girl band S.H.E. and singer Pan Weibo潘玮柏, and Wilber Pan.

its wide circulation. Compared with other Chinese expressions that denote "territory," such as *lingtu* 领土 "territory," *lingyu* 领域 "area," "domain," "territory," *quyu* 区域 "region," "area," *dipan* 地盘 refers to a territory under one's control or sphere of influence, often through rivalry. A common collocation as exemplified in several Chinese dictionaries is *zhengduo dipan* 争夺地盘, "vie for *dipan*." In Chinese (popular) literature, *dipan* is often used in association with characters, such as outlaws and gangsters, and forces that are perceived as anti-establishment, deviant, and nonconformist. The connotations of rivalry and anti-establishment thus add indexical oomph to the slogan. *Wode dipan, wo zuozhu* 我的地盘, 我做主 "my turf, I decide" not only can index self-decision and individualism, characteristics that are shared with the "international youth culture" (Hooper, 1991, p. 267) but it is also an especially effective resource to index disalignment from a deep-rooted image of a *tinghua de* 听话的 — "obedient," literally "listening to the words of someone" — *Chinese* youth who is expected to "listen to the words of" or be obedient to authorities, in both public and private spheres. Hence, the utterance of "*wode dipan wo zuozhu*" 我的地盘, 我做主 contests the familiar mantras that an obedient Chinese youth should adhere to, for instance, *ting dangde hua* 听党的话 "obey the Party," *ting lingdao de hua* 听领导的话 "obey the leadership," *ting laoshi de hua* 听老师的话 "obey the teacher," *ting zhangbei de hua* 听长辈的话 "obey the elders," and last but not least, *ting fumu de hua* 听父母的话 "obey the parents." Such a disalignment affords the slogan an applicability to a wide range of contexts where Chinese youth express their own voices.

In addition, M-Zone has created an extremely mobile or transportable slogan by virtue of its highly productive and repeatable syntactic paradigm, [possessive pronoun + NP, personal pronoun + decide].[6] The original first person possessive pronoun and its corresponding first person personal pronoun can be replaced with second and third person possessive pronouns, and virtually any noun phrase would fit in the paradigm. Hence, compared with the metapragmatic radio discourse segments in Spitulnik's (1996) study, the

---

[6] Tannen (2007, pp. 48–67) observes that repetition may occur along a scale of fixity in form, ranging from precise repetition (exactly the same words) to paraphrase (similar ideas but in different words). In the midway of the scale are cases of repetition with variation, such as a repetition with a single word altered.

M-Zone slogan has an even greater repeatability and more general applicability such that the slogan and its variants are transportable to virtually any contexts. As the following analysis show, the slogan is widely circulated across online contexts and has become a powerful resource for stancetaking among Chinese online youth users.

5. Google Search of "My Turf, I Decide"

Following contentions of Subrahmanyam *et al.* (2009), it is believed that online authors project offline themes to their blogs or cyberspace, which indicates that their online life and offline life are connected. The data for the analysis of the recontextualization and circulation of the slogan were collected by employing the technique of "Google intertextuality" (Bauman, 2005, p. 146), as demonstrated in Hill's (2005) study of *mañana* as an element of mock Spanish. We performed Google searches of the original slogan, *wode dipan, wo zuozhu*, "my turf, I decide," and the text string "*wode *, wo zuozhu*" ("my *, I decide") which searched the variants of the original slogan with a shared syntactic form of "my Noun Phrase, I decide." As shown in Table 1, Google searches with different time ranges demonstrate the impact of Zhou Jielun and his rap song "My Turf" on the wide distribution of the slogan and its variants in the form of "my NP, I decide." The use of the phrase "my turf, I decide" was minimal (12,300 occurrences in Row 1) in the seven-year period

Table 1: Results of Google search based on time periods.

Row number	Phrase searched	Range of time period specified	Search result (entries)
(1)	我的地盘, 我做主 *wode dipan, wo zuozhu* Gloss: my turf, I decide	01/01/1996–04/15/2003 (Zhou Jielun 周杰伦becoming the spokesperson for M-Zone)	12,300
(2)	我的地盘, 我做主 *wode dipan, wo zuozhu* Gloss: my turf, I decide	04/15/2003–05/21/2010 (data collection for this study completed)	2,410,000
(3)	我的*, 我做主 *wode *, wo zuozhu* Gloss: my *, I decide	04/15/2003–05/21/2010	177,000,000

prior to Zhou Jielun becoming the spokesperson for M-Zone (April 15, 2003) when compared with its use over the same time span after (2,410,000 occurrences in Row 2). The slogan has been heavily recontextualized, generating an intertextual series in the form of "my NP, I decide" (or "your NP, you decide") that has grown to an enormous size: 177 million occurrences over the seven-year period from April 15, 2003 to the time when data collection for this study was completed on May 21, 2010. The data discussed in the rest of the chapter are mainly from personal blogs and social networking sites which combine blogs, profiles, music/photo/video-sharing, and guest books, etc. Other sources include online forums, news reports, and commercial websites. Some examples are presented in Table 2.

Table 2: Examples of "My/Your NP, I/You decide."

Category		Example
Titles of blog sites	1	我的地盘，我做主
		wode dipan wo zuozhu
		My turf, I decide
	2	我的博客,我做主
		wode buoke, wo zuozhu
		My blog, I decide
Titles of blog entries/articles	3	我的人生，我做主
		wode rensheng, wo zuozhu
		My life, I decide
	4	我的美丽,我做主
		wode meili, wo zuozhu
		M beauty, I decide
	5	我的青春，我做主
		wode qingchun, wo zuozhu
		My youth, I decide
Titles of online forums	6	我的健康,我做主
		wode jiankang, wo zuozhu
		My health, I decide

(Continued)

Category		Example
Titles of commercial websites	8	你的地板,你做主
		nide diban, ni zuozhu
		Your house-floor, you decide
		(Website for interior design)
	9	你的留学，你做主
		nide liuxue, ni zuozhu
		Your studying-abroad, you decide
	10	你的美丽,你做主
		nide meili, ni zuozhu
		Your beauty, you decide
		(Website for a skin care clinic)
	11	我的王国，我做主
		wode wangguo, wo zuozhu
		My kingdom, I decide
		(Website for online games)

6. Circulation and Recontextualization of the Slogan in Online Discourses

The above Google search results have shown that the slogan and its variants have been circulating widely in the cyberspace, mostly in blogs. When limiting the search category to "blogs," the original slogan alone was found in as many as 579,000 blog entries by May 25, 2010. Examples of titles of personal blogs or online journals include, "My blog, I decide," "My life, I decide," "My emotions, I decide," "My youth, I decision," and so on. As Stern (2008) observes, personal sites such as blogs and home pages provide young people both a space and a stimulus to express themselves, through which they "feel entitled to engage in public address." (2008, p. 104) In this sense, the slogan and its variants are deployed as a linguistic resource by online authors to claim their own space for self-expression and entitlement to self-decision, both of which may be more limited in their offline lives. In our following analysis of the recontextualizations of the slogan, the term "intertextual series" (Hanks, 1986) is used to highlight the interrelatedness between the slogan and its variants. As Bauman and Briggs (1990) point out, the recontextualized linguistic material inevitably carries with it traces from its earlier contexts. Coupland also notes, "speakers often quote or reconstruct the words of other people, and in so doing they can inflect those source voices in various ways, giving them particular identity traits and qualities" (2007, p. 114).

Evidence is found for the intertextuality being part of the users' knowledge as sometimes they explicitly identify Zhou Jielun's song or the M-Zone advertisement slogan as the "source utterance" (Bauman 2004, p. 130). The following is an example from a blog of a college freshman about his first semester, entitled "我的生活，我做主！" "My life, I decide."

(1) 第一学期就在新鲜多彩而又紧张严肃中一晃而过。好的开头是成功的一半，回首留下的足迹，我快乐，我欣喜，我充实，我的生活我做主！……周杰伦的一句"我的地盘，我做主"唤起了每一颗年轻的心。大学更是我们成长的自由天地，每个人的生活更应该由自己当家作主。四年的流金岁月正是我们创造自我价值的黄金时代，振翅高飞吧！活出属于自己的那份精彩！

"The first semester, filled with fresh, diverse as well as nervous, experiences has flown by in the blink of an eye. A good start is halfway to success. Looking back, I feel happy, delighted, and enriched. **My life, I decide!** ... **Zhou Jielun's "my turf I decide"** touches the heart of every young person. College is a land of freedom where **we develop**. **Everyone's life should be decided by themselves**. Four fleeting years in college is indeed the golden time for **us** to create our self-value. Flap your wings and fly high! Live the excitement that belongs to yourself/yourselves!"
Source: http://student.ustb.edu.cn/%5Cpage/life/list.asp?sid=49&id=2397

In the opening paragraph of the blog, the author captures his first semester in college life by recontextualizing the ad slogan in the form of "my life, I decide!" As elaborated in the rest of the blog, this single sentence highlights the first semester of a college freshman's life as a period of developing individuality and independence. In the final paragraph, the author invokes the original slogan. The statement that Zhou Jielun's slogan "touches the heart of every young person" explicitly presupposes a shared knowledge of the source utterance among the author's fellow students. The use of first personal plural pronoun noun "we" and "us" in this paragraph also assumes an alignment from other fellow students. Although in most cases the source utterance is not explicitly acknowledged, the recontextualization of the slogan positions the users in broad alignment with the attributes and attitudes projected through Zhou Jielun 周杰伦 as mentioned earlier (see Jaffe (2009, p. 20)). As a result, the intertextual series connects the users into a community of shared understanding and allows them to relate to other relevant persons and group in particular ways. The following are a few examples where the intertextual series is drawn on to take a stance.

6.1. *Taking a stance of independence and self-determination*

(2) "My life, I decide"
我的人生，我做主！
我想我本来是要按照父母的意思念完大学，有能力呢就考个本校的研究生，不行就在他们的帮助下找一份工作，然后再谈恋爱再结婚生子……可是现在不同了，我要自己计划自己的人生，就算苦一点也没有什么，因为心中有梦有理想所以我什么都不怕。……我不要这样碌碌无为的活着，才不要在父母给画好的图纸上走来走去，我要我自己。也不要像一些女孩子一样把希望寄托在自己的男朋友或未来的老公身上，我就要靠自己。
"My life, I decide!
Originally I thought I was going to follow my parents' plan for me to finish college, take the postgraduate examination if I can, or if I cannot, I will find a job with their help, and then I will go out with someone, get married and have a child. … But now, things are different. **I want to make my own plans for my life**. Even though there may be much hardship, it does not matter. I am not afraid because I have dreams and ideals. … I do not want to lead a vain and humdrum life, **nor do I want to follow the blueprint drawn up by my parents. I want to rely on myself. Also, I do not want to be like other girls who either rely on their boyfriend or future husband. I want to depend on myself.**"
Source: http://blog.readnovel.com/article/htm/tid_415722.html

In this example, the female author declares her decision to pursue her ideals and dreams regardless of possible hardship. In addition, she also firmly articulates her determination to rely on herself to do what she wants to achieve. As suggested by the title of her blog, "My life, I decide," she takes up a stance of independence and self-determination. At the same time she disaligns herself from those who depend on their parents and from women who rely on their romantic partners. The latter are associated with a stereotype of the single-child who is always dependent on others.

Compared with the previous writer, the tone of the blogger in (3) is more confrontational in his plea for freedom and independence from one's parents, especially, the mother. Contemplating the similarity between his own personal experience and that of a main character in a popular television drama entitled "My youth, who decide," the author writes in his blog entry with the title "**My youth, I decide**":

(3) "My youth, I decide"
我的青春，我做主
可是伟大的母亲难道你还想象70年代一样为儿女们安排那些不知道结局生活吗？
现在年代不同了我们都要为自己的青春去努力为自己今后的生活负责，我们已经有为自己今后的生活选择的权利也有这个能力！为什么不能放手让我们自己去独立自己去追求属于我们的感情和生活呢？我感觉伟大父母你们不够理智，不服从你安排的生活就说我们不孝顺不懂事，那什么才是孝顺呢？难道接受你们的安排让我们彼此都或的很痛苦就是孝顺吗？……我们的青春需要我们自己来做主要我们自己来选择，而你们只是需要为我们指导建议而不是强加和干预。致天下伟大的母亲们求你们放手让我们自己来做主，长期在母鹰保护下的雏鹰是很难长大的！我们的青春要我们自己来做主！

"My youth, I decide
But great mother, you still want to arrange your children's lives like in the 1970s? … Time is different now. We all have to strive for our own youth and take responsibility for our lives in the future. **We have the right to make choices for our own lives and we also have the ability to do so! Why cannot you let go of your hand and let us be independent, let us pursue our emotions and lives that belong to us?** I feel that great parents, you are not reasonable enough. If we do not obey the life that you arrange for us, you will say that we do not show filial obedience and that we are not sensible. Then what is filial piety? Is it considered filial piety if we accept your arrangement so that we both live miserably? … **Our youth is supposed to be taken charge of by ourselves and we make our own choices**. You [mothers] only need to offer us advice but not to interfere and impose on us. To the great mothers on earth, please let go of your

hand and let us make decisions by ourselves. There is no way for a young eagle always under the wings of the mother eagle to grow up! **Our youth should be decided by ourselves!**"
Source: http://weixingcheng2008.blog.163.com/blog/static/388271572009438233148/

From the first paragraph of the blog, not shown here, it can be seen that the author may be involved in a romantic relationship that is not approved by his parents, especially his mother. In the second paragraph, translated above, the author emphasizes his independence and the right to self-decision. He juxtaposes independence and self-decision to the traditional Chinese virtue of filial obedience, challenging the assumption that independence and self-decision from a child equates nonfilial obedience. In addition to advocating for independence, he also takes an oppositional stance against parental control, thus showing his defiance against the traditional norm of unconditional filial obedience. Similar to the previous example, the taking up of a stance involves showing the speaker's positioning, that is, alignment and/or disalignment, with relevant others. In this example, by saying that in the 1970s parents arranged their children's lives, the author — who is 25 years old — aligns himself with the other youth readers of his generation, the so-called *baling-hou* 八零后, or the "post-eighties" generation. This alignment is indexed through his use of the first person plural pronoun in the rest of the blog and the final declaration, "our youth should be decided by ourselves!"

It is also shown from the above example that the author is taking a stance of defiance against the traditional value of filial obedience and consequently against the control of one's parents. The slogan and its variants are ready to be used to index such a stance as the indexicality of rebellion again authority is already imbued in the source utterance. The following is another example of this kind.

6.2. *Taking a stance of defiance against authority*

(4) "My turf, I decide"
问题：家里的意见能决定我的自由,我该如何解决？
回答：年轻人有点个性好不好啊 这个是靠你自己去争取的！要努力斗争现在我同你一样 我正在革命努力吧！我 的地盘我做主!!!!!!!!
"Question: My family's opinions constrain my freedom. How can I deal with this situation?

Response: Young person, show some character! You have to strive for your own freedom! You have to fight hard.
Now I am in the same situation as you. **I'm rising in revolt. Make great efforts! My turf, I decide!!!!!!!!"**
Source: http://women.zhishi.sohu.com/question/72930582.html

In (4), from Sogou Q&A website, where people submit questions and others offer opinions or suggestions, the person responding to the question encourages the questioner to fight for his/her freedom, which positions both of them in defiance against their families, presumably their parents. By taking such a stance, the speaker defies the traditional Chinese practice of *xiaoshun* 孝顺, or "filial piety," which highly values deference and obedience to one's parents. "My turf, I decide" at the end of the response not only directly indexes self-decision but also evokes a youthful defiant stance that is carried over from Chou's original slogan. That such a stance is particularly one associated with youth is made clear from the beginning of the response where the responder addresses the questioner as *nianqing ren* 年轻人 "young person." Furthermore, by revealing that she/he is in the same situation as the questioner, the responder aligns her/himself with the latter.

6.3. *Taking a stance of individuality and (bold) self-expression*

(5) "My blog, I decide"

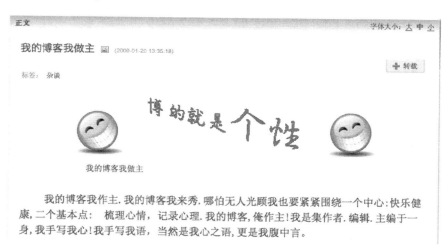

In the above blog page entitled "My blog, I decide," an animated headline reads: **"what is blogged about is individuality."** The author writes:

我的博客我作主。我的博客我来秀。哪怕无人光顾我也要紧紧围绕一个中心：快乐健康⋯我手写我心！我手写我语，当然是我心之语，更是我腹中言。

"**My blog I decide**. In my blog I do the show. Even if nobody visits my blog, I still want to focus on one central theme: happiness and healthiness. ... **I write with my heart! I write in my own words. Of course, these are words from the bottom of my heart.**"
Source: http://blog.sina.com.cn/s/blog_46ee80bb0100boz6.html

6.4. *Taking a stance of individuality and audacity*

6) "My life, I decide"
在家憋闷了1个多星期，终于在发霉前走出家门，跟朋友相聚一刻。 …… 由于都是一些"生活忒无聊，刺激难寻求"的闲人，于是乎，我们决定创建一个富有我们风格的'独特社团'。 …… 勇于拼搏才是我们'新人类'的个性。青春是青涩的，是激情的，是积极的，是无惧的，是狂妄的，是纯粹的，既然我们正身处于这个黄金年龄段，有何畏惧？大胆去追求足以，就算失败又如何，我的人生我做主！

"Staying in the house for a week, I finally went out before turning moldy to get together with some friends. ... Because we are all people who live 'boring lives' and 'avoid seeking excitement', we decide to create a 'unique community' of our own style. ... Daring to go all out is the distinguishing characteristic of us 'neo-tribes.' ... Youth is immature, passionate, active, fearless, impudent, unadulterated. As we are at this golden age period, what are we afraid of? Audaciously pursue (self-) satisfaction. It does not matter if we fail. My life, I decide!" *Source*: http://blog.sina.com.cn/s/blog_69e1b6c00100m7mt.html

In this example, the writer and her friends decide to create a "unique community" of their style. Identifying herself and her friends as belonging to *xin renlei* 新人类, "neo-tribe," she describes the unique characteristics of youth as "immature, passionate, active, fearless, impudent, unadulterated." She is also displaying an audacious attitude. "My life, I decide" at the end recaptures her stance of individuality and audacity. Implicitly, she disassociates herself and her friends from those who are overcautious and indecisive, a stereotype associated with people of older generations.

7. Titles of Commercial Web Pages

The intertextual series has been not only widely used by youth online writers but also taken up by businesses targeting youth consumers. Such cases are illustrated by examples (8)–(11) in Table 2. By using the intertextual series, the businesses position themselves, and by extension, their products, in alignment with youth consumers, projecting themselves as participants of youth culture. At the same time, by using the catchy phrase and its variants, the businesses entice youth consumers to make their own purchasing decisions and promises attractive trendy youthful attributes such as individuality and trendiness through consumption. The following is an example from a website that sells *gexing liwu* 个性礼物 "presents/gifts of individuality," or DIY presents/gifts.

(7) 个性T恤：喜欢什么就印什么；我的T恤我做主
个性时代个性自我，个性T恤印上你喜欢的图案，想怎么印就怎么印，喜欢什么就可以印上什么。我的X　我做主已经成了年轻网友在网络上的口头禅，我的T恤　我做主，我的空间　我做主……
印制有自己独特图案的T恤，让你的T恤不走寻常路，真正的独一无二，其中透露出自己的个性文化又寄托了一种感情的宣誓，让新时代的你避免了"撞衫"的尴尬出现。… 非同网络告别千篇一律，告别时尚个性的禁锢。在追求个性化、自我风格上，可谓不遗余力 …

"**T-shirts of individuality; Print whatever you like; My T-shirts, I decide**
The era of individuality and a self with individuality, T-shirts of individuality are printed with the patterns that you like. Print whatever you want, whatever you like. **My X, I decide has become a catchy phrase among young online friends. My T-shirt, I decide, My space, I decide** …
Print T-shirts with your unique designs, let your T-shirt be out of the ordinary and truly unique. It shows your individuality and is imbued with your

feelings. It enables the new-era you to avoid the embarrassing situation of "clothes clashing" [i.e., accidentally wearing the same garment as another person].... Feitong Web bids farewell to repeated patterns and to confinement of fashionable individuality. **We spare no effort in pursuing individualization and individual styles....**" *Source*: http://www.feitong18.com/

"My T-shirt, I decide" in the title is used to project the youthful stances of individuality and self-decision. The company also explicitly demonstrates that it is in tune with youth culture by displaying knowledge of the intertextual series: "'My X, I decide' has become a catchy phrase among young online friends." The use of the first person pronoun in "my t-shirts, I decide" and addressing the reader with the second person pronoun as the "new-era you" are strategies of synthetic personalization "to give the impression of treating each of the people 'handled' *en masse* as an individual" (Fairclough, 1989, p. 62; see also Talbot (1995)). The intended consumer is constructed as a youth of the "new era" who pursues individuality and independence. The company is projected as the enabler and provider of resources for such youthful pursuits.

8. Conclusion

The enormous size of the intertextual series inspired by M-Zone's slogan "My turf, I decide" demonstrates that it has become a salient semiotic resource for stancetaking among Chinese youth. As shown in the previous examples, a particular set of stances are indexed through recontextualizations of the slogan. These include individuality, independence, opposition against authorities, audacity, and above all, they are *youthful* stances. The intertextual series has become a staple of youth talk and an "emblem" (Agha, 2007, p. 235) to which a set of youthful personae are attached. They allow online users to align themselves with others taking similar stances and disalign with people of older generations, negative stereotypes of their own generation, and entrenched traditional Chinese values, such as collectivism, filial piety, and modesty. Thus, similar to the "public words" investigated in Spitulnik (1996) and the intertextual series of *mañana* in Hill (2005), the intertextual series of "my NP, I decide" have become a salient linguistic resource that can be drawn on for discursive purposes and to mediate community membership. The use of this intertextual series makes one's speech immediately recognizable as "youth talk." Hence, it can be used either by a young person to index his or her alignment with the current youth culture, or by adults, marketers, and corporations to make their speech appealing to a youth audience as demonstrated in example (7). While the stances of individualism, defiance against authorities, and independence displayed by Chinese youth are shared among youth cultures in the context of globalization, the resources — linguistic and nonlinguistic — to index such stances are a creative combination of global as well as local elements. The linguistic resource focused on in this chapter is quintessentially Chinese. Zhou Jielun's song "My Turf," which propels the spread of the intertextual series, is such a combination. The music is a mixture of hip hop and *Gangtai* 港台 pop (see de Kloet (2006)). His commercial images and those of M-Zone's other four spokespersons are also a blend of local and global elements including their clothes and gestures (see, e.g., his hip-hop-influenced clothing style and gesture in Figure 3). It is the bricolaging of the local and global semiotic resources that make the stances trendy and cool for Chinese youths, who, as Wang (2005) describes, are constantly exploring new styles. Finally, the wide circulation of the intertextual series play a crucial role in the conventionalization and habituation of such stances (Jaffe, 2009) associated with a new Chinese youth style.

Appendix

Lyrics of "*Wode Dipan*" 我的地盘 (My Turf) and its English Translation[7]

在我地盘这你就得听我的，
把音乐收割用听觉找快乐，
开始在雕刻我个人的特色，
未来难预测坚持当下的选择。

在我地盘这你就得听我的，
节奏在招惹我跟街舞亲热，
我灌溉原则培养一种独特，
观念不及格其他全部是垃圾。

---

[7] English translation is provided by Qing Zhang.

My Turf, I Decide

用态度扩张地盘到底什么意思怎么一回事?
广场的鸽子占领头版的报纸,
一种全新的解释标题关于这座城市,
关于一种学习考试和年轻就该有的本事,
动感地带的交通标志到底离我有几公尺?
我说老师我是不是真的不懂事?
听我念饶舌歌词欣赏我打拳的样子,
我站在教室练拳方式你的样子线条一致,
隔壁的小姑娘公开表演需要勇气,
别人玩线上游戏我偏耍猴戏。
我用形意猴拳在练习,
引你注意, 如果觉得有趣,
不要吝啬示个好意。
青春是干净的纯白,
像一片绿地的窗外,
我将记忆的门打开,
把所有发生的事记下来。

那弹钢琴的孩子正用他们的手指,
弹奏未来的历史, 我用手机传中文字,
那传输的速度绝对会让你们竖起大拇指,
生活不该有公式, 我可以随性跳芭蕾舞,
照节拍手放开静下来,
像一只天鹅把脚尖掂起来,
讲究快餐的这年代也可以很天真地说爱。

Here on my turf, you have to listen to me,
Harvest the music, use my auditory sense to search for happiness,
Starting to carve out my individuality,
The future is difficult to predict, adhere to the choices at the moment.
Here on my turf, you have to listen to me,
The beats are provoking, I flirt with street dance,
I irrigate my principles, nurturing a kind of uniqueness,
If ideas fail to make the grade [if ideas are not up to date], everything else is garbage.

Using attitudes to expand the turf, what does it really mean? What is going on?
Pigeons in the square occupy the newspaper's front page,
A completely new interpretation of the headline about this city,
Regarding the ability for studying, taking exams and what a youth should have,
How far away is the traffic signal of M-Zone from me?
I say, Teacher, am I really not sensible?
Listen to the lyrics of my rap songs, appreciate the style of my shadowboxing,
I stand in the classroom, your style of shadowboxing is consistent.

The little girl next door needs courage to perform in public,
Others play online games, whereas I play monkey opera,
I practice with monkey-style Shape/Will Boxing,
To catch your attention, if you feel it is interesting,
Do not be stingy, show some fondness.

Youth is clean pure white,
Like a patch of green lawn outside the window,
I open the door to memory,
Record everything that happens.

The kid playing the piano is using his or her fingers,
To play the history of the future,
I use the cell phone to transmit Chinese characters,
The speed of transmission is surely to get your thumbs up,
Life should not have formulas, I can dance ballet at will,
Let go of your hands according to the beat, quite down,
Tiptoe like a swan,
We can innocently talk about love in the fast-food era.

References

Agha, A (2003). The social life of cultural value. *Language & Communication*, 23(3–4), 231–273.

Agah, A (2007). *Language and Social Relations*. Malden, MA: Cambridge University Press.
Allen, G (2000). *Intertextuality*. New York: Routledge.
Bailey, B (2000). Language and negotiation of ethnic/racial identity among Dominican Americans. *Language in Society*, 29(4), 555–582.
Bakhtin, MM (1981). *The Dialogic Imagination: Four Essays*, Michael Holquist (ed.), Caryl Emerson and Michael Holquist) (trans.). Austin, Texas: University of Texas Press.
Bakhtin, MM (1986). *Speech Genres and Other Late Essays*. by Vern W. McGee Austin, (trans.) TX: University of Texas Press.
Bauman, R (2004). *A World of Others' Words: Cross-Cultural Perspectives on Intertextuality*. Malden, MA: Blackwell.
Bauman, R (2005). Commentary: Indirect indexicality, identity, performance: Dialogic observation. *Journal of Linguistic Anthropology*, 15(1), 145–150.
Bauman, R and C Briggs (1990). Poetics and performance as critical perspectives on language and social life. *Annual Review of Anthropology*, 19, 59–88.
Bucholtz, M (1999). "Why be normal?": Language and identity practices in a community of nerd girls. *Language in Society*, 28(2), 203–223.
Bucholtz, M (2002). Youth and cultural practice. *Annual Review of Anthropology*, 31, 525–552.
Bucholtz, M (2009). From style to stance: Gender, interaction, and indexicality in Mexican immigrant youth slang. In *Stance: Sociolinguistic Perspectives*, A Jaffe (ed.), pp. 146–170. Oxford: Oxford University Press.
Chau, YA (2006). Drinking games, karaoke songs, and "yangge" dances: Youth cultural production in rural China. *Ethnology*, 45(2), 161–172.
China Mobile (2005). <http://www.chinamobile.com/en/mainland/products/brands.html>, accessed on September 8, 2005.
Chun, E (2009). Speaking like Asian immigrants: Intersections of accommodation and mocking at a U.S. high school. *Pragmatics*, 19, 17–38.
Coupland, N (2007). *Style: Language Variation and Identity*. Cambridge, U.K.: Cambridge University Press.
de Kloet, J (2006). Sonic sturdiness: The globalization of "Chinese" rock and pop. *Critical Studies in Media Communication*, 22(4), 321–338.
Drake, K (March 3, 2003). Cool Jay. Time Asia. http://www.time.com/time/asia/covers/501030303/story.html, accessed on April 4, 2006.

Du Bois, JW (2007). The stance triangle. In *Stancetaking in Discourse: Subjectivity, Evaluation, Interaction*, R Englebretson (ed.), pp. 139–182. Amsterdam: John Benjamins.

Fairclough, N (1989). *Language and Power*. London: Longman.

Fairclough, N (1995). *Media Discourse*. New York: Edward Arnold.

Farrer, J (2002). *Opening Up: Youth Sex Culture and Market Reform in Shanghai*. Chicago: University of Chicago Press.

Goodwin, MH and C Goodwin (1987). Children's arguing. In *Language, Gender, and Sex in Comparative Perspective*, S Philips, S Steele and C Tanz (eds.), pp. 200–248. New York: Cambridge University Press.

Hanks, W (1986). Authenticity and ambivalence in the text: A colonial Maya case. *American Ethnologist*, 13(4), 721–744.

Hill, J (2005). Intertextuality as source and evidence for indirect indexical meanings. *Journal of Linguistic Anthropology*, 15(1), 113–124.

Hooper, B (1991). Chinese youth: The nineties generation. *Current History*, 90(557), 264–269.

Jaffe, A (2009). Introduction: The sociolinguistic of stance. In *Stance: Sociolinguistic Perspectives*, A Jaffe (ed.), pp. 3–28. Oxford: Oxford University Press.

Liechty, M (2003). *Suitably Modern: Making Middle-Class Culture in a New Consumer Society*. Princeton: Princeton University Press.

Mendoza-Denton, N (2008). *Homegirls: Language and Cultural Practice among Latina Youth Gangs*. Malden, MA: Blackwell.

M-Zone. <http://www.sc.chinamobile.com/mzone/profile/>, accessed on September 8, 2010.

Moore, R (2005). Generation Ku: Individualism and China's millennial youth. *Ethnology*, 44(4), 357–376.

Ochs, E (1992). Indexing gender. In *Rethinking Context: Language as an Interactive Phenomenon*, A Duranti and C Goodwin (eds.), pp. 335–358. Cambridge: Cambridge University Press.

Phipps, G (2004). CD reviews (August 29, 2004). *Taipei Times*. <http://www.taipeitimes.com/News/feat/archives/2004/08/29/2003200785>, accessed on May 21, 2010.

Rampton, B (1995). *Cross: Language and Ethnicity among Adolescents*. London: Longman.

Roth-Gordon, J (2007). Youth, slang, and pragmatic expressions: Examples from Brazilian Portuguese. *Journal of Sociolinguistics*, 11(3), 322–345.

Spitulnik, D (1996). The social circulation of media discourse and the mediation of media discourse and the mediation of communities. *Journal of Linguistic Anthropology*, 6(2), 161–187.

Stern, S (2008). Producing sites, exploring identities: Youth online authorship. In *Youth, Identity, and Digital Media*, D Buckingham (ed.), pp. 95–118. Cambridge, MA: The MIT Press.

Subrahmanyam, K, E Garcia, LS Harsono, J Li and L Lipana (2009). In their words: Connecting online weblogs to developmental processes. *British Journal of Developmental Psychology*, 27, 219–245.

Talbot, M (1995). A synthetic sisterhood: False friends in a teenage magazine. In *Gender Articulated: Language and the Socially Constructed Self*, K Hall and M Bucholtz (eds.), pp. 169–182. New York: Routledge.

Tannen, D (2007). *Talking Voices*, 2nd Ed. New York: Cambridge University Press.

Wang, J (2005). Youth culture, music, and cell phone branding in China. *Global Media and Communication*, 1(2), pp. 185–201.

Willett, R (2008). Consumer citizens online: Structure, agency, and gender in online Participation. In *Youth, Identity, and Digital Media*, D Buckingham (ed.), pp. 49–70. Cambridge, MA: The MIT Press.

Yan, Y (1999). Rural youth and youth culture in north China. *Culture, Medicine, and Psychiatry*, 23, 75–97.

CHAPTER 5

CHINESE VIA ENGLISH: A CASE STUDY OF "LETTERED-WORDS" AS A WAY OF INTEGRATION INTO GLOBAL COMMUNICATION

KSENIA KOZHA

Institute of Oriental Studies, Russia

The so-called "lettered words" 字母词 *zimuci* are a significant part of Modern Chinese vocabulary. Lettered words are foreign words and their abbreviations, spelled in Modern Chinese texts with foreign alphabets' letters. There are also abbreviations of Chinese words transcribed in pinyin, and a variety of their combinations with Chinese characters. This kind of graphic blend, which is evident in the Chinese language today, is actually a surface representation of integral phonological and morphological processes. This indicates a series of transformations in Chinese native speakers' perception of what a written sign is: how it corresponds to the phonetic and semantic appearance of a word; how it assists Chinese native speakers in expressing themselves in the most updated manner and in due correspondence with the native language's typological and logical nature. These phenomena are analyzed in the chapter in terms of linguistic integration: phonetic, morphological, and communicative. This analysis, along with the supporting examples, is aimed at better understanding the origins of the topic proposed, its scale and spread degree.

1. Introduction

> "The biggest potential setback to English as a global language, it has been said with more than a little irony, would have taken place a generation ago — if Bill Gates had grown up speaking Chinese."
>
> (David Crystal, 1997, p. 112)

The globalization processes and phenomena are naturally reflected by languages the people speak. What we witness today is not only the great influence cultures have on one another but also a new turn in the development of communicative forms. Changes can be seen both in our everyday conversations and in deep layers of our language structures.

Pondering upon the linguistic projection of globalization, we will hardly evade speaking of the English language's worldwide presence as the key factor, influencing contemporary linguistic climate on the planet.

David Crystal, the author of *English as a Global Language* (1997), reports that 85% of international organizations make official use of English, at least 85% of the world's film market is in English, and about 90% of published articles are written in English. Du Hui point out that "more than 80% of all scientific papers are first published in English and over half of the world's technical and scientific periodicals are in English. Furthermore, five of the largest broadcasters in the world (CBS, NBC, ABC, BBC and CBC) reach a potential audience of about 300 million people through English broadcasts. In addition, computer software and manuals are often supplied only in English, 85% of the international telephone conversations are conducted in English, and English is the language of medicine, electronics, space and the Olympics" (Du, 2001, p. 130).

Meantime, national languages continue to exist and develop, adapting to new communicative circumstances and providing linguists with new existential data on languages' contacts, change, and future. Special attention has been paid recently to the perspectives of English interference with morphologically, syntactically, and phonetically distinct languages. A number of scientific quests have been taken in search of the most updated knowledge about local languages' lexical store uploading, their word compounding innovations, and phonetic and grammar development in times of globalization.

Being part of this general trend, this chapter is focused on global English in what could be called "a narrower interpretation," i.e., on global English in a local environment. We will try to point out some peculiar ways of dealing with challenges of modernity through the circumstance of the modern Chinese.

The "Speak English" boom that has been evident in China in recent decades resulted in an overall increase in the number of people who are able to read, write, and communicate in English, i.e., to go outside conversational boundaries and to join the global communicative network.

To keep up with the times, native speakers, who are forced to acquire rapidly distributed knowledge of new technical facilities or mental know-how, are at the same time naturally acquiring new linguistic means to express themselves relevantly in their mother tongue. What could be regarded as a quite natural course of events for many European languages, most of which emerged out of tight linguistic interactions, has, actually, not been so natural for the Chinese language up till recent times:

> "The historical events in modern times prompted reform-minded scholars, educators, and politicians to take a critical examination of the Chinese language in close connection with the social, political, economic, educational, and cultural aspects of the country, and at the same time created a society that was more receptive to changes and innovations initiated into the language" (Chen, 1999, p. 202).

And, of course, there is the Internet, which, as it is widely admitted today, has produced a new communicative reality, or rather *virtuality*, within a couple of recent decades. The language of the Internet in any country, and China is not an exception, is flooded with foreign terms, abbreviations or set expressions — most of them loaned from English or produced under its influence, inductively.

The most common feature shared by Asian languages, borrowing from "global vocabulary," is the use of English words in everyday conversations of non-English native speakers.

The following examples have been picked up from popular TV series/TV dramas, both Chinese and Korean; the latter translated into Chinese subtitles. These onscreen replicas are read and understood by a huge audience of TV-dramas' spectators in China:

> 就在这儿 Thank You 吧!
> "Well, right here to say thank you!"

你不 PASS, 她PASS.
"You cannot pass [in the night club], she can pass"

我跟他要组个BAND.
"I am going to organize a band with him"

不是EVERYBODY HAPPY吗?
"Isn't everybody happy?"

咱们开始PARTY吧!
"Let's begin our party!"

What is so striking about all these examples, seeming quite common in a pure conversational sense? Most probably, it is a *Chinese–English graphic blend* — a mix of Chinese characters and English letters, appearing in the same lines of text as natural components of a single utterance.

If we look deeper in order to find the origins of the phenomenon, we will see that this graphic blend is, actually, a surface representation of integral phonological and morphological processes. The fact that such a synthesis of scripts is possible, and that, moreover, lots of alphabetic words are not loans, but originate in Chinese, indicates that a certain transformation has taken place in Chinese native speakers' perception of what a written sign is, and how it corresponds to phonetic and semantic appearance of a word.

2. Lettered-Words as Transfer Factor

The so-called "lettered-words," or *zimuci* 字母词 in Chinese, are a significant part of Modern Chinese vocabulary. Lettered words are foreign words and their abbreviations, spelled in Modern Chinese texts with foreign alphabets' letters and not with Chinese original characters (Liu, 1994, p. 21; Markina, 2007, p. 121). This is how this phenomenon appears in magazines, newspapers, on websites, and on TV screens:

(a) pure loans: a number of loaned abbreviations or nonabbreviated words, used by Chinese native speakers in their original English writing:
WTO — World Trade Organization;

ATM — automatic transfer machine;
kiss, call, ball, smile, etc.

(b) lettered words (both abbreviated and not) in combination with Chinese hieroglyphic components. According to Chinese linguistic terminology, such words are normally called *hunxuer* 混血儿 "metis-words" or "blend-words":

三G手机 "the third generation mobile phones" (三 san "three," G "generation," 手机 *shouji* "cell phone");
TV族 "generation, grown-up after the invention of television" (TV "television," 族 *zu* "kin, race, group");
call台 "informational phone service" (to call + 台 *tai* "counter, bar"), etc.;

A number of Chinese lettered words is created in China and based on the Chinese official phonetic alphabet *pinyin* (拼音). Most of them are abbreviations:

GB — 国家标准 guojia biaozhun "state standard";
PSC — 普通话水平测试 Putonghua shuiping ceshi "*Putonghua* (the standard Mandarin) skill tests";
YM — 圆满 *yuanman* "completely successful" (Internet word);
FB — 腐败 *fubai* "to spend time eating, drinking, and having fun" (*Internet word*, originally means "corruption," etc.)

The formation of lettered words based on the *pinyin* alphabet in Chinese, as well as their independent functioning in the language, is the direct consequence of the broad popularization of *pinyin* in the territory of China, aimed at standardization of the *Putonghua* pronunciation norms in the multidialect society.

Appearance of foreign lettered words and abbreviations in the Chinese context is naturally linked with the increasing role of English in contemporary Asian society, which became especially evident during the preparations for the Beijing Olympic Games in 2008.

2.1. *Why lettered words?*

Why have they been chosen as the present study case? The arguments in favor of this choice are all to do with the specific nature of the phenomenon, which appears to be a clear demonstration of both new global trends in communicative forms' development and of their natural reflection in the course of the development of Modern Chinese.

Graphic appearance in letters distinguishes lettered-loans from those of earlier times, borrowed with the use of traditional writing, i.e., in characters. For instance, "golf" appeared as 高尔夫 *gao'erfu* in Chinese, "chocolate" appeared as 巧克力 *qiaokeli*, and "shopping" appears as 烧瓶 *shaoping* on the Chinese web today.

Emergence of *pinyin*-lettered words, originated in Chinese, demonstrates that changes affect basic principles of Chinese words graphic representation, and lexical structure modifications.

In retrospect, there have been no precedents for such massive circulations of lettered-words in a hieroglyphic language's history. This implies necessity of further linguistic inquiry into surface displays of this interference, as well as deeper analysis of its consequences for the Chinese language's development.

Lettered-words in Chinese have been studied recently by a number of Chinese linguists: Liu (1994, 2001), Jia (2000), Dejing (2001), Jianmei (2002), Hu (2002), Yuan (2002), Zezhi and Pu (2005); by American researcher Hansell (1989, 1994); by Russian linguists Skorobogatyh (1998), Solntseva (2002), Markina (2007, 2008).

Detailed linguistic investigations, carried out by these and other authors, fruited a range of precious observations on the problems of loaned items' interference with the Chinese language structure: difficulties of loans phonetic adaptation to the Chinese pronunciation norms; ways and principles of lettered-words classification; effects of lettered-element's mass penetration into the Chinese writing system; questions of lettered-words vocabulary status.

Nevertheless, it has to be admitted that the lettered-words phenomenon has not yet been examined at a wider theoretical angle and there still remain fascinating questions to explore: what is it so specific about the mechanism of the two languages' (Chinese and English) increasing interaction? What do the crucial marks of this interaction indicate? Is the Chinese words' new appearance in letters a real instrument for the Chinese language's integration into worldwide communicative network, or is it just a compromise to keep a linguistic balance in situation, where "languages of identity need to be maintained, while access to the emerging global language — widely perceived as a language of opportunity — needs to be guaranteed" (Crystal, 1997, p. 22)?

3. Integration: Its Context and Contents

Integration is normally understood as the intermixing of parts or elements previously segregated. This is often interpreted as process of minor elements joining as a coherent whole. Thus, it could be expected that integration of a certain language or its native speakers into global communicative network happens via a situation when more and more people in a certain country learn English, go abroad, or connect to the Internet. This interpretation may be accepted with a proviso that it is not the only one.

In this chapter, "integration" is interpreted as an *internal bi-vectorial* process that implies integration of new elements with the Chinese language structure, forming a new image of the language, supplying it with new conversational facilities, and, based on replenished phonetic, lexical, and morphological resources, its further integration with the contemporary communicative environment.

Indeed, the process of foreign elements integration into the Chinese language's matrix is double-vectorial.

On the one hand, the Chinese language itself influences loanwords: it is adapting words of foreign origin to its original phonetic and morphological structure, in accordance with its typological nature, which makes it possible to consider new loans to be a legitimate part of the Chinese vocabulary.

On the other hand, massive spring-up of lettered elements, both borrowed and original, is interfering with the language's system, which allows us to regard the process of lettered elements' integration as the main cause for unforeseen metamorphoses at the deeper layers of the Chinese language's structure.

Transformations within the new sphere of loans are of a special linguistic interest, since they are the result of contacts between typologically different languages.

In next several paragraphs, the specifics of lettered-words' functioning on variant levels of the Chinese language's structure, to follow the ways of lettered-elements integration into both verbal and nonverbal communication in Chinese, and to analyze how loaned and newborn vocabulary is used by Chinese native speakers to ensure their full-scale participation in crossborder communicative activities are discussed.

3.1. *Phonetic integration*

As is generally recognized in literature (Gorgoniev *et al.* 1960), among dominant typological features of Chinese, there are its syllabic structure, supersegmental role of tone and morpheme-syllable correspondence. In isolating languages, such as Chinese, syllables coincide with morphemes, a morpheme (or simple word), being associated with a certain meaning, is normally read with a toned syllable, and not with a separate sound.

Being represented in letters, abbreviations are pronounced in syllables, according to the name of each letter they consist of: A [ei], J [dʒei], H [eitʃ], Y [wai], T [tiː], etc. Probably, it is the syllabic structure of lettered abbreviations that makes their penetration into Chinese far easier than acquiring non-abbreviated loans from nonisolating languages (Markina, 2007).

Moreover, an abbreviation is read in syllables, adjoining each other in an agglutinative technique, i.e., with no fusion involved. This enhances the analogy between an abbreviated complex and the Chinese syllable arrangement within polysyllabic structures.

3.1.1. *Phonetic experiment*

Our observations on the lettered-items phonetic assimilation in Chinese have been confirmed by a special field study — phonetic experiment. The study resulted in demonstration of the predominant role of the Chinese pronunciational norms over phonetic invaders — foreign syllables, represented by letters.

What we can positively claim today is that all loaned letters' names (pronounced in syllables) in all possible combinations in Chinese bear tones. This is, evidently, the utmost of the Chinese influence on loaned elements within its phonological system.

The whole range of Modern Standard Chinese tones has been applied in toning syllables of foreign origin by Chinese native speakers involved in the experiment.

Evidently, the presence of tone is tightly bound to a sound segment in Chinese native-speakers' linguistic subconsciousness, just as each syllable is bound with meaning. As Chinese linguist Jia Baoshu notes: "VCD (video compact disk) in Chinese differs from VCD in English with *the tones* it bears."

With this single feature only, this word can already be regarded as assimilated by the Chinese language" (Jia, 2000, p. 79).

At the same time, it should be noted, that not all of the experiment participants read the same syllables with the same tones. Moreover, the study demonstrates that there are disaccords in ways of pronouncing this or that letter name, i.e., syllable, most of them being different from those that can be found among original Chinese sounds or syllabic structures (Markina, 2007).[1]

A significant part of foreign syllables' phonetic invasion is shared by original Chinese *pinyin* abbreviations. Three tendencies in reading *pinyin* words have been revealed:

(a) in accordance with Chinese reading of syllables:
GG [gege] 哥哥 "elder brother";
RPWT [renpin wenti] 人品问题 "a person with some problems/defects in character or morality" (*Internet word*);
BXCM [bingxue congming] 冰雪聪明 "very clever";

(b) in accordance with English reading of *pinyin* letters' names, which is a clear evidence of interference:
HSK (汉语水平考试 *hanyu shuiping kaoshi* "Chinese language standard examination") as [eitʃ]-[es]-[kei];
WSK (外语水平考试 *waiyu shuiping kaoshi* "foreign language standard examination") as [ˈdʌb(ə)ljuː]-[es]-[kei], etc.;

A number of abbreviations, standing simultaneously for an English and Chinese word, allow two possible readings in Chinese:

LG = [laogong] 老公 "husband", or LG = [el dʒi] "Life is Good" (famous brand name and slogan);
FBI [fenbei'ai] 粉悲哀 (= 很悲哀) "very sad"; FBI [ef bi ai] "Federal Bureau of Investigation."

---

[1] Based upon Xiandai Haunyu Cidian (1979), the whole syllabary of Modern Standard Chinese comprises about 420 syllables, if the tonal differentiations are not counted and about 1,300, if they are counted (Cheng, 1999, p. 36).

Examples, shown above, suggest a conclusion: acceptance of lettered-items by the Chinese phonetic system contributes to enriching its phonetic resources, bringing in new sound combinations in new phonetic environments, as well as new syllabic structures, different from the original Chinese structures.

3.2. *Morphological integration*

The key arguments of the next several paragraphs are with the Chinese language's broadening and varying morphological appearance, which becomes more and more complicated with lettered-words integrating into the Chinese grammatical environment, both on morphological and syntactic levels. A great deal of the motivation for this has come from the necessity for Modern Chinese to support its native-speakers' strivings for their full-scale participation in global communication with the language's morphological resources.

Morphological integration of lettered-elements is realized through a peculiar *verbarium* — formation of new compound and derivative *metis*-words or loan-blends, where lettered and hieroglyphic components are combined.

> "The concept of hybridization may be understood both in the broad and in the narrow sense. The former understanding of this term includes all combinations of heterogenous lexical constituents, i.e., native and borrowed root-morphemes and word-formatives in one word, while the latter refers only to such combinations of native and borrowed constituents which involve discoverable foreign model. We adhere to the broader understanding of the concept of hybridization, as it offers complete leisure to investigate the behavior of borrowed constituents, not only as regards the mechanism of their importation and assimilation, but also as regards their word-formatting ability in the borrowing language" (Novotna, 1969).

There are three main ways in which letter-character hybridization is realized in Chinese:

First, new lexical items are formed by means of word composition, in accordance with Chinese basic word-compounding models.

Combining synonymous stems is one of the main word-composing instruments in Chinese: 朋友 *pengyou* "mate + friend" = "friend"; 互相 *huxiang* "each other, mutual + similar, mutual" = "mutually"; 美丽 *meili* "beautiful +

beautiful" = "beautiful"; 欺骗 *qipian* "to cheat + to cheat" = "to cheat", etc. (Dragounov, 1962, pp. 131–132). It is significant, that many lettered-words involved in word compounding processes in Chinese are composed by a similar method, which lays emphasis on their structural correspondence with Chinese original vocabulary, as well as with loans of previous periods:

MBO 管理 "Management by Objectives," where 管理 *guanli* "management" duplicates "M" = "management" in abbreviation;

API 指数 "Air Pollution Index," where 指数 *zhishu* "index" duplicates "I" = "Index" in abbreviation;

HSK 考试 "Chinese Language Standard Examination" 汉语水平考试 *hanyu shuiping kaoshi*, where 考试 *kaoshi* "examination" duplicates "K" *kaoshi* "examination" in abbreviation.

The attributive model is also widely used in compounding new *metis*-words, or blends:

IP 电话 "Internet-phone" = "Internet Protocol" + 电话 *dianhua* "telephone";

VIP 卡 "special guest's card" = "Very Important Person" + 卡 *ka* "card," which is formed by analogy with Chinese 信用卡 *xinyongka* "credit card," 生日卡 *shengri ka* "birthday card," etc.;

W 时代 "wireless generation," where "W" stands for "wireless," and 时代 *shidai* is "generation, or era" in Chinese;

call 台 "call-center, reception" = "to call" + 台 *tai* "counter, bar";

Second, lettered-elements integration is possible by applying Chinese affixes or affix-like formatives (in Novotna's terminology, 1967) to loans, with new derivatives as the result:

E 化 *e-hua* "electronization";

IT 化 "process of information technologies (IT) embedding": 电影IT化 *dianying IT-hua* (equipment of cinematography with IT facilities), 汽车IT化 *qiche IT-hua* (equipment of cars with IT facilities), etc.[2];

IT 界 "the sphere of information technologies," where IT "information technologies" and 界 jie is the Chinese word-formative with general meaning "world, sphere";

SOHO族 "home office workers," where SOHO means "small office/home office," and 族 *zu* is the Chinese word-formative with original meaning "kin, race" and grammaticalized meaning "a group of people";

CtrlCV族 "web-editors," working with web-materials, copying them and pasting with the use of CtrlCV keys.

Moreover, lettered words referring to animate objects appear to be used with the plural suffix 们 *men*, just like Chinese nouns that indicate animate objects:

MBA们 = "Masters of Business Administration";
PR们 "public relations officers"/"permanent residents";
boy们 = "boys";
little boy们 = "little boys";
star们 = "celebrities," there are also "super star 们," etc.

A reverse trend, which does not necessarily refer to lettered-loans only, is that borrowing foreign words comes along with borrowing foreign affixes, which is normally regarded as the utmost degree of languages' interference. One of the consequences is the induced grammaticalization of certain Chinese morphemes, which have never been used as affix-like formatives before.

---

[2] It is interesting the suffix 化 *hua* is again among "rather productive formatives which colligate with borrowed morphemes," as described by Novotna in regard with loan-blended derivatives in Chinese: "expressing the change of state, it corresponds to the English verb-suffixes -ize, -ify or noun-suffixes -ization, -ification" (Novotna, 1969).

For instance, Chinese morpheme 客 *ke* "guest," used in a phonetic loan 黑客 *heike* "hacker," was transformed by analogy with English suffix "-er," in a functional component, meaning "a person, doing something":

朋客 *pengke* "punk";
威客 *weike* "wit-key," "a person, using his wits (phonetic 威 *wei*) to achieve something";
博客 *boke* "blogger," etc.
(Zhang, 2010, p. 107)

Here we arrive to the third display of lettered-loans' morphological adaptation, which refers to new words appearing through conversion, or functional shift. Conversion may be applied to both abbreviated and non-abbreviated loans, which normally results in their verbalization with further morphological integration by means of tense-aspect affixation: -了 le (perfect aspect), -过 guo (iterative aspect), -着 zhe (continuous aspect):

那天,　　我们,　　真的,　　crazy,　　了
natian,　　women,　　zhende,　　crazy,　　le
"We really went completely crazy that day"

昨夜,　　他们,　　卡拉,　　OK,　　了,　　一番
zuoye,　　tamen,　　kala,　　OK,　　le,　　yifan
"They sang karaoke yesterday"
(karaoke is used in verbal function and is adjoined with suffix 了 le — perfect aspect marker; 一番 *yi fan* 'one time/a bit' — momentary aspect marker)

他,　　DCC,　　了,　　一张,　　照片,　　给,　　我
ta,　　DCC,　　le,　　yizhang,　　zhaopian,　　gei,　　wo
"He sent me a photo through DCC (document control center)"
("DCC" abbreviation is verbalized and followed by suffix 了 le)

As the examples show, lettered abbreviations, being compound nouns by definition, may move, by means of conversion, to the class of verbs. This functional shift, affecting abbreviations in Chinese, implies broadening our perception of abbreviations' status as of a class of compound nouns only.

Chinese tense-aspect formatives may also be applied to non-converted lettered-verbs of foreign origin:

她, 时时, call, 着, 我
ta, shishi, call, zhe, wo
"She is calling me all the time"

没人, call, 过, 我
meiren, call, guo, wo
"Nobody has called me"

And again, as in the case with loaning affix-like formatives for Chinese nouns, verbal suffixes may also be borrowed, especially in Net-speech (or the language of the Internet):

大哭ing "crying" = 大哭 *daku* "to cry" + "-ing" (continuous aspect marker in English);
开会ing "having a meeting or conference" = 开会 *kaihui* "to have a meeting or conference" + "-ing";
恋爱ing "Loving" = 恋爱 *lian'ai* "love" + "-ing";
(Zhang, 2010, p. 130)

他吃饭ing "He is eating" (吃饭 *chifan* "to eat");
我上网ed "I went online" (上网 *shangwang* "to go online" + "-ed", past tense suffix in English)

What can be positively claimed today is that the sphere of affixation in Chinese is broadening not only through arranging new lexical items (lettered-loans) with Chinese affixes/affix-like formatives but also by applying loaned affixes to original Chinese stems/morphemes in the process of word-formation.

This type of morphological blend is normally regarded as most complicated stage of the process of borrowing, indicating that the languages' interaction has approached its utmost degree.

The examples above show evidence of morphological assimilation of loaned items, application of a broad variety of integration devices, as well as the fact of the massive spring-up of *pinyin*-words in Chinese, allowing lettered-words to be a legitimate part of Modern Chinese vocabulary. Indeed, as one of Chinese Net-bloggers noticed: 阿Q不再孤独，让我们为他高兴吧! "— A Kiu is not lonely anymore, let us rejoice for him!"³

4. Communicative via Syntactic

In the above paragraphs, the essence of lettered-elements' integration has been interpreted through its phonological and morphological appearances. This analysis, along with the supporting examples, was aimed at better understanding the origins of the topic proposed, its scale and spread degree.

The next step is to elaborate on the phenomenon's verbalization — to see in which communicative forms it is shaped, how it is used in everyday conversations, and to what extent it helps Chinese native speakers to integrate with contemporary communicative society.

These days, any consideration of communication leads inevitably to a consideration of the role of the media. Indeed, development of public relations, the press, broadcasting, the Internet, motion pictures, advertising, etc. has gone far beyond geographic boundaries. To gain a larger audience's attention, media companies have to provide an English version of their paper on the web or English subtitles to their picture on DVD. This, to varying degrees, influences local communicative environments in all countries providing media services to their population, and China is not an exception. At the other end of this vector there are non-English native speakers, faced with the necessity to acquire proficiency in English as means of communication and as part of a successful social image, as well.

The following considerations result from large-scale observation of the Chinese press, advertising and TV dramas, as well as the websites and chatrooms. Lettered-vocabulary appearances in Chinese contexts comes along with lettered-words' syntactic functioning. Analysis of lettered-words' colloquial

---

[3] From 人民网 www.people.com.cn 2002/2/22, editor: 夏爱平 Xia Aiping. 阿Q is the major character of Lu Xun's famous novella *The True Story of Ah Q* (1921). The author of this sentence claims 阿Q to be the first combination of a Chinese character and a letter (a hybrid-word) used in Chinese literature.

representations allows for the determination of their positions within Chinese syntactic structures, which are as follows:

(a) Subject:
年轻, 的, CEO, 比, 前几天, 开心, 了, 许多
nianqing, de, CEO, bi, qianjitian, kaixin, le, uduo
"The Young CEO (Chief Executive Officer) seemed much more cheerful than in the past several days"

当前, 中国, 的 PR们, 必须, 明确 一点:……
dangqian, zhongguo, de PRmen bixu mingque yidian
"At present, Chinese PR-specialists have to realize the following:…"

(b) Predicate:
我, 肯定, 是, 你的, 男朋友!, 我们 kiss 过, 那么, 多次!
wo, kending, shi, nide, nanpengyou, women, kiss-guo, name, duo, ci
"Of course, I am your boyfriend! We kissed so many times!"

公司, 帮, 他, pay, 所有, 的, MBA, 课程
gongsi, bang, ta, pay, suoyou, de, MBA, kecheng
"His company helped him to pay for his MBA (Master of Business Administration) courses"

In this example, the lettered-word is part of the compound verbal predicate, the first part of which is represented with the Chinese verb 帮 *bang* "to help".

(c) Attribute:
By analogy with Chinese original attributes, lettered-words in this syntactic function are normally followed with the attributive marker 的 *de*:

不必, 费心思, 方式, 是, OK, 的, 主人
bubi, feixinsi, fangshi, shi, OK, de, zhuren
"Behind an OK-expression there hides the idea that it is better not to be bothered with anything"

很多, 俱乐部, 都是, lady, free, 的
henduo, julebu, doushi, lady, free, de
"Many clubs are lady free"

Apart from that, lettered-attributes may be combined with Chinese adjectives. For instance, with 很 *hen* "very," such as

很Hi/high
很cool
很Q[4]
很In

Lettered-elements appear to be involved in adjectives comparison degrees paradigm or in peculiar plays on words. This is, for example, a loaned lettered-adjective, used in superlative degree in Chinese:

那里, 是, 年轻, 时代, 最, Hi, 的, 地方
nali, shi, nianqing, shidai, zui, Hi, de, difang
"That is the most popular/trendy/high-class (Hi [hai] = high [hai]) place for young people's meetings"

This is how a lettered-adjective in comparative degree is used in advertising in Hong Kong:

G更
好O
D的

In this example, pinyin letters (initials "G" and "D," and final "O"), partially transcribing Chinese syllables 更 *geng* "even more," 好 *hao* "good" and 的 *de* "attribute marker" correspondingly, are used to form an abbreviation GOD "Goods of Desire" — the name of the shopping mall.

Along with the abovementioned syntactic features, lettered-words appear in combinations with Chinese classifiers (count words), which assign them to different semantic groups of the Chinese original vocabulary. Most of these lettered-loans are functioning in combination with the general objectifying

---

[4] See Professor Victor Mair's blog for more meanings of "Q" in Chinese: http://languagelog.ldc.upenn.edu/nll/?p=2252.

classifier 个 *ge*. However, a wide range of other classifiers is involved in the sphere of the lettered-words' functioning:

他们, 要, 去, 一, 个, Party
tamen, yao, qu, yi, ge, party
3PL + "will" + "to go" + "one" + CL + party
"They are going to a party" (个 *ge* — general counting word for objects)

他, 收到, 了, 一, 封, SMS
ta, shoudao, le, yi, feng, SMS
"he" + "to receive" + PERF + "one" + CL + "SMS"
"He has got one SMS (Short Message Service) [by cell phone]" (封 *feng* — counting word for letters)

第, 一, 台, VCD, 诞生, 在, 中国
di, yi, tai, VCD, dansheng, zai, zhongguo
ORD NUM + "one" + CL + "VCD" + "to be born" + "in" + "China"
"The first VCD appeared in China" (台 *tai* — counting word for flat objects)

450, 位, CEO, 之间...
450, wei, CEO, zhijian
450 + CL + "CEO" + "among"
"Among 450 CEO (Chief Executive Officer) [there are...]" (位 *wei* — counting word for people).

All of this evidence of lettered-items' circulations in the Chinese hieroglyphic context, being representative of the vocabulary, being spontaneously selected, being part of the growing lettered-vocabulary, allows certain estimations on the scale and tempo of Chinese native speakers' comprehension of contemporary communicative instruments.

These instruments are concerned with the use of English as a global communicative medium, and yet, the Chinese language's interface nowadays demonstrates that there is no evident *switch to English* in China, but rather a gradual integration. This integration is realized through Chinese native speakers' intentions to master English as part of one's professional image construction, or as means to express oneself in the most up-to-date or trendy manner, or simply as means of communication when traveling the world or chatting online.

The results of these communicative intentions are naturally reflected in the native language, which produces a variety of neologisms and activates its assimilation resources to react properly.

5. Conclusion

The overall presence of English in the global communicative space may hardly be denied nowadays. Nevertheless, other languages continue to live their own lives, adapting to a new communicative reality. Rapidly growing populations in China and some other countries provide the international communicative society not only with a great number of potential learners of English as a second language but also, and more importantly, with a greater number of native language speakers. Thus, the future of English as a global language still seems rather vague in this everchanging perspective. The present state of affairs might be considered a natural segment in the historical chain of sociolinguistic events:

> "The overwhelming impression must be that the language is alive and well, and that its global future is assured. But linguistic history shows us repeatedly that it is wise to be cautious, when making predictions about future of a language. If, in the Middle Ages, you had dared to predict the death of Latin as the language of education, people would have laughed in your face — as they would, in the eighteen century, if you had suggested that any language other than French could be a future norm of polite society" (Crystal, 1997, p. 113).

Indeed, notwithstanding the fact that the phonetic, morphological, and graphic systems of the two languages — English and Chinese — differ significantly, which shows itself in the specifics of integration of borrowed elements with the original ones, foreign items are widely accepted by the Chinese linguistic environment, as well as by Chinese native speakers, who reproduce borrowings in everyday conversations, produce a broad variety of loan-blends, as well as producing original Chinese *pinyin*-words.

This flexibility of the Chinese language, balanced with its fundamental features dominance (its syllabic structure, isolating syntax, etc.), allows the assumption that loaned elements are assimilated and used by the Chinese language not only as means of its integration with a broader communicative network, but also as a source of new linguistic devices, facilitating the language's development in contemporary course, strengthening its presence on the global linguistic map.

References

Chen, P (1999). *Modern Chinese: History and Sociolinguistics*. Cambridge, U.K.; New York, NY: Cambridge University Press.

Crystal, D (1997). *English as a Global Language*. Cambridge: Cambridge University Press.

Du, H (2001). The globalization of the English language: Reflections on the teaching of English in China. *International Education Journal*, 2(4), 126–133.

Dragounov, A (1962). *Grammaticheskaya Sistema Sovremennogo Kitayskogo Razgovornogo Yazyka (Grammatical System of Modern Spoken Chinese)*. Leningrad: University Press.

Gorgoniev, Y, Y Plam, Y Rozhdestvenskiy, G Serdyuchenko and V Solntsev (1960). Common features of Sino-Tibetan and typologically similar languages of South-East Asia (discussing monosyllabism). In *Proc. XXV World Sinologists Congress*, Moscow.

Jia, BS (贾宝书) (2000). Guanyu gei zimuci zhuyin wenti de yidian sikao yu changshi 关于给字母词注音问题的一点思考与尝试 (Analyzing the problem of lettered-words transcription). *Yuyan Wenzi Shiyong*, (3), 77–79.

Liu, YQ (刘涌泉) (1994). Tantan zimuci 谈谈字母词 (On lettered-words). *Yuwen Jianshe*, (10), 21–24.

Liu, YQ (刘涌泉) (ed.) (2001). *Zimuci Cidian 字母词词典 (The Dictionary of Lettered-words)*. Shanghai: Shanghai Cishu.

Markina, K (2007). Lettered-words in Modern Chinese: Foreigners or fellow citizens? *Asian and African Studies*, 12(1), 121–128.

Novotna, Z (1967). Linguistics factors of the low adaptability of Chinese loan-words to the lexical system of Modern Chinese. *Monumenta Serica*, 26, 103–118.

Novotna, Z (1969). Contributions to the study of loan-words and hybrid words in Modern Chinese. *Archiv Orientalni*, 37, 48–71.

Zhang, YH (张云辉) (2010). *Wangluo Yuyan Yufa Yu Yuyong Yanjiu* 网络语言语法与语用研究 (*Internet Language Grammar and Pragmatic Study*). Shanghai: Xuelin.

Zhang, ZZ (张泽志) and P Zhang (张普) (2005). Several discussions on Chinese letter-word phrases. *Journal of Chinese Language and Computing*, 15(3), 161–171.

CHAPTER 6

LEARNING ENGLISH TO PROMOTE CHINESE — A STUDY OF LI YANG'S CRAZY ENGLISH

AMBER R WOODWARD

Washington University in St. Louis School of Law
University of Pennsylvania, Pennsylvania, USA

English as second language (ESL) mania has swept the Chinese nation, especially for young adults seeking to study and work abroad or accept better-paying positions in foreign companies within China. Urban Chinese students begin English instruction in grade school and must demonstrate proficiency throughout college. Some feel that the push for English endorses Western hegemony or emigration. Others, however, like celebrity ESL mogul Li Yang 李阳, capitalize on the profitable ESL industry and purportedly promote Chinese nationalism, as exemplified in Li's slogan "Conquer English to make China stronger! 征服英语，让祖国更强大!" (*Zhengfu yingyu, rang zuguo geng qiangda*!). Li's "Crazy English" (*Fengkuang Yingyu*, 疯狂英语) method requires confidently and quickly shouting English while blasting techno music or gyrating. The pedagogical gains made through Li's emphasis on properly pronouncing English are dubious, though his insistence on forgoing fear and embracing confidence may be successful in positively transforming students' psyches. Although Li's incorporation of nationalism (and racism) into his Crazy English program may ease anxieties over the disadvantages of English promotion in China, it is uncertain how long these political and hate-inducing messages will be tolerated by the international community or even by the Chinese government.

1. Introduction

English is the current *lingua franca* of the international community. Nations without English as a native language push to promote English as a second language (ESL) in their schools and workplaces in order to compete with economic and diplomatic demands. In China, the ESL movement has boomed over the last decade. According to the official news service Xinhua News Agency, the ESL industry in China profited 300 billion yuan (44 billion USD) in 2010 (Wang, 2010). Of the many ESL outlets, one stands out as the most popular, though highly controversial. The name of the game is Crazy English and its purveyor is Chinese superstar Li Yang. Droves of Chinese citizens buy into Li Yang's unorthodox program to improve their spoken English and combat their personal fears. Li tells his audiences that English is the language of international commerce and foreign affairs, so let us master it and use it to spread the word of the greatness of the *Chinese* language and culture! Crazy English employs gesticulation and shouting exercises to improve pronunciation and confidence. The concrete gains made through these pedagogical techniques are dubious. However, many attest to the gains made in erasing students' fears of losing face and, at the very least, in encouraging students to practice speaking English and challenge the traditional focus on only reading and writing.

In addition to Li Yang's unorthodox English-learning methods, Li spins his Crazy English program in another unique and seemingly ironic way. As a businessman seeking profit, Li emphasizes the importance of learning English, especially focusing on speech, for career enhancement. But in order to quell national insecurities that China's best and brightest will prefer living in the West and leave the motherland permanently, Li declares that learning English will allow Chinese people to spread the word of the greatness of China, as well as make money internationally to strengthen the Chinese economy. He cries out, "One-sixth of the world's population speaks Chinese. Why are we studying English? ... Because we pity [foreigners] for not being able to speak Chinese!" (Osnos, 2008). His nationalist messages also serve to win him favor with the Chinese government, an undoubtedly important connection for a nonofficial who gives mass lectures and discusses politics in a country that forbids such suspicious activity. However, Li Yang's patriotic commentaries often go beyond what would be necessary to meet his goals.

Within his nationalist message, he weaves racist and hate-inciting threads, leading some to question whether Li is a megalomaniac and whether the international community will continue to tolerate his activities.

2. Background

"Li Yang Crazy English" utilizes a highly unconventional method of language learning — a combination of shouting and wild gesticulation — which Li developed to combat his own failures in college English courses. Li's rags-to-riches legend is well known: when Li was young, he was a terribly shy student with nearly failing grades. Li attended Lanzhou University to study mechanical engineering and English, but his achievements remained lower than average (in his first year he failed 13 exams, most of those in English). Embarrassed and frustrated with his record and desiring to remain at the university, Li made a major change to his ineffective study habits and introverted lifestyle. One day, Li went to a park and began reading English aloud. He would shout English passages and class exercises, focusing his vocal energy on trees, light posts, or even the unsuspecting pigeon (Zhan, 2002). The more he practiced and the louder he spoke, the more confident he became. Li found himself practicing everywhere, including rooftops, dormitories, and deserted fields. After using his shout-aloud method of learning English for only three or four months, Li received the second highest score in his class for the mandatory Test for English Major Level 4 (TEM 4) National English Exam (Zhan, 2002; Spaeth, 1999). Li felt inspired to share his unique study techniques with his friends and classmates, giving his first English lecture in Room 201 of a Lanzhou University building (Lee, 1998). Li's career as a speaker of English escalated under his self tutelage; he became a radio disc jockey, TV English advertisement reader, and English news announcer for Guangdong People's Radio, Hong Kong television, and a Guangzhou Canton TV station. In 1994, Li turned his unorthodox language learning method into a profitable enterprise. He established the Li Yang Crazy English Promotion Studio, known as "Li Yang Crazy English."

Li now demonstrates his Crazy English method in mass lectures that he presents across the country. Some compare the lectures to rock concerts, wherein thousands of people congregate in large school auditoriums or open public spaces to watch Li "perform" English on stage. It is estimated that tens of millions of Chinese have attended a lecture or purchased his products. During the lectures, the audience is actively engaged in Li's program, reciting his English slogans and madly waving their limbs in imitation. They clap their hands and stomp their feet to rap or techno music while shouting phrases such as "Mike likes to write by the bright light at night" at rapid speed (Li, Y. Performance). These touring lectures may accommodate 20,000 to 30,000 spectators for a single event (Spaeth, 1999). Li has a record of performing before 100,000 people in a single day at Chengdu, Sichuan, exceeding that of Mao's 90,000. Li also conducts lectures to small assemblies, such as a group of government officials or a private company's employees. He has given specialized presentations to the People's Liberation Army and the 2008 Beijing Olympics volunteer corp. In addition to the profits made from lecture ticket sales, Li Yang Crazy English products (audiotapes, videos, computer programs, and books) are major revenue drivers. Li's products have even spawned pirated materials with names like "Crack English" and "No. 1 English Crazy."

3. Methodology

3.1. *Pedagogy*

Criticism of foreign language classes in China is directed at the emphasis on preparing for the English examinations (the CET 4/6, TEM4/8, and TOEFL), rather than learning English comprehensively and practically. As these national English exams only recently added oral components, traditional classroom emphasis was only on reading, writing, and, sometimes, listening skills. Li Yang Crazy English seeks to counterbalance this failure of the educational system by concentrating on oral ability. Li believes that Chinese students "have no problem writing, they have no problem reading. That's why I trigger their power of speaking" (interview with Kirpal Singh, 2003).

Li Yang has three rules for participation in Crazy English: "Speak Loud, Speak Fast, and Speak Clearly" ("大声, 快速, 清晰"). To improve pronunciation, Li emphasizes the repetition of phrases, words, and syllables. He calls this "Tongue-Muscle Training" or working the "International Muscle." He says, "The tongue is an important organ for speaking. Some muscles in the tongue used to pronounce English sounds have withered in Chinese so we need to shout to restore them" (Liu, 2001).

During lectures, Li yells out in English and asks that the audience recite after him by shouting strings of words such as "lucky, nice, face, no, no smoking, talk, famous, dangerous, enjoy your stay (Li, Y. Performance)." Words are repeated until Li is satisfied that the audience has accurately replicated the proper pronunciation. Li teaches pronunciation with a general American accent (neutral Midwest). Sometimes, however, Li impresses his audience with his pronunciation skills by exaggerating the American accent of words, particularly with his favorite phrase "very good," in which he draws out the "y" and the vowels in both words. Li will occasionally speak in another English accent, such as British English or vocalizations common to those in the American ghetto ("gangsta-speak"), but this is done in jest, merely to entertain the audience. Li Yang's talent for pronunciation includes his ability to reproduce the accent of an American speaking Mandarin. For example, he mocks Americans speaking Chinese for saying "Ni H**ow**," instead of the accurate "Ni H**ao**" (你好) (Li, Y. Performance).

In addition to demonstrating proper (and not-so-proper) English pronunciation, Li employs approximately 20 hand/arm movements that are supposedly coordinated to specific vowel and consonant sounds. In Crazy English lectures, Li introduces a vowel or consonant sound by vocal repetition as well as gesticulation. Students mimic Li by attempting to coordinate their voices and hands to produce an accurate pronunciation. Following is a table that lists some of the most frequently used pronunciation and hand/arm movement synchronizations:

Sound	*Hand/Arm Movement*
"a" in "What"	With the right hand held above the head, make a hand puppet and open it when vocalizing the "a" (For the word "what," slowly open the puppet mouth on "wha" and close it on the "t")
"a" in "Made"	With the right hand held above the head, bend at the wrist with a flat palm, move arm from front to back over one's head
"e" in "Better"	With the right hand held above the head, pointer and middle fingers make a scissor cutting motion, opening on the "eh"
"ea" in "Meat"	Make the OK sign with the right hand, move in straight line across body from left to right

"i" in "Like"	With the right hand's pointer finger, draw a small complete clockwise circle
"o" in "Go"	With closed fingers and a cupped palm, dip the right hand from up right, down center, and then up left
"ow" in "Brown"	With the right hand pointer and middle fingers, draw a large circle that moves toward the body, then away
"th" in "Three"	With the right hand held above the head, bend at the wrist with a flat palm, move arm from right to left over one's head

These movements are not based in any academic theory that acknowledges their pairing or usefulness. Indeed, the arbitrariness of the pairings is even more apparent when one realizes that Li changes the gestures in some of his lectures, puzzling students who previously memorized the coordination and believed them to be important. This alteration may be inadvertent, but such a mistake indicates that Li does not take the gestures as seriously as he professes.

Many nonconsumers of Crazy English associate the method with wild hand clapping and arm waving, unaware that there is a purpose to this movement. One native English speaker (a Canadian) claims that when he performed a Korean Television Shopping Network infomercial for Li Yang Crazy English, he was required to say that Canadians learn English by waving their hands in the air while speaking (Surridge, 2003). The Canadian was further obligated to wave his arms whenever he spoke English in response to the questions asked by the Korean actors. As the Canadian actor was uninformed as to the designated movements, he merely flailed about as he spoke. Obviously, neither the actors nor those marketing the products understood the importance or the denotation of the Crazy English movements. This too undermines the educational significance that Li accords his movements.

Another flaw in Li's method is that it does not address coherency or fluidity of speech. Even though improvement in speaking English is the primary goal of Crazy English, it only examines the problem of pronunciation. If Crazy English followers do not have a pre-existing knowledge of English grammar and vocabulary, they will not learn to speak coherent English from Crazy English. In lectures, Li teaches the pronunciation of single words or words within a sentence, without giving any context. Many of Li's sentences seem perfectly useful, such as "How are you doing?" but they become less practical because he does not teach the follow-up responses ("I'm fine."). Moreover, many phrases that Li teaches are unknown or uncommon in English-speaking countries, such as "she's as fine as frog's hair," "Hainan is the Hawaii of the Orient," or "don't worry about the horses being blind, just load the wagon." Li also teaches uncommon colloquialisms, such as "there are no flies on me" (indicating an active mind) and "the walls have ears." (Li, 2005a) The attention that Li gives to such sentences would lead a student to believe that the sentences were important or useful. Furthermore, without context, the student is left to imagine where and when to use the sentences that he or she labored to pronounce perfectly. Combining words that are unrelated in meaning and pronunciation is another problem of Crazy English. For example, Li may string together words like, "great, make, dangerous, famous" and "good, city, busy." Usually the words are chosen to emphasize a similar pronunciation, like the "ā" sound in the first set of words here; yet, at other times, the words seems to have no similarities in pronunciation, as with the second set. In one computer program, Li asks the user to repeat, "Lucky, nice, face, no, no smoking, talk, famous, dangerous, enjoy your stay." (Li, Y. Performance) Some Westerners are bewildered by encounters with Crazy English students, who try to move at high speed from one random topic to the next, leaving their conversation partners in a daze ("Crazy Place, Crazy English," 2004).

Crazy English is not meant to improve reading or writing comprehension, and the lectures certainly will not do so for a beginner. The vocabulary and grammar used in Crazy English lectures are simple and rarely translated. English demonstrations rarely contain full English sentences, and Li will often give the motivational portions of his lectures in Chinese. The emphases in Crazy English products do differ from the lectures to cover reading comprehension. These may teach the meaning, proper pronunciation, and vocal personality of English colloquialisms, such as "not have a penny to one's name," and "don't lose heart." Each colloquialism is followed by one or two examples of its use, as the colloquialism "Don't talk to me like that!" is demonstrated in: "A: You're fat and ugly and I hate you. B: Don't talk to me like that!" (Li, 2005a) Li has refined his lectures over the years, tending toward a more comprehensive learning system. But buyers beware: Li only guarantees gains in the pronouncing English, and success is doubtful in that regard, anyway.

3.2. *Psychology*

The psychological message of the Crazy English program is closely related to its didactic emphasis on pronunciation improvement. A familiar Li Yang motivational phrase is "Enjoy losing face," a shorter version of "Put your face in your pocket and cry out in English with me, so that you do not lose it in the future!" Li uses these slogans with his students to combat common psychological obstacles like bashfulness and introversion, because, as Li says, "Chinese are typically shy. Shouting can help erase their mental obstacles, excite their mouths and ears, and strengthen their confidence and concentration" (Liu, 2001).

"Crazy English! Crazy life! Crazy world! I love this crazy game, so let's go!" (Zhang, 1999). According to Li, the "Crazy" in Crazy English signifies the desire for students to have passion and to fulfill the dreams of their country and parents by giving 100% of themselves to their goals, without the fear of failure. This message is especially important in East Asian countries, as one of the major hindrances to activities such as learning foreign languages is the fear of losing face (Ho, 1976). The fear of losing face is so great for many Chinese that it becomes debilitating. In Chinese classrooms, students are expected to speak English at a certain level of fluency. If they personally feel that their spoken English skills are not up to par with the standards set by the teacher, then they may be so afraid of failure that they decide to forgo speaking in class (Ho, 1976). The same fear is also reflected in encounters with foreigners. If a Chinese person feels that his or her English is too poor, he or she may not converse with a native English speaker for fear of poorly representing the Chinese people as a whole. Common English teaching methods in China accommodate this fear of failure by deemphasizing speech in the classroom. The goal is to avoid embarrassment, even at the cost of learning to speak accurately and effectively. By denying speaking practice, the student enters a vicious cycle, wherein language skills deteriorate due to fear, and fear increases due to deteriorating capability.

Giving students the confidence to succeed in school is not an innovative message, but with Crazy English, Li has been able to popularize and market the message more successfully than ever before. Journalist Kerim Friedman (2005) reflected, "From what I see, self-confidence is the real product that Li is selling." Many consider Li Yang a motivational speaker due to his emphasis on personal empowerment in Crazy English lectures. Li chants, "I love humiliation! I embrace hardship! I welcome failure! I pursue success!" (Zhang, 1999). Li disagrees with the traditional accommodation of fear in the classroom, because he believes that embarrassment can be a great motivator to learning and improvement.

During lectures, Li uses two activity structures that assist students with breaking out of their shell. One of the activities is clapping, sometimes to loud techno music, while screaming Crazy English phrases as quickly and as loudly as possible. The noise of the clapping (and the loud music, when used) drowns out the individual voices, creating anonymity for speaking practice. The students are more comfortable because they do not fear that others will overhear their potential mistakes or shortcomings. Clapping can also encourage students to speed up the repetition of phrases. Li's second activity is a confrontational shouting game. Li will bring a student or several students up to his stage and, with the students on one team and Li on his own team, the two groups jab their fingers in their opponents' faces while shrieking sentences like "You had better study hard!" If taken out of context, this activity would be highly emotionally abusive, but in the Crazy English setting, Li hopes that it will ignite passion and courage within students' hearts.

Dr Weiguo Qu, a sociology lecturer and English professor at Fudan University, discussed the contribution of the Crazy English method to dispelling the fear of losing face. He notes, "Li Yang's way of doing things is you shout and speak collectively, so basically it's anonymity. So when you shout this way, [making mistakes] doesn't matter at all. . . . People acknowledge Crazy English lectures as a place where they should shout English, even if their English is poor." Dr Qu is skeptical that successful strides made by students during the Crazy English lectures will carry over once the lecture has ended. Once the anonymity is lost, he says, the bravery disappears (personal interview, November 6, 2006).

4. Infusion of Chinese Nationalism

In addition to its "innovation" in providing an ESL program that caters to Chinese students' didactic and psychological needs, Li Yang Crazy English provides yet another twist: it premises the need to learn English upon the need to promote China and the Chinese language. Li's Crazy English blog displays the heading: 征服英语, 让祖国更强大! (*Zhengfu yingyu, rang zuguo geng qiangda!* Conquer English to make China stronger!)

In order to sell tickets and products, Li must encourage English language learning by emphasizing that English is the *lingua franca* of commerce and foreign relations. Li says, "If China is to be an economic power, its citizens must speak the language of global commerce well enough to be understood" (Meijdam, 1999). Once Chinese students have perfected their pronunciation and speaking abilities, Li touts that they will be able to succeed abroad. But to relieve the common Chinese insecurity that students studying or working in the West will prefer to remain abroad (and the fear that pushing English in schools tacitly endorses Western hegemony), Li frames the reasons for learning English thus: students should not learn English to better themselves, but rather to serve as Chinese missionaries. Chinese people must learn English so that they can communicate with foreigners to tell them of the greatness of the *Chinese* language and culture (Zhang, 1999). Li tells students they can do this by becoming Chinese language teachers abroad or merely by speaking English to as many foreigners as possible to advocate tourism and study abroad in China. At minimum, Chinese abroad should educate foreigners about Chinese culture and the Chinese language. For Li, it is even better if they promote the superiority of the Chinese people. "I want [the Chinese] to use English and spread Chinese as a world language. . . . Mastering English and therefore enriching our country is an act of patriotism," Li says (Yamane, 2005).

Li says, "I promote the love-thy-country angle because I don't want our people to forget China after they acquire English" (Friedman, "Crazy English"). He tells the students that it is their filial duty to their country and to their parents to help China's economy rise above the top three economies — American, European, and Japanese. Li cries, "What is the most concrete way to love your country? To make yourself qualified for the twenty-first century, to make yourself strong mentally and physically, to make more money internationally — that's the way to love your country" (Walsh, 1999). This invocation of a modern filial piety seems rather effective; when the students hear this and begin to repeat Li's phrases "Never let your parents down! Never let your country down! Never let yourself down!" some of them, especially the female students, begin to sob (Zhang, 1999).

Li Yang's nationalist message also includes a bit of tough love. Although Li uses patriotism and love of China to support his political ideals, he emphasizes his disgust with the country's current state of affairs (hence, the need to buy his products and learn English to build up the country!). In 2000, Japanese news source *Asian Political News* discussed Li's point of view:

> The Chinese government, apparently favoring his nationalistic approach, has allowed Li to use historic spots such as the Great Wall, the Marco Polo Bridge, and the Forbidden City, helping stir media interest in his classes. But Li said during the interview [with Kyodo News] that his real purpose in using those places is to make Chinese people realize that China is no longer the great country it used to be, and that learning English is the only way to regain national prosperity. "We have a splendid ancient civilization, but we should not be proud of it," he said. Printing, papermaking, gunpowder and the compass are known as the four great ancient inventions of China, but "now we are importing all our machines from foreign countries," Li said. "We should not just be proud of something glorious in the past. We should be ashamed of the distance we lag behind." ("'Crazy English' teacher in pursuit of Chinese dream," June 12, 2000)

Li bolsters his Chinese nationalist commentary by infusing it with racist messages. The racist messages promoted in Crazy English lectures are generally more subtle than the themes of Chinese nationalism. In lectures, Li is particularly critical of the Japanese, Europeans, and Americans (despite his Caucasian American wife and employees). His resentment toward Americans and Europeans is primarily based on their economic dominance over China: "America, England, Japan — they don't want China to be big and powerful!" (Osnos, 2008). Li's feelings toward the Japanese, however, run deep. In his lectures, he derides the Japanese as "thieves" of Chinese innovation and culture and as "stupid" because they cannot speak Chinese and even their English is poor (Zhang, 1999). Li advocates that Chinese should be embarrassed and horrified that their economy has fallen behind the Japanese economy. And while Li usually avoids teaching English to elementary school students (he believes that children should not learn English until they are old enough to have mastered Chinese), he visits primary schools to lecture about the history of Japanese animosity toward the Chinese. In one scene of film, Director Zhang Yuan's documentary, *Crazy English*, Li Yang and reporter Mia Turner from *Time Asia* discuss Li's anti-Japanese sentiments (author's translation for Chinese portions, see Appendix 1 for original transcript):

LY: "I collect a lot of photos about the Japan's invasion in China. I took scenes of the Japanese murdering people. I collect these photographs. That is to say, I print them out. I want to show them to Chinese elementary school students, to let them know that we absolutely cannot forget the events of 1937, about 60 years ago. Because now [Chinese children] are already indifferent, because they use Japanese products, think that Japanese things are great. It already feels like [the events are] largely forgotten. If you are old and bring up these things, they think it is very weird. We absolutely cannot forget this. This is already the Chinese nation's humiliation, Japan's savagery and cruelty; a lot is revealed. So I am really not asking that everyone — I am really not encouraging everyone — to hate the Japanese. I encourage them to hate themselves. So I want to make — I — the reason I collect these picture to show to the elementary school students is that — I do not want to promote hate into Japanese and Chinese people, I want to encourage Chinese people to hate themselves."

Times: "Why?"

LY: "Because you're weak. You were weak, so you were invaded. If you are strong no one can, no one dare to do that to you. So, the best way to show you love your country, the best way to show you hate Japan — or to show you remember that terrible history 60 years ago — is try to make yourself strong. So, that is my way to remember history."

Although Li tries to mitigate the reporter's revulsion with his comments and deny being labeled as racist by asserting "I do not want to promote hate," moments later Li forgets himself and says that "the best way to show you hate Japan ...." After saying this, Li jumped in his seat and rushed to correct himself by amending his words, "... or to show you remember that terrible history 60 years ago," but his message is clear. At a separate event, a Chinese student who disliked the Japanese confronted Li and sought his advice. Li told him, "If you really want revenge against Japan, then master their language" (LoBaido, 2001). Li later claimed that he did not intend to advocate Chinese revenge against the Japanese, but these numerous candid statements against the Japanese undoubtedly qualify Li as an advocate of anti-Japanese sentiment or, at the very least, a patriot who is willing to risk the possibility of promoting hate so long as it increases nationalist sentiment.

Some of Li's nationalist (and racist) commentary may be more than a way to create a niche in the ESL market and remain in the good graces of those wary of English language promotion; it is possible that Li is a megalomaniac on a sort of political campaign of his own. In one Crazy English lecture DVD, although containing a professional and uncontroversial lecture, the four-minute-long introduction to the lecture portrays a mad mob leader and seemingly violent masses. The black, white, and red scenes are set to coming-to-war music and drumming, as well as women's terrified screams. Pictures of Crazy English mobs and scenes of Nazi gesticulation give the undeniable impression that the DVD is about social unrest and political upheaval. The audience is surprised when the scene that follows this dramatic introduction is that of a funny language learning exercise! Li's marketing department may have hoped the introduction's dramatic effect introduces the craziness of Crazy English, but to a Western eye, it is too intense and horrifying to pass it off as merely a marketing ploy.

Li has been likened to Mao and even Hitler. With such accounts, it is easy to picture the man as a scary demagogue, but Li shares the charismatic, attractive, and personal likeable qualities commonly attributed to despots. There is no doubt that he is a captivating motivational speaker, and nothing about his character seems phony or rehearsed. Indeed, Crazy English products and other media and entertainment sources depict Li as enthusiastic, hard-working, sincere, and kind. Li's wife, a Caucasian American who sometimes performs with him, staunchly defends Li against claims of megalomania and racism. But there are still skeptics. Famed author Wang Shuo wrote of Li:

> I have seen this kind of agitation .... It's a kind of old witchcraft: Summon a big crowd of people, get them excited with words, and create a sense of power strong enough to topple mountains and overturn the seas....
> I believe that Li Yang loves the country. But act this way and your patriotism, I fear, will become the same shit as racism (Osnos, 2008)

In September 2007, another controversy over Li's intentions for his political messages began to surface. During a trip to the Crazy English Training Base in Baotou, Inner Mongolia, Li insisted that approximately 3,000 students kneel before him and their teachers. Many accused Li of attempting a form of cult leadership. One reporter, Bob Chen, wrote, "No one can definitely tell whether Chinese are too sensitive with the past servile age, or it's just a stunt by BSP Sina.com, or even a trick by Li Yang to catch eyeballs in an unusual way." (Chen, 2007) Li responded twice to the controversy and accusations. In his September 8, 2007 blog entry, Li wrote, "Here, I would like to state my point of view: first, it was I who suggested that the students kneel in gratitude to their teachers; second, I think that is a common [but] great kneel." Two days later, Li was again compelled to comment on the situation. He wrote, "The pictures of the kneeling are real, I am already accustomed to this frequent [kneeling], the students kneeling is respectful of their teachers. In a few days I will go to Chengdu to give a lecture, [and] I believe that I can make all of those among Chengdu's best middle school students kneel" (author's translations, see Appendix 2 for original transcript).

So far, Li's patriotic themes have created a close relationship between himself and the CCP. In fact, he was appointed to head the English campaign for the 2008 Olympics and has received permission to hold mass lectures at the most sacred of Chinese locations. However, Li did not always enjoy universal approval. In 1996, two years after Li established Li Yang Crazy English, the Crazy English method became popular in Guangdong province against the will of traditional English teachers there. In response, the local government prohibited Li from giving seminars in the area for six months. The government in Chengdu, Sichuan, also banned Li from teaching for an extended span of time (Spaeth, 1999). For now, however, Li's popularity remains high. Even if Li's nationalist (and racist) themes are purely in place to alleviate the general concern that ESL promotion encourages emigration of China's best and brightest, only time will tell if such themes will continue to appease the Chinese government or eventually lead to the intolerance of the international community.

5. Conclusion

The Li Yang Crazy English program is dynamic and multifaceted. For one, the focus on speech and the way in which pronunciation is taught through shouting and movement are unique among ESL programming in China, even if the gains made are dubious. The desire to increase student confidence is also special and perhaps more viable. Equally unique is Li's emphasis that Chinese students should master English in order to serve as missionaries for China, promoting their country and the Chinese language, as well as making money internationally to rebuild the Chinese economy. Li's program and nationalist messages are well known and clearly popular with the general public as Li is one of the most successful entrepreneurs in China. But whether Li's purported pedagogical gains are real and whether his national purpose is as innocent as stated, remains unanswered.

Appendix 1

The following contains a transcript of the interview between Li Yang and Mia Turner of *Times Asia*, as captured in Zhang Yuan's documentary, *Crazy English*. The reporter and Li switched between English and Chinese when speaking (errors retained; ellipses indicate pauses).

Times: So yesterday when you were talking, you mentioned about Japan, and you said, you know, "日本就是偷我们东西。"

LY: 对.

Times: "偷世界上的…"

LY: 是.

Times: What did you mean by that?

LY: Japanese people are just a … Japanese people … I, I did one thing … I collect a lot of photos about the Japans invasion in China. 我把日本杀人的很多镜头全部。… 照片都收集起来。说起,我把它印起来。我要给中国的小学生看,知道一九三七年,应该是六十年前,发生的事情。是绝对不能忘记的。因为他们现在已经无所谓了。因为他们用的是日本的产品,觉得日本东西很好了。已经觉得大忘了。你老提那东西,他们觉得很奇怪。它是绝对不能忘记了。那已经是中国中华民族的耻辱,日本的残暴残酷。多能显现出来。那么我并不是要求大家,我并不是鼓励大家去恨日本人,我要鼓励大家恨自己。So I want to make … I … the reason I collect these picture to show to the elementary school students is that … I don't want to promote hate into Japanese and Chinese people, I want to encourage Chinese people to hate themselves.

Times: Why?

LY: Because you're weak. You were weak, so you were invaded. If you are strong no one can, no one dare to do that to you. So, the best way to show you love your country, the best way to show you hate Japan — or to show you remember that terrible history sixty years ago — is try to make yourself strong … So that's my way to remember history.

Appendix 2

The following contains the original transcript Li Yang's responses to media attention over the kneeling incident in Inner Mongolia, as posted on his blog at http://blog.sina.com.cn/lyce

"在这里,我要申明我的观点: 第一,是我提议学生给他们的老师跪下感恩的; 第二,我认为这是普通的、伟大的一跪!" Li Yang, September 8, 2007.

"下跪的照片是真的,我已经习以为常了,学生下跪是对老师的尊重。过几天我还要去成都讲课, 相信可以让成都最好中学的全体学生下跪。" Li Yang, September 10, 2007.

References

Ho, YF D (1976). On the concept of face. *The American Journal of Sociology*, 81(4), 867–884.

Lee, E (1998). Let's Go Crazy. *Beijing This Month*, 59, 26–27.

Li, Y. Performance. *Li Yang Ying Yu (Li Yang English)*. DVD. Digide A.

Li, Y (ed.) (2005a). *Blurt Out, 5*. Guangdong Audio-Video Publishing: Guangzhou.

Meijdam, A (1999). Pumping up the volume (July 30, 1999). *Asia Week*, p. 25.

Osnos, E (2008). Letter from China: Crazy English (April 28, 2008). *The New Yorker*.

Qu, W (2006). Personal interview. Shanghai, China (November 6, 2006).

Spaeth, A (1999). Method or madness? (January 18, 1999) *Time Asia Magazine* 153(2).

Woodward, AR (2008). A survey of Li Yang Crazy English. *Sino-Platonic Papers*, No. 180 (April 2008).

Yamane, Y (2005). Chinese patriots burn with English fever (July 2, 2005). *The Asahi Shimbun*.

Zhang, Y (1999). *Crazy English*. DVD. Xian Film Studio.

Online Resources

Chen, B (2007). Has Crazy English gone crazy? (October 16, 2007) *China Digital Times*, <http://globalvoicesonline.org/2007/09/17/china-has-crazy-english-gone-crazy/>.

Crazy Place, Crazy English (January 7, 2004). *China Teachers* <http://www.china-teachers.com/article31.html>.

Friedman, PK (2005). Crazy English (July 3, 2005) *Keywords*, <http://keywords.oxus.net/archives/2005/07/03/crazy-english/>.

Li, Y (2003). Strategic minds. *Channel NewsAsia*. Interview by Dr Kirpal Singh, <http://www.smu.edu.sg/news_room/smu_in_the_news/2003/200306.asp>, accessed December 2007.

Li Yang Crazy English Blog <http://blog.sina.com.cn/lyce>.

Liu, YM (2001). Li trains crowd to loosen their English tongues (August 9, 2001) *21st Century*, <http://www.21stcentury.com.cn/article.php?sid=1932>.

LoBaido, AC (2001). Return to Babel (July 18, 2001). *World Net Magazine*, <http://wnd.com/news/article.asp?ARTICLE_ID=23667>.

Surridge, GQ (2003). The infomercial (September 11, 2003) *The Big Electra Kurva (in Korea)*, <http://surridge.blogspot.com/2003_09_07_surridge_archive.html>.

Walsh, D (1999). Films from Taiwan and China (October 2, 1999). *World Socialist Web Site*, <http://wsws.org/articles/1999/oct1999/tff3-o02.shtml>.

Wang, GQ (2010). Rush to learn English fuels quality issues (August 5, 2010). *Xinhua News Agency*, <http://news.xinhuanet.com/english2010/culture/2010-08/05/c_13430861.htm>.

Zhan, N (May 2002). Li Yang Crazy for English. *China Today*. <http://www.china-today.com.cn/English/e20025/li.htm>.

CHAPTER 7

MORE THAN ERRORS AND EMBARRASSMENT: NEW APPROACHES TO CHINGLISH

Oliver Radtke

Institute of Chinese Studies, Heidelberg University, Germany

This chapter deals with Chinglish as Chinese–English translations found on public bilingual signage in the People's Republic of China. It traces back the origin of the term Chinglish and summarizes existing academic and nonacademic commentaries on the phenomenon. In Chinese academia, Chinglish is regarded as a deficiency that needs to be corrected whereas among the non-Chinese commentators, Chinglish enjoys a slightly Orientalist reputation of belonging to the "charming side of China." This chapter further focuses on Chinglish in four fields, i.e., history, sociolinguistics, sociology, and political science. These four methodological approaches highlight Chinglish as a useful tool of analysis, which helps to shed light on the existing relationship between China and the English language. Chinglish research also enables researchers to critically reflect official administrative processes and the Chinese government's efforts of positioning the nation in a global English-speaking context.

1. Introduction

Under the title "Shanghai is Trying to Untangle the Mangled English of Chinglish" in May 2010, the *New York Times* opened yet another round of discussion on the efforts of China's glitzer city to get rid of something that is boon and bane for many residents in China: Chinglish (Jacobs, 2010). The resulting four-month-long newspaper debate, which is just one of many during the last decade (BBC, 2001), was brought to an — at least momentary — end when in September the same year the *Global Times*, which is owned by the governmental mouthpiece *People's Daily*, spoke a rather drastic verdict: "Chinglish sentenced to death" (Fang, 2010).

On the other hand social media platforms such as Facebook or Flickr are registering thousands of members for groups such as "Chinglish — save China's disappearing culture." Private websites such as www.engrish.com are enjoying steady traffic and regular Chinglish picture contributions by the respective visitors, often accompanied by a style of writing that tries to be entertaining or witty.

The idea of this chapter is to shed light on Chinglish beyond the dichotomic attribution of "it is fun" or "it is shameful." The chapter traces back the origin of the term and summarizes existing Chinese and non-Chinese academic and nonacademic commentaries on the phenomenon. It goes on to suggest a new look on Chinglish as a research tool in four main approaches and shows preliminary results by dealing with existing data collected by the author.

One might ask, what is Chinglish anyway? The Oxford English Online Dictionary (dictionary.oed.com, 2010) defines Chinglish as "colloq. (freq. depreciative), a mixture of Chinese and English; esp. a variety of English used by speakers (*sic*) of Chinese or in a bilingual Chinese and English context, typically incorporating some Chinese vocabulary or constructions, or English terms specific to a Chinese context. ..." The first usage of the term "Chinglish" dates back to the 1950s. Maurice Freedman's *Chinese Family and Marriage in Singapore* in 1957 reads: "The noun 'keep' is sometimes used in Chinese–English. [Note] Sometimes jocularly referred to as 'Chinglish.'" (Freedman, 1957, p. 101) The first academic usage of Chinglish is likely to be a book review in *The China Quarterly* in 1970 by Adie in which he writes: "The author explains (...) in English that is both straightforward and readable — a change from the Chinglish which sometimes creeps into scholarly writing on the new China." (Adie, 1970, p. 188)

In this chapter, Chinglish is defined, not as a deficient oral usage of English in the process of learning the language, but as an interchangeably creative or plain wrong occurrence on bilingual (or sometimes trilingual with Japanese or Korean) Chinese–English public signage in the People's Republic of China. Public signage is treated very broadly and includes all kinds of bilingual text that is publicly available,[1] which could appear from commodity packaging to T-Shirts.[2]

2. Previous Studies

This section deals with existing studies on Chinglish, when and where they have been made and what conclusions might be drawn from this particular set of data. The section also shows the different attitudes toward Chinglish and concludes with a comprehensive compilation of governmental acts in the fight against Chinglish.

What has been said and researched about Chinglish before needs to be considered within the context of an existing English fever (*yingyu re*, 英语热) in China, which has been growing into a highly profitable industry of English teaching and training. The former teacher and self-made millionaire Li Yang, for his star appeal aptly coined by *Newsweek* "the Elvis of English" (McCrum, 2010), has made a business empire out of successfully commercializing China's fixation on learning the idiom that during the Great Proletarian Cultural Revolution (1966–1976) came under fire for its association with "the running dogs of capitalism" (but was nevertheless continued to be taught with a revolutionary twist). Li Yang comes three decades later but displays a similar patriotism. One of Li's slogans is "Conquer English to Make China Strong." Chapter 6 takes a closer look at Li's business model and how it links language training with nationalist sentiments. Knowledge of English has become "cultural capital" (Bourdieu, 1984, p. 47) *par excellence* and may easily be regarded as one of the most influential forms of symbolic capital in China. As Hu (2009, p. 49) puts it: "Access to such knowledge [of English]

---

[1] Public means that no entrance or other kind of fee has to be paid in order to see the signage.
[2] Chinglish research is not to be confused with research on China–English, i.e., correct English with endemic terms such as "Three Representatives" or "The Gang of Four," research that has grown into an extensive corpus of academic publications since the term was coined in 1980 by Professor Ge Chuangui (Ge, 1980).

is intertwined with the availability and deployment of other types of capital, creates relations of power, and leads to both symbolic and material profits."[3]

One might assume that in a country grappling (again) with learning and displaying English since at least the beginning of the reform and opening-period, extensive research on Chinglish should be available. Studies on how to improve English learning pedagogy and avoidance of oral Chinglish exist widely, but figures for Chinglish understood as public signage and approached as a social phenomenon are surprisingly low.

2.1. *Previous studies abroad*

The following two sections focus on academic publications, blogs/virtual collections showing that there exists not only rather substantially varied research in China and abroad but also diverted public interest in the subject matter.

2.1.1. *Academic publications*

There is only one PhD thesis that mentions Chinglish in its historical research on Chinese Englishes: Zhang (2003) offers a historical review of Chinese Englishes from early Pidgin English to the most recent codemixing by analyzing a number of representative texts from newspapers, textbooks, and creative writings from Chinese contemporary authors who publish in English.

Pinkham (1998, p. 1) identifies Chinglish on two levels: word choice and sentence structure. The cited materials are mainly from the political genre, such as official documents and announcements. For Pinkham, who worked as a copy editor in China, "Chinglish, of course, is that misshapen, hybrid language that is neither English nor Chinese but that might be described as 'English with Chinese characteristics.'" Pinkham states that "almost every

---

[3] The perseverance of this English fever is insofar puzzling, as being an English major can, according to the "2010 Annual Report on the Employment of Chinese College Graduates," no longer be regarded as the stepping-stone to a fast track career in the PRC. For the last three years, the maximum number of jobless graduates majored in English, computer science, and law (Chinese Academy of Social Sciences, 2010).

English text that has been produced by a native speaker of Chinese contains unnecessary words," which she classifies into five categories: (1) unnecessary nouns and verbs; (2) unnecessary modifiers; (3) redundant twins; (4) saying the same thing twice; and (5) repeated references to the same thing.

Bolton (2003) and Adamson (2004) have been crucial in compiling and researching the history of English and English teaching in China. The most active journal in terms of discussions on *China–English is English Today*, published with Cambridge University Press with more than three dozen articles on the topic. In terms of public signage, though, current research again has been scarce. One paper has been done on the linguistic landscape of Taiwan only recently: Curtin (2009) focuses on the relationship between social identity and properties of indexicality of language scripts in the public space of Taibei and for that purpose analyzes different types of public signage.

2.1.2. Blogs/virtual collections

Besides the occasional picture slide show on Chinglish in Western media (e.g., Jacobs (2010)), there are several blogs and websites that deal with the phenomenon more continuously. Engrish.com and Chinglish.de (the latter is run by the author) are entirely devoted to displaying Japlish and Chinglish in their existing context. Other private websites (such as "The Chinglish Collection" or "Chinese English a.k.a 中式英语") are showcasing their own collection as a searchable photo album with little or no own commenting or contextualization of the shown examples.

Two groups on the social media platforms Facebook and Flickr are worth studying in terms of Chinglish. The Facebook group as of October 27, 2010 displays 2,949 pictures and has 9,026 members and for the same date the Chinglish group on flickr.com lists 4,699 pictures and 955 members. Both groups offer a constantly growing pool of Chinglish pictures that users take themselves all over China. The Facebook group is tellingly called "Save Chinglish — China's disappearing culture" and many comments in the group showcase a clear tendency toward keeping Chinglish. The group's self-description reads: "This group is for all of those people who love to giggle at poor grammar, wrong context, and embarrassing spelling of the English language" (www.facebook.com/group.

php?gid=4441472314&v=info). The Flickr pool description simply states: "Fine examples of Chinglish (Chinese–english)" (www.flickr.com/groups/chinglish/). Obviously there are a growing number of Chinglish aficionados active on the Web.

2.2. *Previous studies in China*

2.2.1. *Academic publications*

First, most writers of academic articles and theses dealing with Chinglish and/or bilingual Chinese–English signs come from universities or academies that do not feature very high on the current university ranking. Until October 2010 the Chinese academic papers database *Wanfang shuju* 万方数据, accessible through the China Academic Journals database hosted at Staatsbibliothek Berlin, listed 64 MA and 1 PhD theses dealing with Chinglish (*Zhongshi yingyu*, 中式英语). About 28 theses or 43% of those were *not* coming from the current top 100 universities (CUAA, 2010).

Since research on public signage is not necessarily done under the keyword "Chinglish," another search was done with the term "*gongshiyu*" 公示语 (public sign language) and similar results were found: 36 out of 56 theses are produced at universities inside the top 100 ranking. About 20 theses or 36% are coming from universities outside the top 100. It would be exaggerated to conclude that the research quality on Chinglish is low because it is not dealt with at the current top-ranked universities, the influence of lower-ranking universities and their respective research on a nationwide scale might be regarded as lower, though. It needs further research to substantially draw conclusions on why Chinglish research does not meet the interest of China's top universities.

Lü and Dan (2002, 2007) is the only researcher who has published monographs on English–Chinese bilingual signs. His focus is on compiling standardization lists and dictionaries that serve as a reference compendium, instead of doing sociologically or sociolinguistically motivated research.

The stand of the abovementioned Chinglish theses can be summarized as follows: Chinglish is regarded solely as a problem; it is hindering effective communication with foreign visitors. The English translation is to be read by foreigners and overseas Chinese who cannot speak Chinese. As stated in the majority of the MA theses compiled above, the writers wish to assist China's

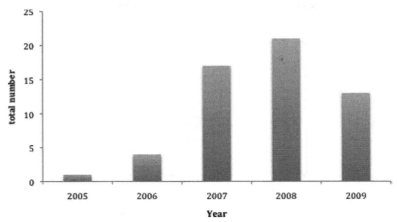

Figure 1: The rise and fall of MA theses on public signs between 2005 and 2009.

rapid economic development and help promote China's international image be searching for effective methods to standardize Chinglish into English. Second, most previous studies echo a global tendency of advocating bilingual signs as a means of communication and a sign of social sophistication, and strongly suggest that China has to follow. That is why the theses' focus is on problem solving and correction. Third, most thesis writers are more interested in "the response of the foreign receiver," rarely is Chinglish regarded as a phenomenon with a sociological or sociolinguistic connotation.

Furthermore, when one takes a look at the time span in which the *gongshiyu* studies were produced (see Figure 1), it is reasonable to speculate about a possible influence of the Chinese government, eager to promote the correction of, in their eyes faulty, bilingual signage on the growing interest of academic research in this topic. The following chart has made use of the same set of data as Figure 1, but looks exclusively at the time of publication. There is a steep increase of theses produced between 2006 (4) and 2007 (17) with the most theses on this topic (21) produced in 2008, followed by a visible decrease the following year (13).[4]

---

[4] The database search query did not display any hits for 2010. While the possibility exists that not even one single thesis was produced this year, it seems more likely, though, that data of 2010 has not been entered into the database yet.

It is worth deliberating a possible connection between the growing number of rather pragmatic, correction-oriented theses and an event that China was highly motivated to present in a flawless fashion: the 29th Olympic Games in Beijing. This hypothesis is indicated by the drastic change of numbers after 2008, when the public interest (and the interest of the Western media) shifted away from bilingual signage to other more pressing topics, for example, growing social unrest or rising unemployment rates.

What conclusions can be made from this set of data? Research on Chinglish is not as sloppy as a huge number of public bilingual signs, but it obviously does not rank very high on the nationwide university agenda either. It might be speculated, that research was pushed when it was necessary to deliver pragmatic, correction-oriented statements from academia how to improve the nation's public bilingual signage standard and was offstage again when the Olympics and Paralympics were over.

2.2.2. *Blogs/virtual collections*

There is no existing substantial collection of Chinglish signs from a Chinese collector. There are solely occasional blog posts on the main blog portals such as sina.com or sohu.com (e.g., http://t.sina.com.cn/maxray) or mass mails with an anonymous collection of rather well-known examples (often taken from websites such as engrish.com).

2.2.3. *Official acts*

For many local and central governmental offices, presenting the country in a flawless bilingual manner has become an industry of its own. The following overview is just a small compilation of official activities.

In August 2004, delegates of a "Chinese–English public signs investigation group" (*Hanying gongshiyu yanjiu keti zu*, 汉英公示语研究课题组) under the guidance of Beijing Second Foreign Language University Professor Lü Hefa toured eight European countries, investigating how the local governments deal with public sign translation (Wang, 2006). In September the same year (and in 2009 one year prior to the Shanghai EXPO), the Shanghai Language Committee organized an expert committee to deal with Chinese–English sign translation (Smithstreet Solutions, 2010). In

May 2005, the China Daily website held a press conference to announce a campaign on "Use Accurate English to Welcome the Olympics — Public Bilingual Sign Standardization Drive" at Beijing's University of International Business and Economics (China Education and Research Network, 2005). The Beijing Speaks Foreign Languages Committee, run by Beijing Municipality, issued month-long correction campaigns to eradicate Chinglish.[5]

Similar acts were carried out before the Shanghai EXPO. A Beijing-style campaign to replace Chinglish (or "shocking English," *leiren yingyu* 雷人英语 as the site called it using a popular youth term) from street signs (jointly run by the Communist Youth League Committee, Microsoft's web portal MSN, and the Chinese language version of Microsoft's search engine Bing) has been online at http://engkoo.msn.cn/expo/ since April 2010 with prizes like free online English courses.[6] The latest campaign was held in Guangzhou in November preparing for the Asian Games 2010.[7]

The list of the abovementioned official campaigns and activities is long; the changes are clearly visible in China's metropolitan cities but, as the growing number of picture contributions to Facebook's photo group shows, Chinglish is far from becoming extinct, thus questioning the effectiveness of the above-listed governmental acts.

3. Suggestion for Further Studies

The uncovered aspects of both Western and Chinese academic research includes questions on the political nature of Chinglish, its sociohistorical

---

[5] There even is a website, "e-signs.info 汉英公示语站," http://online.e-signs.info/, founded by the Beijing Second Foreign Languages University to display its work. It does not seem widely used, though.
[6] The appeal of this campaign or its prizes for participants cannot be named overwhelming, though. Since its inauguration in April 2010 till its offical closing in June, in three months the site has generated 320 entries only, a substantial part is copied from other already existing websites and is not even dealing with Shanghai but other cities.
[7] Volunteers from Guangdong University of Foreign Studies 广东外语外贸大学 posted their findings on a sina.com-blog named 迎亚运规范羊城英语公示语, http://blog.sina.com.cn/zhongxinzy.

potential for insights into the acceptance of English in Chinese society. Further questions could deal with the studying of process organization and the fact that governmental actions are mostly only shortlived correction campaigns that are announced in grand manner but have little sustainable and long-term effect. Besides dealing with the rather largely looming question "why does Chinglish exist in the first place?" the following suggestions argue for a new kind of academic research on Chinglish.

3.1. *New fields of research*

The question is: if it is not about a pragmatic focus on translation theory and correction, how to approach Chinglish? First, the prevalent approach to view Chinglish negatively in the previous studies needs to be amended. The focus on pragmatic translation correction and patriotic contribution to the motherland's progress is lacking balance. What is missing (or not generating enough research interest) in the existing studies is an exploration into the multilayered meaning that is behind Chinglish, whose very existence is a statement about contemporary China concerning her current and historic relationship with the West. The daily Chinglish production is a meaningful set of data from a sociolinguistic point of view. The analysis of Chinglish as an application of the Bourdieuan sense of "distinction" is a helpful auxiliary discourse for a partial analysis of contemporary Chinese society. And finally, the production and the official battle against Chinglish is a rich source for analyzing governmental administrative processes. In the following, these four aspects will be dealt with a bit more in detail:

(1) Chinglish as a source for statements about contemporary China and her current and historic relationship with the West

An important aspect of Chinglish research must be to analyze the "proactive side" and the "receptive side" of the Chinese public in terms of English. "The proactive side" is using English to cope with a perceived asymmetry between itself and Western English-speaking countries. The "receptive side" of the Chinese public deals with the image of the West versus a self-perceived underdog image of China, both of which is closely interlinked with the English language. Initially, the reception by force through the Opium Wars later underwent a change of attitude: with the building of the International

Settlements in Shanghai old town residents realized that English is a profitable language to be learned in terms of employment opportunities and income. The international competition about the "metropolitanness" of a city is mirrored in an intranational ranking among Chinese cities. Bilingual signs are part of that metropolitan appeal and need to be fostered. This attitude, though, has recently been taking into consideration again with governmental actions swinging against the use of too much English (Chen and Zhao, 2010).

(2) Chinglish as a source for sociolinguistic statements

The error variety on public signs ranges from simple typos to total gibberish, but also includes completely legible English grammar with highly "unconventional" wording in a corresponding social register. The style and variety of errors hint at existing social attitudes toward foreign languages and how to work with them in a non-native setting. If the majority of signs is analyzed, one would spot simple typos or jumbled letters, this might indicate a certain sloppiness during the sign production process, but not in terms of the general translation quality. If a substantial amount of signs display word-for-word translations that can be traced back to the usage of machine translations, this might indicate a lack of interest in a correct English translation. The error analysis leads to a newly established typology of Chinglish.

(3) Chinglish as a source for an auxiliary discourse for a partial analysis of contemporary Chinese society

Many shop signs, for example, with a clearly misplaced English translation, such as this fashion shop (Image 1) in Beijing's Haidian District called "Decay" or *tuibian* (蜕变, metamorphosis) displays English not as a translation helper. In this no sense-making form, English is clearly a sign of ornamentational distinction, giving the shop an aura of cosmopolitanism, even if the attempt fails from a Western point of view. It is rather likely to be a success or without impact on the shopping behavior of its Chinese clientele.

(4) Chinglish as a source for analyzing administrative processes

Seeing Chinglish signs one can ask: who is in charge of official and governmental sign productions? Why is there a need to produce bilingual signs even in remote areas? Sociologist John W. Meyer (1994) researched why international organizations under the real or assumed influence of outside

Image 1: Shop sign in Beijing's Haidian District.

demands show remarkably similar structural change. Using what he called the theory of isomorphism provides a helpful discourse to try to understand why Chinese governmental and official institutions feel compelled to issue bilingual signage all over the country. This feeling of compulsion is feeding back to point (1) and China's self-understanding and self-positioning in an international arena.

3.2. *Dealing with data*

As stated above in this study, Chinglish is approached as a source for a variety of information. In the following preliminary findings are listed.

3.2.1. *Statistical analysis*

The corpus of Chinglish signs that is the basis for statistical analysis consists of more than 2,000 examples collected by the author and contributors to the website www.chinglish.de over the course of 10 years. A randomly selected preliminary sample of 150 Chinglish pictures taken across the nation was taken for this chapter's survey. In total, nine categories were set up to differentiate the signs: Commercial Products, Company Signs, Don'ts, PR Gibberish, Public Education, Public Signs, Restaurant, Tourism, and Warnings.

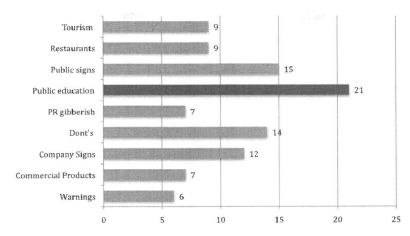

Figure 2: Chinglish categories in percent.

The category "Public Education" is leading by far (cf. Figure 2), followed by other "Public Signs" and "Don'ts." "Public Education" contains specimen such as "Be careful, don't be crowded" or "You can enjoy the fresh air after finishing a civilized urinating." The "Tourism" and the "Public Signs" part are relatively small since all signs that feature an educative tone or educative content were put in the "Public Education" category.[8] The number of Chinglish signs at tourist destinations seems low, since many of them follow the tone of "The beautiful scenery comes from your care" and thereby falling into the category "Public Education." One might ask, though: whom do Chinese authorities want to educate — Chinese or foreigners?

The general outcome of this survey can be challenged with a different set of data. Had I only visited restaurants throughout China, the category "Restaurants" would have looked much bigger. Nevertheless, the survey gives further fuel to the following assumption: Chinglish in the form of public signs ("Educative signs," "Warning signs," and "Don'ts") make up a substantial part in the corpus (in the survey more than 50%) and fuels the assumption that Chinglish might be, first, a form of anonymous communication, often between official institutions and the public. Chinglish with its educative tone,

---

[8] This outcome hints at the likely necessity to generate a new set of categorizations.

its anonymous top-bottom setting (we educate, you follow) can be closely related to the communications approach of mass education campaigns, such as the Great Proletarian Cultural Revolution (1966–1976). White characters on red banners where used as much as they are used nowadays.

With the existing and growing "language contact zone" between China and English-speaking visitors, expats, and students, the pressing question is: why is nobody checking the accuracy of these signs? Is the "contact zone" not wide enough yet? Is there even a lack of interest in correct translations? The following approximating model tries to offer preliminary thoughts in an increasing order of relevance:

(1) Nobody speaks English in China.

Although research on the proficiency in English suggests that the overall EFL competency is low — Yang (2006, p. 7) demonstrates that "the majority of English language learners in China, who have graduated from high school or college in the past few years, do not reach a level where they are able to communicate effectively in English" — this approach is clearly wrong. Tens of thousands of students graduate from Chinese universities majoring in English every year. Among them are enough graduates with excellent language skills, not to mention returnees from abroad. Young graduates who speak and write fluent English usually do not work as translators, though. "The number of people who actually practice translation or interpretation is estimated (very conservatively) to be at around 500,000, most of whom are part-time translators who hold a regular job elsewhere" (Huang and Huang, 2009). Doing translations as a side job might not be enough in terms of qualification, when it comes to the sophistication of public signs.

(2) We do not care.

This theoretical approach might come from a line of thinking similar to "No matter if it is right or wrong, as long as it looks foreign, cool or different, we are fine with it." This approach is appealing because of the many unintelligible Hanyu *pinyin* signs and many examples of what in the survey is termed "PR Gibberish." This, of course, cannot be called translating, but must be coined decorating. English words are placed on billboards, road sign, and product labels solely for the purpose of appearing bilingual and attract domestic consumers. They are meant for ornamentation, not for information. Tellingly, it is the Translator's Association of China that shows dissatisfaction over the state of mind of some of its customers: "The sad thing for translators is that when people discover wrong translations, they invariably pinpoint their fingers at the individual translators who have done the particular translation job, not aware that the root cause lies with the ignorance of the need for professionalism on the part, first and foremost, of administers or those who have failed to give out translation jobs to the professional translator." (Huang and Huang, 2009)

(3) We do not know any better.

A lot of restaurant menus are translated by friends of the owner's extensive family or recent high school graduates, who do not possess a very good grasp on the English language. This rather self-apologetic explanatory model does not match well with the ambitious goal of continuously attracting foreign investment and portraying cities as international metropoles and comes close to an "anything goes" — mentality at work which to assume and prove needs rock-solid data.

(4) We want to do it ourselves.

A fourth option would be the discussion about "losing face" and a certain unwillingness to accept the help of foreign experts. This discussion is about self-reliance and lacks a convincing argument since China clearly has invited a stream of foreign experts since the beginning of its Reform and Opening Policy in 1978. As Brady (2000, p. 943) put it: "foreigners have played a crucial role in this latest phase of the country's modernization." If they played such a crucial role, why were not they also crucial in the implementing and controlling of English translations?

(5) Let the machines do it.

It is quite likely that many sign manufacturers (and forced-to-be translators like the inexperienced employee in charge of public relations) are actually relying on free online software to generate the characteristic word-by-word translations. The general problem here is that "much of the language used on the Internet is colloquial, incoherent, 'ungrammatical,' full of acronyms and abbreviations, allusions, puns, jokes, etc. — this is particularly true for electronic mail and the language of chat-rooms and mobile telephones. These types of language use differ greatly from the language of scientific and technical texts for which MT [machine translations] systems have been developed." (Hutchins, 2007) Since this is not necessarily the case with official signs, another problem nevertheless might have a considerable impact on machine-based translations. As Hutchins (2007) puts it: "The Internet has also encouraged somewhat less scrupulous companies to offer online versions of electronic dictionaries (or phrase books) as 'translation systems.' Anyone using such products for translating full sentences (and text) is bound to get unsatisfactory results — although if users do not know anything of the target languages they will be unaware of the extent of the incomprehensibility of the results."

To further substantiate the last point, eight of the existing Chinglish collection's more prominent phrases are selected and translation quests are run on five popular websites that offer free online translation services.[9] As can be seen from the table below, the outcome[10] is not only pure Chinglish, but sometimes quite similar to what has been found on the corresponding public signs (see images of the respective sign in the appendix).

Example 1

---

[9] Used online services (1) http://fanyi.cn.yahoo.com/, (2) http://trans.godict.com/, (3) http://www.iciba.com/, (4) http://translate.google.com/, (5) http://www.onlinetranslation.cn/.

[10] Garbled translation output is the case with most other languages run through a translation software at the moment, although efforts by Google's ambitious translation project "Google Translate," which is based on statistical machine translation, are promising, see "Inside Google Translate" (Google a).

More Than Errors and Embarrassment **161**

Original Chinese: 先下后上，文明乘车
Original English: After first under on, do riding with civility

(1) After first under on, the civilization rides in a carriage.
(2) Go down upper, civilized riding of queen first.
(3) After descending first up, the civilization goes by car.
(4) After the jump, civilized ride.
(5) Under on, the civilization rides in a carriage after first.

Example 2

Original Chinese: 青青的草 怕你的脚
Original English: Green grass dreading your feet

(1) The blue grass fears your foot.
(2) Green grass is afraid of your foot.
(3) The very green grass fears your feet.
(4) Green grass afraid your legs.
(5) The blue grass fears your foot.

Example 3

Original Chinese: 小草有情 你当有意
Original English: Love the litter grass

(1) The grass feels emotion you when intends.
(2) Small grass has feeling you should have a mind to.
(3) The small grass has feeling you to be to have intention to.
(4) When you intend to large and enthusiastic. (!)
(5) The grass feels emotion you when intends.

Example 4

Original Chinese: 注意安全 请勿戏水
Original English: Noticing security Don't play water

(1) Pays attention safely please do not play with water.
(2) Pay attention to safety not play with water please.
(3) Noticing the safety pleases not drama water.
(4) Do not playing in the water safety.
(5) Pays attention safely please do not play with water.

Example 5

More Than Errors and Embarrassment **163**

Original Chinese: 向自觉维护公共卫生的游客致敬
Original English: Salute to the tourist who keeps the public hygience.

(1) Salutes to the aware maintenance public health tourist.
(2) Salute to the visitor who defends public health conscientiously.
(3) Pay respects toward the visitor who aware of self to support public hygiene.
(4) Tourists pay tribute to consciously safeguard public health.
(5) Salutes to the aware maintenance public health tourist.

Example 6

Original Chinese: 文明参观 讲究卫生
Original English: Visit in civilization, Pay attention to hygiene

(1) Civilized visit Is fastidious the health.
(2) Civilization is paid a visit to Pay attention to hygiene.
(3) Civilization visit Pay attention to hygiene.
(4) Civilization tour Stress health.
(5) The civilization visits Is fastidious hygienic.

Example 7

Original Chinese: 请勿忘随身物品
Original English: Please don't forget to carry your thing

(1) Please do not forget along with the goods.
(2) Do not forget please with self article.
(3) Please don't forget personal luggage.
(4) Do not forget belongings.
(5) Please do not forget along with goods.

Example 8

Original Chinese: 残疾人厕所
Original English: Deformed men toilet

(1) Disabled person restroom
(2) Deformed man toilet (!)
(3) Disable and sick person's toilet
(4) Disabled toilet
(5) Disabled person restroom

This is, of course, not a representative sample. In any case, in the order of increasing likelihood, the translation software approach has to play a considerable role. Another possible way of making use of software support is the following approach of georeferencing programing.

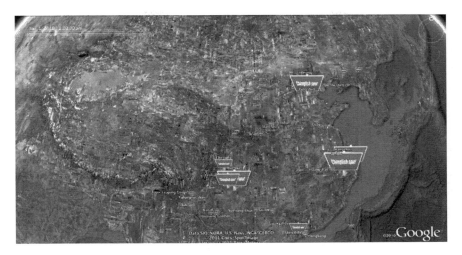

Figure 3: Using GeoTwain to visualize Chinglish findings across the PRC.

3.2.2. *Geographical analysis*

In conjunction with the History Department of Heidelberg University and external programmer Konrad Berner, a software program is being developed under the name of GeoTwain.[11] In its current version 0.3b runs as a small, efficient georeferencing program that produces kml-files that can be opened with the software GoogleEarth.[12] The Heidelberg research tool is helpful not only to produce maps that are layered over the globe to show historical sites but also to indicate time frames and changes within them. A cooperation between the author and the initiators at Heidelberg University are currently probing into options to apply the program to Chinglish research. The tool is not only providing georeferencing data for each Chinglish sign but can also produce a timeline to show where and when the sign was spotted (not produced). Figure 3 shows all 100 images listed in a recently published volume of Chinglish pictures (Radtke, 2009).

---

[11] Freely accessible at http://kjc-fs2.kjc.uni-heidelberg.de/GeoTwain/.
[12] Self-description: "Google Earth allows you to travel the world through a virtual globe and view satellite imagery, maps, terrain, 3D buildings, and much more" (Google b).

The distribution shows a clear focus on the east coast of China with most signs being spotted in Beijing and Shanghai. Moving further away from the coastal areas shows a clear decrease of Chinglish findings. Whether this is an indication for the analogy "the more foreigners, the more Chinglish" awaits further research.

4. Transculturality

In terms of a transcultural product, Chinglish itself is not transcultural, but the reactions toward it are. How do Chinese and foreigners, respectively, react to Chinglish and how this is consciously or subconsciously forming their image of China? Judging from the comments on Facebook and Flickr it is often not only the intended meaning of bilingual signs that is different from the actual translation, but the reactions toward the sign are different than the intended ones. The question remains to be researched whether Chinglish is creating a form of hybrid linguistic variety that is being used for fun or a means to make fun of China, to belittle Chinese efforts of speaking English and how the Chinese public, steered (or not) by official media reports, might react toward it.

Regarding transcultural studies, one might wonder what kind of study exists where the researcher comes from a cultural context different from the context of his or her research topic and the study results are *not regarded* as transcultural. Arguably, *all* studies where the cultural backgrounds of the topic and the researcher are *nonidentical* should be regarded as transcultural studies. In the process of looking at something from the outside, the researcher immediately adds something not only from his or her theoretical but also from his or her cultural background to the research. I cannot see how cross-cultural research can be conducted without the conscious or unconscious addition of cultural connotations, therefore inevitably leading to a result which has to be regarded transcultural.

During the content analysis of a particular research, one should be aware of his or her own cultural background and in how far this vintage point is influencing one's own research results. To make it concrete: the analysis of Chinglish signs done by a non-native English speaker from Germany inevitably leads to a slightly different analysis than the one done by an English native speaker. In any case, the view from the outside creates a methodological threshold that one needs to overcome but always leads the researcher into a transcultural realm of results.

5. Conclusion

The phenomenon of Chinglish is not new but has intensified with the use of machine translation software and the Internet. Research on Chinglish, on the other hand, is a rather unchartered area once moving away from a focus on correction and standardization. With an assumed link between academic research and governmental interest in sign correction prior to large-scale events, such as the 2000 Beijing Olympic Games or the Shanghai EXPO, research on and above MA thesis level increased visibly during the Olympic Year and decreased sharply after the big event was over.

The nationwide English fever that is still sweeping across China and found peculiar forms such as Li Yang's Crazy English teaching method, is obviously not elevating the translation competence on bilingual public signs to a level high enough that it is not constantly picked up by local and foreign media reports. Low English competence is only one side of the story, though. It is valid to speculate about whether governmental agencies and private companies are actually seeing the necessity to hire professionals for high-quality translations.

There is a visible divide between Western and Chinese media reports on Chinglish. There are quite a few Western websites in favor of keeping Chinglish in one way or the other; it seems, though, that the goal of these sites is different from the Chinese official statements available, which are in favor of standardizing bilingual signs. Online groups such as Facebook or Flickr are more or less solely concerned about taking away the "giggle" or Chinese characteristics in public garden warning signs such as "Little grass has life, please watch your step."

Judging from the existing preliminary data visualized in the software GeoTwain, there is a decrease in Chinglish density once one starts to move away from China's coastal areas. This observation still awaits more statistical backup. Whether the existence of Chinglish can or cannot be directly linked to the density of foreigners in certain Chinese metropoles needs further research. It is safe to say, though, that Chinglish signs are often not intended as a direct means of communication, but as a carrier of a different kind of meaning, i.e., that of distinction. The symbolic capital (Bourdieu) of Chinglish is clearly visible.

This chapter tried to show that research on Chinglish is not only helpful to reveal the "mysteries" surrounding the actual sign production but can also be employed to shed light on existing social attitudes toward the English language and the positioning of China in a global English-speaking context. Research on Chinglish offers a useful tool to think about existing asymmetries and the ways in which layers of Chinese society try to cope with it. Certainly, more research and proper fieldwork needs to be done to work out questions such as why foreign experts were obviously not that intensively employed in the production and proofreading of public signs as they were in many other fields of Chinese society since the beginning of *gaige kaifang* in 1978.

References

Adamson, B (2004). *China's English: A History of English in Chinese Education*. Hong Kong: Hong Kong University Press.
Adie, WAC (1971). Review of *Asia Awakes, A Continent in Transition* by Dick Wilson. *The China Quarterly*, 45, 188–189.
Bolton, K (2003). *Chinese Englishes: A Sociolinguistic History*. Cambridge: Cambridge University Press.
Bourdieu, P (1984). *Distinction — A Social Critique of the Judgement of Taste*. London: Routledge.
Brady, AM (2000). Treat insiders and outsiders differently: The use and control of foreigners in the PRC. *The China Quarterly* (164), 943–964.
Chinese Academy of Social Sciences (2010). *2010 Nian Zhongguo Daxuesheng Jiuye Baogao* 2010年中国大学生就业报告 (*2010 Annual Report on Chinese College Graduates' Employment*). Beijing: Shehui kexue wenxian chubanshe.
Curtin, ML (2009). LANGUAGES ON DISPLAY: Indexical signs, identities and the linguistic landscape of Taipei. In *Linguistic Landscape — Expanding the Scenery*, E Shohamy, and D Gorter (eds.), pp. 221–237. New York: Routledge.
Freedman, M (1957). *Chinese Family and Marriage in Singapore*. London: Her Majesty's Stationery Office.
Ge, CG (1980). Random thoughts on some problems in Chinese–English translations. *Chinese Translator's Journal* (2), 1–8.

Hu, GW (2009). *The craze for English-medium education in China: driving forces and looming consequences*. *English Today*, 100(4), 47–54.

Lü, HF (吕和发) and LP Dan (单丽平) (eds.) (2002). *Hanying Gongshiyu Cidian* 汉英公示语词典 (*A Chinese–English Dictionary on Signs*). Beijing: Shangwu yinshuguan.

Lü, HF (吕和发) and Y Wang (王颖) (eds.) (2007). *Gongshiyu Hanying Fanyi* 公示语汉英翻译 (*Chinese–English Translation of Public Signs*). Beijing: Zhongguo duiwai fanyi chuban gongsi.

Meyer, JW and WR Scott (1994). *Institutional Environment and Organizations: Structural Complexity and Individualism*. Thousand Oaks: Sage Publications.

Pinkham, J (1998). *The Translator's Guide to Chinglish*. Beijing: Foreign Language Teaching and Research Press.

Radtke, OL (2009). *More Chinglish — Speaking in Tongues*. Salt Lake City: Gibbs Smith.

Wang, HF (王海凤) (2006). Ouzhou biaoshi shangxi" 欧洲标识赏析(Appreciation and Analysis of European Signage). *Guanggao Daguan (Biaoshiban)* (2), 48–53.

Yang, J (2006). Learners and users of English in China. *English Today 86*, 22(2), 3–10.

Zhang, H (2003). *Chinese Englishes, History, Contexts, and Texts*, PhD thesis, University of Illinois at Urbana-Campaign.

Online Resources

BBC Online (2001). *Beijing Clamps Down on "Chinglish"* (August 14, 2001), <http://news.bbc.co.uk/2/hi/asia-pacific/1491288.stm>.

Chen, J and YN Zhao (2010). Chinese TV stations told to stop using English phrases (April 7, 2010) *China Daily*, <http://www.chinadaily.com.cn/china/2010-04/07/content_9692983.htm>.

China Education and Research Network (2005). *Welcome the 2008 Games with Correct Bilingual Signs* (May 26, 2005), <http://www.edu.cn/Newswin_1547/20060323/t20060323_127180.shtml>.

Chinese University Alumni Association (CUAA) (2010). *2010 Zhonguo Daxue Pingjia Yanjiu Baogao* 2010中国大学评价研究报告 (*Evaluation of the Chinese Universities ranking in 2010*), <http://www.cuaa.net/cur/2010/>.

E-signs.info, <http://online.e-signs.info>.

Facebook group. *Save Chinglish — China's Disappearing Culture*, <http://www.facebook.com/group.php?gid=4441472314>, accessed on October 27, 2010.

Fang Y (2010). Chinglish sentenced to death (September 29, 2010). *Global Times*, <http://www.globaltimes.cn/www/english/metro-beijing/update/top-news/2010-09/578288.html>.

Flickr photo group. *Chinglish*, http://www.flickr.com/groups/chinglish/>, accessed on October 27, 2010.

GeoTwain, <http://kjc-fs2.kjc.uni-heidelberg.de/GeoTwain/>.

Google (a). *Inside Google translate*, <http://translate.google.com/about/intl/en_ALL/>.

Google (b). *About Google Earth: What is Google Earth?* <http://earth.google.com/support/bin/answer.py?hl=en&answer=176145>.

Huang, YY and CQ Huang (2009). *The Translation Industry in China: Current Development and Potential for International Cooperation* (October 13, 2009), <http://www.tac-online.org.cn/en/tran/2009-10/13/content_3182787.htm>.

Hutchins, JW (2007). Machine Translation: A Concise History, <http://www.hutchinsweb.me.uk/CUHK-2006.pdf>.

Jacobs, A (2010). Shanghai is trying to untangle the mangled English of Chinglish (May 2, 2010). *New York Times*, <http://www.nytimes.com/2010/05/03/world/asia/03chinglish.html>.

McCrum, R (2010). "Glob-ish — powered by the Internet and the global media, English has evolved into the world's language (June 12, 2010). *Newsweek*, <http://www.newsweek.com/2010/06/12/glob-ish.html>.

Oxford English Dictionary Online, "Chinglish," <http://dictionary.oed.com/cgi/entry/00335104?single=1&query_type=word&queryword=chinglish&first=1&max_to_show=10>.

Smithstreet Solutions (June 17, 2010). *Shanghai Government Partners with SmithStreet to Work towards a Chinglish-free Expo*, <http://www.smithstreetsolutions.com/topics/topic_expo.htm>.

CHAPTER 8

WRITING CANTONESE AS EVERYDAY LIFESTYLE IN GUANGZHOU (CANTON CITY)*

JING YAN

Columbus Academy, Columbus, Ohio, USA

This chapter reports on part of a larger sociolinguistic study based on a written survey conducted on 116 Cantonese–Mandarin bilingual speakers in Guangzhou who are biliterates in Standard Written Chinese (SWC) and Vernacular Written Cantonese (VWC). Both quantitative and qualitative analysis is conducted in this chapter to explore how and to what extent of the Guangzhou regional identity is reflected in the everyday writing in Guangzhou local community. The findings of the correlation analysis between Cantonese lifestyle in Guangzhou and VWC elements reveal that VWC is positively viewed as an indicator of Guangzhou regional identity. In addition to the correlation analysis, the critical discourse analysis on the use of VWC as Cantonese lifestyle suggests that mass media and Hong Kong culture play important roles in strongly promoting the use of VWC in Guangzhou area. Everyday lifestyle other than using VWC in Guangzhou community also plays a key role in the maintenance of VWC.

---

* The research reported here is part of the author's PhD dissertation, supported by Dr Marjorie KM Chan's Seed Grant received from the Ohio State University.

1. Introduction

Regional identity is established through local people's everyday lifestyle, including their literacy practice in daily life. In the present study, Cantonese identity is defined as a kind of regional identity in contrast to a common Chinese national identity. It emphasizes on the willingness of the people living in Cantonese communities, especially in Ling-nan (岭南) area,[1] to distinguish themselves from the people living in the other areas in the nation. According to Snow (2004, p. 189), "use of Cantonese (in written as well as spoken form) is one way in which the Hong Kong speech community (and also the Cantonese-speaking regions of Guangdong identity) celebrates its ethnolinguistic vitality and distinctiveness within the broader Chinese ethnic and cultural community." As the core part of the regional identity of Ling-nan area, Hong Kong identity is highlighted through the use of written Cantonese. Given the important cultural function of written Cantonese in the Cantonese-speaking regions in China — Ling-nan area, the concern of the present study is how and to what extent of Cantonese identity in Guangzhou (hereinafter called **Guangzhou identity**), another significant part of the Ling-nan identity, is reflected in the everyday writing in Guangzhou community.

To answer these questions, both quantitative and qualitative analysis is conducted in this chapter. First, Guangzhou identity is quantified through measuring the favor of the **Cantonese lifestyle in Guangzhou** (hereinafter called as **Guangzhou lifestyle**). The preference for the Guangzhou lifestyle is examined in a regional lifestyle survey conducted toward 116 SWC–VWC biliterates.[2] It is proposed that the more a SWC–VWC biliterate subject favors

---

[1] Ling-nan area in this chapter includes all Cantonese-speaking regions in China. "Ling-nan culture" is a term that covers all aspects of Cantonese life in southern China such as Cantonese cuisine, Cantonese art, and Cantonese language.

[2] According to Yan (2008, pp. 1–2), SWC refers to Standard Written Chinese, while VWC refers to Vernacular Written Cantonese. SWC written form reflects spoken Mandarin Chinese and is based on the lexicon and grammatical structure of Mandarin Chinese. VWC is a "Chinese-character-based" writing system to record spoken Cantonese. VWC includes the standard stock of Chinese characters and a considerable number of dialectal vernacular characters. However, setting norms with regard to the registers of the spoken language (colloquial Cantonese), VWC is largely unreadable by a Mandarin speaker who is not trained in using Cantonese.

the Guangzhou lifestyle, the stronger he or she holds a Guangzhou identity, and *vice versa*. Based on the data collected from the survey, a correlation analysis is conducted between the Guangzhou lifestyle and the use of the VWC lexical and syntactic variables, and between Guangzhou lifestyle and language attitudes toward VWC. The aim is to explore the extent that VWC is viewed as indicator of Guangzhou identity. In addition to the correlation analysis, the qualitative approach of critical discourse analysis (CDA) is employed to study the VWC discourses generated by the 116 Cantonese–Mandarin biliterates in the survey. The focus of the discourse analysis is on the role of Guangzhou identity in acquiring and using VWC in the life experience of the biliterates. Looking into the details described in the discourses, the survival of VWC as a kind of Guangzhou lifestyle under the power of the national language policy, and how the use of this vernacular writing shapes and strengthens the Guangzhou identity at the meanwhile can be better understood.

2. Data Description: Guangzhou Lifestyle

In the survey of Guangzhou lifestyle, a written questionnaire consisting of 55 items is designed as the survey instrument to collect data from the 116 SWC–VWC biliterates.[3] All the 55 items are about the preference of Guangzhou lifestyle, such as self-identification as a member of Guangzhou Cantonese community, preference to Cantonese cuisine, appreciation of career development opportunities, willingness to make Cantonese friends, appreciation of Cantonese arts and entertainments in Guangzhou, etc. A four-scale ranking scheme is provided for the participants to choose the degree of their agreement/disagreement with each item in the questionnaire: SA (Strong Agree), A (Agree), D (Disagree), and SD (Strongly Disagree). For example, item 1 states as: 我认为我是广州社会的一分子 (I think I am a member of Guangzhou society). The survey participants need to choose SA, A, D, or SD to describe their situations.

We use three steps to describe the preference of the 116 biliterates toward Guangzhou lifestyle. The first step is to transfer the inverse questionnaire items. There are two types of questionnaire items in the survey of

---

[3] Refer to Yan (2008) Appendix D, for the details on the questionnaire of Guangzhou lifestyle.

Guangzhou lifestyle. The majority of the items in the questionnaire are stated in a positive way, such as item 1 mentioned previously. Some items, purposely, are stated in a negative way such as item 9: 我很少吃粤菜 (I rarely eat Cantonese cuisine). The aim of using negative items is to test the internal consistency and reliability of the questionnaire. In present analysis, the order of the results for the negative items was an inverse. That is, "SA" in item 9 equals to "SD" in item 1, "A" in item 9 equals to "D" in item 1, and *vice versa*.

After the questions of inverse are transferred, a Likert score is assigned respectively to the four-pointed scheme:

SA = 3
A = 1
D = −1
SD = −3
Missing = 0

Adding the total score of the 55 questionnaire items of each individual subject as the raw score with range from −165 (−3*55) to 165 (3*55), we propose a "PercentScore" that calculates the raw score for each subject through the following formula:

(original score − min possible score)/(max possible score − min possible score)

Whereas the minimum possible score is −165, the maximum possible score is 165. The PercentScore ranges from 0 to 100. The score of 100 indicates the most favor toward Guangzhou lifestyle, while the score of 0 shows the strongest disliking of the Guangzhou lifestyle. Figure 1 reports the distribution of the PercentScore in the 116 Guangzhou SWC–VWC biliterates. The majority of the survey subjects have the PercentScore ranging from 60 to 70, indicating an overall positive attitude toward Guangzhou lifestyle. Nevertheless, for certain amount of the participants, the PercentScores are either below 60 or above 70. In the present study, it is proposed that the participants with PercentScore below 60 hold a weaker Guangzhou identity, whereas those with PercentScore above 70 hold a stronger Guangzhou identity.

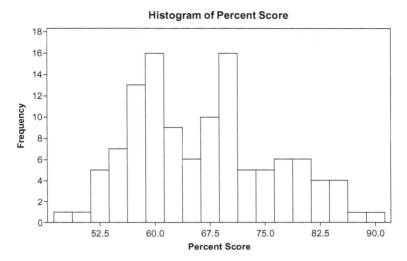

Figure 1: PercentScore of Guangzhou lifestyle among 116 SWC–VWC biliterates.

3. One-Way ANOVA of Guangzhou Lifestyle and VWC Literacy Practices

One-way ANOVA[4] is conducted to analyze the correlation between the PercentScore of Guangzhou lifestyle and the VWC literacy practices of general lexicon, classifier, and sentences. Since the PercentScore of lifestyle reflects the strength of regional identity, this study aims to explain the influence of Guangzhou identity on the variation of VWC general lexicon, classifier, and syntax.

Whereas the PercentScore of Guangzhou lifestyle serves as the independent variable in the one-way ANOVA, the dependent variables are selected from Yan (2008) categorization of VWC variables, including 19 sets of VWC lexical variables as shown in Table 1, 3 sets of VWC classifier variables as shown in Table 2, and 5 sets of VWC syntactic variables as shown in Table 3.

---

[4] According to Rietveld and Hout (2005, p. 49), analysis of variance (ANOVA) is a statistical technique which is often applied in the analysis of language data. ANOVA can be applied if two or more groups of participants are compared on the basis of a so-called *dependent variable*. One-way ANOVA is a basic concept of analysis of variance, in which participants belong to a single set of different groups.

Table 1: Seven types of written variants in 19 VWC lexical variables.

Variables (n=19)	Strategy I Type1 (n=10)	Strategy I Type2 (n=17)	Strategy I Type3 (n=9)	Strategy II Type4 (n=10)	Strategy II Type5 (n=2)	Strategy III Type6 (n=4)	Strategy IV Type7 (n=1)
ye5 "Thing"		野		嘢 吔			
me1 "what"	么	物 也	咩		乜		
faan1 "to come back"	返	翻 番					
gam2 "so"		今 敢 甘 禁 感	噉	咁		(口+敢)	
jo2 "verbal particle"		左	佐	咗		(口+佐)	
m4 "negative prefix"		吾	唔				
lak6 "smart, clever"			叻	叻			
fan3 "sleep, sleepy"		训		瞓			
lai2 "to come, arrive"	来	黎		嚟			
mou5 "have not"	无				冇		
hai6 "to be"	是	系	係	喺		(口+系)	
mai1 "don't"	未	米	咪				
ga2 "particle of sound"	嘎	架	咖				
Lau4hei3 "annoy"		劳气	唠气				
ge3 "possessive"		既		嘅			
ngaam1 "right, suitable"		岩		啱			
di1 "a little"	点	地		啲 哋			D
Sai1lei6 "Capable"	犀利	西利					
Gu1han4 "poor, stingy"	孤寒	古寒 姑寒					
	44	82	75	110	48	5	4
Total Tokens		201		158		5	4

Table 2: Ninetten written variants in three sets of VWC classifier variables.

	Variants			
	Approach I	Approach II	Approach IV	
Variables (n = 3)	Type 1 (n = 3)	Type 2 (n = 5)	Type 3 (n = 7)	Type 4 (n = 5)
一把刀	把	张		
一顿饭	顿	餐	歺	
			坡	pō
		条	波	pō
一棵树	棵	颗	科	bo
		把	婆	paul
			碌	P
			朴	

Table 3: Eight written variants in five VWC syntactic variables.

N = 116 Variables	Variants	n	%
S2			
comparative construction			
	比 sentence	38	32.8
	过 sentence	76	65.5
S3			
double-object construction			
	verb + object 1 + object 2	89	76.7
	verb + object 2 + object 1	13	11.2
S4			
dispositional construction			
	将 sentence	18	15.5
S6			
verb negative-complement construction			
	subject + verb + negative-complement + object	100	86.2
	subject + verb + object + negative-complement	16	13.8
S7			
passive construction			
	被 sentence	12	10.3

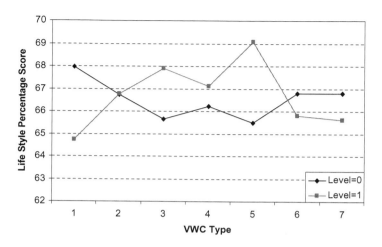

Level 0: Participants who did not use the assigned VWC variant (Type 1 or Type 2 ... or Type 7)
Level 1: Participants who used the assigned VWC variant (Type 1 or Type 2 ... or Type 7).

Figure 2: One-way ANOVA between PercentScore of Guangzhou lifestyle and the seven types of VWC lexical variants.

Level[5]		Type1	Type2	Type3	Type4	Type5	Type6	Type7
Level 0	N	72	66	60	49	76	111	112
	Score[6]	67.97	66.72	65.64	66.21	65.5	66.78	66.78
Level 1	N	44	50	56	67	40	5	4
	Score	64.72	66.76	67.91	67.12	69.08	65.82	65.61
P-value		0.07**	0.98	0.20	0.61	0.05**	0.83	0.81

3.1. *Guangzhou lifestyle and the variation of VWC general lexicons*

Figure 2 summarizes the result of the one-way ANOVA between PercentScore of Guangzhou lifestyle and the seven types of written variants in the 19 sets of VWC lexical variables. As observed, from Type 1 to Type 7, the written variants of the lexical variables become less and less SWC-oriented. The value of Level 0 represents the average PercentScore of the subjects who do not use the assigned type of written variant, while the value of Level 1 represents

---

[5] Level 0 refers to those usages without the VWC type, while level 1 refers to those usages with the VWC type.
[6] Score: lifestyle PercentScore.

the average PercentScore of the subjects who use the assigned type of written variant. The influence of Guangzhou lifestyle on the use of various lexical written variants is explored in the following discussion based on the result of the one-way ANOVA. The statistical difference between the level 0 (N/T)[7] and level 1 (I/T)[8] is marginally significant (p-value < 0.10) based on the ANOVA. Nevertheless, the following correlations between Guangzhou lifestyle and VWC lexical practices are observed.

First, in using VWC lexical variants of Type 1 (the most SWC-oriented variant), the value of level 0 (67.97) is higher than the value of level 1 (64.72), indicating that a weaker Guangzhou identity leads to a convergence of VWC lexicons to SWC lexicons.

The VWC lexical variants of Types 3, 4, and 5, however, are less SWC-oriented than the variants of type 1. The result of ANOVA shows that in using these less SWC-oriented variants, the values of level 1 are all higher than the values of level 0. Based on this finding, it is proposed that a stronger Guangzhou identity would lead to a divergence of VWC lexicons from SWC lexicons.

The subjects who provided the variants of Type 6 "false character" and Type 7 "Romanized symbol" are minority groups,[9] and they both have lower values of level 0 than the values of level 1. Therefore, the role of Guangzhou identity is not positive in using these two types of variants.

Basically, the result of one-way ANOVA reveals that the PercentScore of Guangzhou lifestyle is positively correlated with the use of the less SWC-oriented variants, but negatively correlated with the use of the SWC-oriented variants in the VWC lexical practices of the SWC–VWC bilerates. A strong regional identity of Guangzhou, in this sense, has positive impact on the divergence of VWC lexical variants from SWC.

3.2. *Guangzhou lifestyle and the variation of VWC classifiers*

In the present study, 19 written variants from three sets of VWC classifier variables (一把刀 "one CL knife," 一顿饭 "one CL meal," and 一棵树 "one CL tree") for an ANOVA study with the PercentScore of the Guangzhou lifestyle are

---

[7] Subjects who did not use the assigned VWC variant (Type 1 or Type 2 ... or Type 7).
[8] Subjects who used the assigned VWC variant (Type 1 or Type 2 ... or Type 7).
[9] Five subjects used Type 6 variant and four subjects used Type 7 variant.

Table 4: One-way ANOVA of lifestyle PercentScore and VWC classifier variants.

Variants	CL1 (刀 "knife") Type 1 (把)	CL1 (刀 "knife") Type 2 (张)	CL4 (饭 "meal") Type 1 (餐)	CL4 (饭 "meal") Type 2 (歺)	CL8 (树 "tree") Type 1	CL8 (树 "tree") Type 2	CL8 (树 "tree") Type 3	CL8 (树 "tree") Type 4
Score	65.43	67.82	66.51	66.6	66.75	65	66.68	67.18
P-value	0.18		0.96		0.98			

selected. As shown in Table 2, the variant of Type 1 is the most SWC-oriented variant, whereas Types 2, 3, and 4 are less and less SWC-oriented variants.

Table 4 summarizes the results of ANOVA between Guangzhou lifestyle and the selected VWC classifier variants. No statistical significance ($P > .01$) is found among the VWC variants.

把 *ba*3 and 张 *zhang*1 are the two VWC classifier variants used in the Guangzhou survey for 刀 "knife." 把 *ba*3 is more SWC-oriented than 张 *zhang*1. The ANOVA result shows that the subjects who use 张 *zhang*1 tend to have higher PercentScore (67.82) than those who use 把 *ba*3 (65.43). Guangzhou identity has a positive influence on the divergence of VWC from SWC in this case.

In the case of classifier variants for 饭 *fan*4 "meal," the PercentScores of the users of each variant (餐 *can*1 and 歺 *can*1) are very similar (66.51 and 66.6). This result indicates that the impact of Guangzhou identity is not notable in the variation of VWC classifier for 饭 *fan*4 "meal."

With regard to the set of classifier variants for 树 *shu*4 "tree," the PercentScore for the users of the Type 4 variants (Romanized symbol) is the highest (67.18). This result indicates that a strong Guangzhou identity has positive impact on the divergence of VWC classifier for 树 *shu*4 "tree" from SWC.

In sum, based on the findings in this preliminary study of the correlation between Guangzhou lifestyle and the variation of VWC classifiers, it is suggested that the regional identity of Guangzhou plays a positive role in divergence of VWC classifiers from SWC classifiers.

3.3. *Guangzhou lifestyle and the variation of VWC syntax*

One-way ANOVA is conducted to study the correlation between Guangzhou lifestyle and eight written variants in five sets of VWC syntactic variables. Table 5 summarizes the findings in the one-way ANOVA.

Table 5: One-way ANOVA of lifestyle PercentScore and VWC syntactic variants.

Sentence	S2		S3		S6		S7		S4	
Variants	比- Sentence	过- Sentence	V + O1+ O2	V + O2 + O1	SVO + neg.	SV + neg. + O	被- Sentence	Non-被-Sentence	将- Sentence	Non-将-Sentence
Score	65.9	67.0	66.9	66.5	63.0	63.3	72.8	59.4	67.0	64.9
P-value	$P = 0.56$		$P = 0.88$		$P = 0.97$		$P = 0.17$		$P = 0.41$	

S2: comparative construction; S3: double-object construction; S6: verb negative-complement construction; S7: passive construction; S4: dispositional construction.

The results of ANOVA reveal that in writing VWC comparative construction (S2), the PercentScore of the subjects using fewer SWC-oriented variant (过-sentence) is higher than the subjects using SWC-oriented variant (比-sentence). Similarly, in the case of dispositional construction (S4), the subjects using fewer SWC-oriented variant (将-sentence) are observed to have higher PercentScore than the subjects who do not use 将-sentence. Guangzhou lifestyle is thus positively correlated with the use of fewer SWC-oriented variants in writing VWC comparative construction and disposed construction. In another word, a strong Guangzhou identity keeps VWC divert from SWC in writing the two syntactic structures (S2 and S4).

However, in the case of passive construction (S7), the subjects using SWC-oriented variant (被 sentence) tend to have higher PercentScore than those who do not use the SWC-oriented variant in the writing task. This phenomenon implies that Guangzhou identity has no positive relation with the divergence of VWC passive construction from SWC.

In writing S3 (double-object construction) and S6 (verb negative-complement construction) in VWC, the impact of Guangzhou lifestyle is not notable since the PercentScores for different written variants are very close.

3.4. Summary

Basically, Guangzhou identity, as reflected by the PercentScore of the preference of Guangzhou lifestyle, plays a positive role in the divergence of VWC from SWC in writing VWC general lexicon, classifier, and syntax. Nevertheless, the extent to which Guangzhou identity as an influencing factor has impact on the variation of VWC differs in different linguistic levels.

In writing VWC general lexical items, the Guangzhou lifestyle is positively correlated with the use of the VWC lexical variants that diverts from SWC lexicons, including the variants of Types 2, 3, 4, and 5.

In the case of writing VWC classifiers, the impact of Guangzhou lifestyle is notable with the classifiers for 刀 *dao1* "knife" and 树 *shu4* "tree", but not notable with the classifier for 饭 *fan4* "meal".

In the syntactic level, whereas there is a positive relation between Guangzhou lifestyle and some VWC syntactic variants that are diverted from SWC variants, a SWC-oriented variant "被-sentence" has been found to be positively correlated with Guangzhou lifestyle.

Based on these findings, among different linguistic structures, the impact of Guangzhou identity as an influencing social factor is the most notable in leading the divergence of VWC lexicons from SWC lexicons.

4. Regression Analysis of Guangzhou Lifestyle and Language Attitudes

According to Yan and Chan (2007), regional identity of Guangzhou, reflecting the local solidity, has positive impact on the language attitudes of Guangzhou community to VWC. However, to what extent can a strong local or regional identity strengthen and extend the use of VWC in Guangzhou community, as opposed to the government-sanctioned standard written language, SWC, which is based on Mandarin Chinese? The quantification of Guangzhou lifestyle in this study enables to further explore the correlation between the Guangzhou lifestyle and the language attitudes toward the use of VWC.[10]

PercentScore for language attitudes is calculated for a regression analysis with the Percentscore for Guangzhou lifestyle. Following the same steps using to calculate the PercentScore of Guangzhou lifestyle, the PercentScores for language attitudes are calculated as shown in Table 6. The higher the Percentscore, the stronger is the positive attitude.

Table 6 reveals, among the four dimensions of language attitude of Guangzhou community toward VWC, the attitude toward standardizing VWC has the highest Percentscore, while the general attitude to VWC has the lowest Percentscore. In other words, the SWC–VWC biliterates in Guangzhou are most positive in standardizing VWC, but least positive in using VWC as public media language. The results again reflect the impact of the national language policy on the language attitude toward VWC in Guangzhou community, as discussed in Yan (2008).

The Percentscores for Guangzhou lifestyle and the language attitudes toward VWC serve as the variables for the correlation analysis. As shown in Figure 3, the Pearson correlation between the two variables is 0.525, which is significantly higher than 0 (p-value = 0.000). When correlation = 0, it suggests that there is no linear relationship between two variables. Here the

---

[10] For more details on the questionnaire of language attitudes toward VWC, please refer to Yan (2008) Appendix C.

Table 6: PercentScore for language attitudes toward VWC.

Attitudes	Percentscore (N = 116)
1. Integrative attitude to VWC (Q1–11)	61.4
2. General attitude to VWC (Q12–17)	57.5
3. Instrumental attitude to VWC (Q18–35)	63.7
4. Attitude to standardizing VWC (Q36–46)	66.5

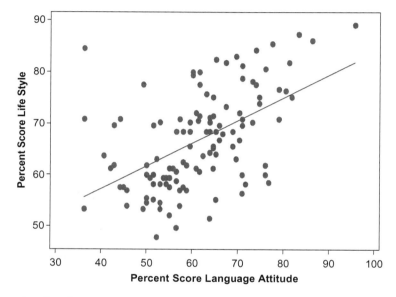

Figure 3: Correlations: PercentScoreLifeStyle, PercentScore Language Attitude, Pearson correlation of PercentScoreLifeStyle and PercentScore Language Attitude = 0.525, *P*-value = 0.000.

correlation is 0.525, which suggests a strong correlation in the research of social science. The positive correlation means that the higher one value, the higher the other value. From the figure (PercentScore Language Attitude versus PercentScore Lifestyle), we can see there is strong positive correlation between language attitude and Guangzhou lifestyle. The higher the language attitude score, the higher is the lifestyle score. Based on this finding, it is concluded that a strong local identity can strengthen the positive attitude to the use of VWC in Guangzhou. The positive attitude toward the use of VWC is highly correlated with a unique Guangzhou identity, an identity that is actually a significant part of a broader Guangzhou–Hong Kong identity of the Ling-nan region.

5. Impact of Regional Identity: Critical Discourse Analysis of VWC Discourse

The findings in the previous quantitative study of the correlation between the use of VWC and Guangzhou lifestyle provide an account of language variation between linguistic aspects and regional identity. To obtain insight on this issue from another side of the coin, that is, "to reveal the way language creates, sustains and replicates fundamental inequalities in societies" (Mesthrie *et al.*, 2000, p. 317), a qualitative analysis of VWC texts is conducted in this section. The approach adopted in the present study is "CDA." This approach is developed from the field of sociology which in an attempt to provide an account for the discourse produced by different social groups or social powers[11] in a critical stance to the position of "language reflects society" in sociolinguistics (Mesthrie *et al.*, 2000, p. 316). In other words, rather than being just a reflection of an "independent" society, language itself is a "reality-creating social practice" (Fowler, 1985, p. 62). Through a critical analysis of discourse samples, the underlying social powers involving in the language use from various perspectives such as language imposition and spread are explored.

As proposed at the beginning of this chapter, Cantonese lifestyle represents Ling-nan identity in a way based on daily life, forming a set of social regulations for the use of VWC in Cantonese communities. Those local regulations, supporting the use of VWC in the Guangzhou community as well, are competing with the institutional regulations enacted by China's government. Guo (2004) examined the three stages of the evolution of the relationship between *Putonghua* (Standard Mandarin Chinese) and

---

[11] Mesthrie *et al.* (2000, p. 320) discussed the account of powers: "At the macro level, they are involved in matters like language imposition and spread. ... Even at the micro level of language structure and use, the effects of power turn up in more areas than is generally acknowledged in linguistics."

Chinese dialect and described the social circumstance in Mainland China as follows:

> The basic official view that Chinese dialects are to be eventually replaced by Putonghua persists until 1980s, without any further change. ... China's view of the relationship between Putonghua and Chinese dialects can be traced to the social concerns underpinning the China's language policy. ... China's promotion of Putonghua is an integrated part of over-a-country continuing efforts at China's modernization. The underpinning social concerns determined, in the early stage, that Putonghua be promoted at any expenses, and moreover Chinese dialects were considered barriers to the modernization effort. ... Under China's then social concerns, dialects were considered harmful to its national unity, national security, and socialist construction, so that these dialects are no doubt target of elimination. The question was whether to eradicate dialects artificially (meaning by strong administrative measures) or to allow them to die out naturally as Putonghua spread to every domain of language use. (Guo, 2004, p. 47)

Under this sociopolitical climate in China, it is not surprising to see that "the dialect-speaking masses had concerns and uncertainty about the future of their dialects and doubts about the role of Putonghua in their daily life" (Guo, 2004, p. 24). Since mid-1990s, China's language planners have redefined the relationship between *Putonghua* and Chinese dialects:

> To uphold the legal status of Putonghua and continue to promote Putonghua vigorously does not mean the prohibition of Chinese dialects, but rather to limit the scope of dialect use. (Guo, 2004, p. 50)

The change of the language policy in recent years brings changes to the way people view the languages or dialects in China. The present study on VWC discourse explores the social concerns of the SWC–VWC biliterates in their learning and use of VWC, particularly how they relate their use of this regional written variety with local or regional identity, as being oppositional to the promotion of the national standard language as well as a national identity in the whole country.

According to the theory of critical sociolinguistics of which the main concern is the impact of power on the use of language, the social regulations built on the daily lifestyle can be defined as the societal bases of power (Mesthrie *et al.*, 2000, p. 318). The focus of present CDA is to criticize how those social regulations have been shaping the VWC literacy practice of the biliterates in the Guangzhou community. With this regard, the framework developed by the critical linguist Fairclough (1992) is used as the basis of the CDA in the present study. Fairclough (1989, 1992, and 1994) propounds a framework for CDA. In his model of CDA, as shown in Figure 4, Fairclough (1992, p.73) proposes that the three dimensions of a discourse involve text, discursive practice and sociocultural practice:

Text (written or spoken), the first layer in Fairclough's model of discourse, is embedded in the second layer of discourse practice involving all the processes of production and interpretation through which the text is created. At the same time, those processes are in turn embedded in the third layer which includes various sociocultural conditions within which the subjects are situated.

According to Fairclough (1992), "discourse contributes to processes of cultural changes, in which the social identities or 'selves' associated with specific domains and institutions are redefined and reconstituted." In other words, social identity is constructed in the context of fluctuating cultural and institutional values, which is represented in text (or discourse). The main

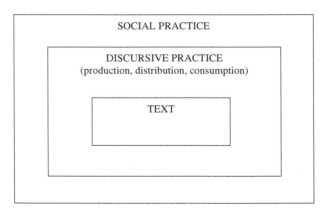

Figure 4: A three-dimensional model of discourse.

Source: Fairclough (1992, p. 73)

Note: Text: a language text, which may be spoken, written or signed; Discourse practice: involving text production and text interpretation; Sociocultural practice: involving wider social and political relations.

concern of the present CDA, therefore, is to reveal how the VWC text derived from an expected relation between the individual experience of acquiring and using VWC and the broader social regulations on VWC — is associated with the regional identity of the Guangzhou community.

Empirically, the model of Fairclough (1992) is applied to examine the VWC discourses produced by 116 subjects by looking into the organization and the content of the VWC text, the producing procedure, and the social conditions (mainly refer to the social powers) to which the subjects relate their use of VWC. The present CDA discusses the impact of Guangzhou identity on the maintenance and spread of VWC from three perspectives: (1) Critical awareness of using VWC in the Guangzhou community contrary to the powerful national language policy and as part of sociocultural practices (the 3rd layer of Fairclough's model of discourse as shown in Figure 4); (2) Regional identity revealed in the language of mass media in the Guangzhou community; and (3) Influence of Hong Kong culture on sustaining VWC in the Guangzhou community.

It is noted that although one of the key approaches of CDA is to address the language matters in a "problematized" view of language,[12] the focus of the present CDA study is not on the misrepresented social relations, but on the language phenomena in the community that shows the effects of sociocultural regulations. The critical point of analysis is the conflict relation between the powers of the national language policy and the local regulations in Guangzhou community. Whereas the use of VWC represents the Guangzhou lifestyle promoted by the local Cantonese culture, the CDA discussion provides some micro-analysis toward the sociolinguistic nature of dialectal writing.

5.1. *Data collection: Composing VWC discourses through writing task*

To obtain samples of VWC texts for CDA, a writing task is conducted as instrument to elicit VWC discourses from 116 subjects in the survey. In this writing task, the subjects are asked to use VWC to describe their experience

---

[12] Mesthrie *et al.* (2000, p. 317) points out that in the critics of CDA, there is an important point about the relation between language and society, i.e., "rather than reflecting society, there is sense in which language misrepresents (or distorts) the key social relation within a community."

of acquiring VWC and the situations under which they use VWC to communicate with the other people. The writing task and the complete text elicited from the subjects are contained in the appendices. An ID number (#1 to #116) is assigned to each VWC discourse for reference purposes.

5.2. *Critical language awareness of using VWC in the Guangzhou community*

The critical awareness of using VWC in the Guangzhou community is explored from two aspects. First, some subjects showed a critical awareness that the literacy practice of VWC is actually in conflict with the national language policy in their VWC discourses. Subject #53 states that his use of VWC is restricted by the social surroundings that all the official languages are based on Mandarin.[13] Subject #28 says that she seldom uses VWC because of the lack of textbooks and dictionaries on VWC.[14] Subject #36 compares the proper social situations for the use of VWC and the use of SWC as follows:

(1) #36: 广东口语文字受生长环境的影响,耳濡目染,自然就学会, 通常在和街坊, 本地朋友, 生活场合的书写下会使用广东口语文字, 这样会比较亲切, 而在比较正规的工作场合, 大型会议, 和同外地的朋友交际时候, 会采用标准的普通话, 这样会得体。
"Imperceptibly influenced by what I saw and heard in my growing environment, I acquired VWC naturally. I usually use VWC to write to my neighbors and local friends under the daily life situations, since it is more intimate. However, **under the formal working situations such as conference and communication with the friends from other places, I will use standard Mandarin because it is proper.**"

---

[13] #53: 广东口语书面使用由于环境的限制, 官方语言都是以普通话为基础的 (The restricted use of VWC is due to the fact that the official language is based on Putonghua Mandarin).
[14] #28: 所学的语文教材中少有广东文字的出现, 字典里也少有批注, 因此, 很少使用广东口语文字 (Little VWC appeared in the Chinese teaching materials that we ever studied. There is little annotation (on VWC) in dictionary. Therefore, I seldom used VWC).

The critical awareness of the use of VWC in Guangzhou community shows their recognition of the official policy that constrains the content of the literacy practices of VWC. Such awareness arises from the unequal relation between the dominant institutions based on national language policy and the local customs based on the need of everyday life. With such a critical awareness of using VWC, it is not surprising to see the biliterates in the Guangzhou community showing a lot of variations in their literacy practices of VWC as discussed in Yan (2008, p. 145).

Second, the use of VWC was related to the local life in Guangzhou community, showing the language awareness of using VWC as a way to express the regional identity. Based on the CDA of the written texts elicited from 116 Mandarin–Cantonese biliterates, it is proposed that the use of VWC is closely attached to the everyday life in Guangzhou community, showing the loyalty to the place where they were born and grew up. For example, many subjects claim that they learned to use VWC from childhood in their daily life as shown in the following examples (2)–(6).

(2) #1: 我从小就学习使用广东口语文字。
 "I learned to use VWC when I was a child."
(3) #10: 本人出生在广州, 系日常生活中经常会使用广东口语文字。
 "I was born in Guangzhou. I often use VWC in my everyday life."
(4) #20: 从小读书习惯看广东口语文字的小说。
 "I used to read fiction written in VWC, since I was a child in school."
(5) #25: 在我成长过程中通过听, 说, 看学会的。
 "As I grew up, I learned VWC through listening, speaking and reading (VWC)."
(6) #30: 从细就识, 日常生活, 与人接触, 发短讯。
 "I learned VWC, since I was a child. I use VWC in my everyday life to get in touch with people and to write text messages."

The written communications in which VWC is used are related to the users' daily life. Basically, those communications include the following:

(1) Writing text messages (Ex. #30);
(2) Writing email (Ex. #1);
(3) Writing instant message on the internet such as QQ, ICQ, and MSN (Ex. #11, #40);

(4) Writing notes (Ex. #12);
(5) Writing letters (Ex. #20);
(6) Writing messages in internet relay chatting room (Ex. #23);
(7) Writing a posting in internet forums (Ex. #53).

With the exception of (4) and (5), most of the written communications mentioned in the discourses rely on the new technologies developed in recent decades. The popularization of the modernized communicating tools in the everyday life of Guangzhou community speeds up the process of information exchange and objectively contributes to the spread and development of VWC. For example, in the statement of Subject #23 in example (7), communication on the Internet is an important channel for her to practice VWC.

(7) #23: 本人从一出生就学习广东话。其实对于广东口语文字了解还不算够，是与朋友通信的时候，上网的时候所认识到广东口语的文字，感觉是既熟悉又陌生，到最后就是由所认识的汉语文字加上"口"字旁，便组成了一个新的文字。通常在办公室内，通信，网上联网聊天，基本上都是与广州人的朋友沟通交流时使用。

"I learned Cantonese as soon as I was born. Actually I do not know enough about VWC. It is when I wrote to friends and surfed on the Internet that I came to recognize the writing for Vernacular Cantonese. As regard, VWC is both familiar and unfamiliar to me. Finally I created new characters through adding radical of 口 "mouth" to the Chinese characters that I have known. I usually use VWC in my office to correspond and chat on the Internet with friends who are basically from Guangzhou for communication."

With regard to the motives of using VWC, there are two important points to be noted. First, the use of VWC in Guangzhou is mostly attributed to the affective factors of intimacy and vividness. This often happens in the inner group communication, that is, both sides are able to recognize VWC. Subject #113 feels that it is more intimate（親切啲啦）to use VWC to communicate with friends or schoolmates in Guangzhou as shown in example (8).

(8) #113: 一般是同广州的同学或者朋友通讯时会写广东口语文字, 親切啲啦。
"Usually I write to my classmates or friends from Guangzhou using VWC, it is more intimate."

Subject #7 enjoys the Vernacular Cantonese words written in Cantonese pop songs and comments that the VWC words of song are vivid and lively (生动又活泼) as shown in example (9).

(9) #7: 很多香港, 广东歌曲都会用广东口语填词, 既生动又活泼, 特别粤曲, 是岭南文化的代表, 我甚是喜欢…
"Many songs of Hong Kong and Cantonese are composed in VWC. They are vivid and lively. Especially Cantonese opera, which represents Ling-Nan culture, is my favorite."

Subject #54 provides a good statement about the motive of using VWC to be intimate in example (10).

(10) #54: 我在和一些关系较密切的亲友之间使用广东口语文字, 例如和家庭成员, 和朋友之间, 感觉更自然, 更亲切。
"I use VWC to communicate with my close relatives and friends, such as my family members and friends. I feel it is more natural and intimate."

Second, the use of VWC is an important strategy to highlight Cantonese identity in certain situation. Subject #29 claims that she tends to use VWC to chat with Guangzhou local friends (广州本土的朋友) on the Internet in order to differentiate themselves from the people from other places (外地人). Subject #56 in example (11) below explains that the motive of using VWC to highlight Guangzhou identity is important in virtual world of Internet.

(11) #56: 伊家有好多网站, 特别是广州的论坛关于广州人生活的都有用广州语文字黎发表留言。如果吾用广州文字留言, 会俾人觉得吾系广州人, 其他网友会对你有甘亲切架。
"Nowadays, in many Internet websites, especially in the Internet forums of Guangzhou, the postings published on the life of Guangzhou people are

in VWC. If I do not use VWC, it will make people feel that you are not a Guangzhou person. The other Internet users will not feel so close to you."

5.3. *Mass media as a key regional promoter to the use of VWC in Guangzhou*

In spite of the restriction of the national language policy against using dialect as public media language, a large proportion of subjects placed mass media as the central topic of their VWC discourse in describing the experience of acquiring VWC. Mass media, including television, newspaper, advertising, and so on, is an important part of modern daily life. As a matter of fact, media text is an inescapable field in the CDA. Although the VWC discourses discussed were not directly drawn from the texts in mass media, the regional identity revealed in the language of mass media proved to be a key promoter to the use of VWC in Guangzhou community. Table 7 summarizes the frequency of the keywords for media appearing in the VWC discourse database. Some examples from the subjects are discussed as follows to examine in detail the regional identity emphasized by the mass media behind the acquisition of dialectal literacy.

5.3.1. *Television*

电视 *dianshi* "television" as a keyword appears 44 times in all the VWC discourse samples (116 pieces). The high frequency reflects the impact of television as a modern media strongly influencing the VWC literacy practices in the Guangzhou community. For instance, Subject #10 emphasizes that watching television news of Guangzhou every day helps in learning VWC.

(12) #10: 如每天睇广州电视台既 "新闻日日睇, 日日倾下计" (口个)[15]个节目就有许多广东口语文字学。

"For example you can learn a lot of VWC through watching the **television** program of *Watch News Daily, Chat Daily* at Guangzhou TV station everyday."

---

[15] (口个) is a pseudo character created by the subjects and is not established in the present VWC.

Table 7: Frequency of key words concerning media in VWC discourses.

Keywords	Frequency
电视 "television"	44
杂志 "magazine"	32
书报, 报刊, 报纸, 刊物 "newspaper"	30
广告 "advertisement"	6
电影 "movie"	5

In addition to television news, television drama is another important source for Guangzhou people to be exposed to VWC. Subject #76 describes the impact of television series on the VWC literacy practices:

(13) #76: 一直都(在)广州这个城市读书与生活, 很容易就能接触到来自于港澳方面的电视, 报刊等资讯, 特别是在读书期间, 同学们相互讨论着电视剧中的情节, 对白, 自然而然就学着使用广东口语来写一些日常交流的小纸条。
"I have been studying and living in Guangzhou city all along. It is very easy to be exposed to the media source from Hong Kong and Macao such as television and newspaper. Especially during the time in school, students discussed with each other about the plots and dialogues of the **television series**, and naturally learned to use VWC to write some notes for daily communication."

(14) #114: (我学广东口语文字)主要通过看香港的杂志或电视连续剧的字幕...
"(I learned VWC) mainly through reading Hong Kong magazines and subtitles in the **television soap opera**."

5.3.2. *Magazine*

The role of 杂志 *zazhi* "magazine" is significant in the spreading of VWC in Guangzhou community. As a kind of media in print, magazines cater to the need of readers not only by providing diverse information and opinions but also by writing in the way the readers appreciate. Subject #82 relates the use of VWC in magazine with the local fashion trend, as shown in the written narration of example (4).

(15) #82: 现在因为在一家本地潮流杂志工作, 所以在编辑稿件时经常会使用广州口语。
"Because I am working for a **local trendy magazine** now, I often use VWC when I edit articles."

Most of the magazines through which the subjects exposed to VWC are from Hong Kong. Examples are given as follows:

(16) #9: 由于生活在珠三角, 经常接触到来自香港既杂志, 电视新闻。
"Because I am living in the Pearl River Delta, I am often exposed to **Hong Kong magazines** and television news."

(17) #15: 平时睇香港杂志睇得多, 有时就学到几个。
"I read a lot of **Hong Kong magazines** ordinarily, (so) at times I learned some VWC."

(18) #63: 真正使用广东口语文字系初中之后, 果时看得香港电视同埋香港的杂志多, 所以就学会使用啦。
"It is after middle school that I actually started to use VWC. At that time, I watched a lot of Hong Kong television and **Hong Kong magazines**. As a result, I learned how to use VWC."

(19) #110: 平时睇香港八卦杂志学到的广州口语文字特别多。
"I especially learned a lot of VWC by ordinarily reading **Hong Kong entertainment magazines**."

Some subjects claimed that it is very common to see VWC in the local magazines and publications. This is shown in examples (20) and (21).

(20) #57: 见惯了报刊杂志等都有广东口语。
"I am used to seeing VWC in newspaper and magazines."

(21) #96: 很多广州的杂志报刊都会用广东口语文字。时间一长, 自然会使用。
"There are a lot of VWC in the local magazines and newspaper in Guangzhou. As time passed, I naturally learned how to use VWC."

To summarize, the social influence of magazines makes the use of VWC in Guangzhou a trendy, common, and fun thing. Especially when Hong Kong culture is involved in the magazine readership, the subjects show a striking consistence on the impact of Hong Kong magazine in describing their experience of acquiring VWC. The impact of Hong Kong lifestyle is discussed in Sec. 4.4.

5.3.3. *Newspaper*

As another type of media in print influencing the Guangzhou lifestyle, the influence of newspaper is the same as magazine, if it is not stronger. The long tradition of newspaper publication in Guangzhou leads to the formation of a very competitive business of journalism in Guangzhou to date. As a result, reading newspapers has become a part of Guangzhou lifestyle. The VWC literacy practice of Guangzhou community is inescapably influenced by such a deep-rooted newspaper readership. In the written narrations on the personal experience of learning VWC, general description about the impact from newspaper as well as the specific impact from some famous newspapers are observed. Below, examples for general descriptions are given in examples (22)–(26), and for special description in examples (27)–(30):

(22) #4: 从书报中得知广东口语文字, 模仿字体, 进而使用广东口语文字。
"I learned about VWC from **newspaper** and imitated the way of writing, and was able to use it finally."

(23) #59: 特别是文革前, 许多书刊, 报纸都有广州方言登载所以学识。
"I learned (VWC) especially before the Cultural Revolution, Guangzhou dialect was published in a lot of books and **newspapers**."

(24) #80: 我是通过阅读香港的报纸学会使用广东口语文字的。
"I learned how to use VWC through reading Hong Kong **newspaper**."

(25) #113: 在广州能读的书, 看的报很多广东口语, 所以认识。
"There are a lot of VWC in the books and newspaper I read, so I learned (VWC)."

(26) #65: 睇电视或睇报纸时间中学习广东文字口语。
"I learned VWC from watching television and reading **newspaper**."

(27) #12: 在香港的《大公报》或者《娱乐周刊》里面学。
"I learned it from Hong Kong's *Takungpao* and *Entertainment* Weekly."

(28) #107: 经常阅读《大公报》, 从香港报刊, 杂志学会不少广东口语文字。
"I often read *Takungpao*. I learned a lot of VWC from Hong Kong newspaper and magazine."

(29) #111: 广东口语文字多数从报刊和杂志上学, 例如《羊城晚报》上有时介绍广东口语文字。
"I mainly learned VWC from newspaper and magazines. For example, VWC was sometimes introduced in *Yangcheng Evening News*."

(30) #114: 例如《新快报》也有"广州话新闻"专栏。
"For example, there is a column entitled 'News in Guangzhou dialect' in ***New Express***."

In short, the newspaper serves as an important source for people to learn VWC in the Guangzhou community. Given the popularity of the local newspaper, it is safe to conclude that a strong readership of newspaper contributes greatly to the acquisition of VWC in Guangzhou.

5.3.4. *Advertisement*

Six subjects note the impact of the advertisement language on their literacy practice of VWC. For example:

(31) #20: 从小读书习惯看广东口语文字的小说, 睇广州语字典, 睇广州话的广告词和电影。

"Since I was a child, I used to read fiction written in VWC, looking up Guangzhou dialectal dictionaries, **advertisements,** and movies [i.e., with subtitles] written in Guangzhou dialect."

(32) #85: 我嘅广东口语文字, 基本上系系日常生活中学会嘅: 同广州人倾计, 体电视, 体亍招, 广告等等。
"My basic knowledge of VWC is acquired during my daily life, such as chatting with Guangzhou people, watching television, reading street postings and **advertisement**, and so on."

(33) #109: 跟住又接触社会上嘅广告和睇过一啲武侠小说咁就学会广东口语文字。
"Further, I was exposed to VWC through the **advertisements** in the society, and reading some martial arts fictions. In that way I acquired VWC."

Basically, advertisement written in VWC is a common scene in Guangzhou community. It wins local customers' favor as well as spreads VWC into the ordinary life of the local community.

5.3.5. Movie

电影 *dianying* "movie" is noted by five subjects in their written narration as an important source to be exposed to VWC. In their description, movies using VWC are all associated with Hong Kong. Hong Kong is one of the major centers of film-making industry in the world (Li, 1996, p. 74). The language employed in Hong Kong movies is mostly vernacular spoken Cantonese, resulting in using VWC very often to write subtitle for the movie speech. Given that Hong Kong movies is a strong social force as a worldwide trademark in all Cantonese-speaking regions, VWC subtitle used in Hong Kong movies promotes the use of VWC in Guangzhou. This is reflected in the following written examples (34) and (35).

(34) #3: 我是看香港电视, 电影, 流行歌词学会使用广东口语文字。
"I learned VWC from **Hong Kong** television, **movies**, and popular songs."

(35) #17: 平时爱看香港电影。以前的香港电影很多时候都会以广东口语做字幕, 所以都学会很多广东口语文字。

"I love watching **Hong Kong movies** at ordinary times. A lot of **Hong Kong movies** in the past used VWC subtitle. Therefore, I was able to learn a lot of VWC."

To summarize, the present discourse analysis provides evidence for the impact of media in influencing and sustaining VWC literacy practice in the Guangzhou community. As a significant part of Guangzhou lifestyle, the activities of watching television and movies, reading magazine, newspaper, and advertisement, contribute greatly to the spread of Guangzhou VWC.

It is noted that the VWC literacy practice of any individual is usually associated with the use of several types of media. In other words, an environment that is suitable for the existence of a vernacular writing is created by the "whole group" of the media. This point of view has been shown repeatedly in the statements of many subjects. For example, Subject #2 argues that both watching television and reading newspaper helps his acquisition of VWC.

(36) #2: 对于广州白话文字, 我是在睇香港电视和报纸时学到的。
"As for Guangzhou VWC, I learned it through **watching Hong Kong television and reading newspaper.**"

In addition to the several types of media previously mentioned, there are some other Cantonese cultural activities that sustain the literacy practice of VWC in Guangzhou such as reading comic books (#39, #44, and #78) and learning Cantonese songs (#3, #7, #40, #62, #102), and Cantonese opera (#7, #57, and #109). Moreover, Internet surfing such as blogging and online chatting shows an overt potential in promoting the use of VWC as stated in the narration of #18, #23, #43, etc. In all, as part of mass media, all those activities contribute to the use of VWC in Guangzhou community.

5.4. *Impact of Hong Kong culture*

Although the present sociolinguistic survey is conducted in Guangzhou community, the impact of Hong Kong culture is observed everywhere in the discourses written about the experience of learning VWC. As discussed in Sec. 4.3, the media containing VWC is often associated with Hong Kong.

The frequency of "Hong Kong" as a keyword appearing in the present discourse corpus is 62 (53% of 116 pieces of discourse). Such a high frequency reveals that the Guangzhou regional identity and the use of VWC in this area are very closely related with Hong Kong culture.

Hong Kong, a flourishing neighbor right beside Guangzhou, actually serves as the cultural capital of Ling-nan area. To describe the historical distinctiveness of the Guangzhou region, Snow (2004, pp. 68–73) draws an outline of Guangdong history which started from Pre-Qin (before 221 BCE) to the period of Nationalist and Republican (1911–1949). The distinct Cantonese (or Ling-Nan) culture and identity with such a long history is held by the whole group of Cantonese-speaking inhabitants of Guangdong area. In this sense, Guangzhou community is sharing a broader Ling-nan identity with Hong Kong community.

The Hong Kong lifestyle represents a kind of modern Cantonese lifestyle which is often tagged as "wealthy," "trendy," "commercialized," and "westernized." Psychologically, pursuing a lifestyle of Hong Kong is natural and even pleasant in Guangzhou community, not to mention that the common Cantonese dialect and culture can be promoted during this process. As a matter of fact, not only in Guangdong area but also in other parts of China, a trend of "northern move of Cantonese" took place during the past several decades (Bruche-Schulz, 1997, p. 311). Zhan (1993, p. 54) points out that the influence of Cantonese opens the door of linguistic diversification which is in line with the trend of modern linguistic life. At the same time, such economics-related influence is also a powerful promoter to the expansion of Cantonese dialect writing.

With regard to the media language, in Hong Kong, the general preference of readers in turn helps to shape the language choice in the Chinese press. Written Cantonese has become a selling point which is no longer an indicator of lower-class writing but a strong indicator of a new cultural identity (Li, 2000, p. 201). As for the case of Guangzhou, the consequence is not so overt, given the language policy of the PRC government and complicated sociolinguistic situations in Guangzhou. The use of Chinese characters to represent (near) homophonous Cantonese morphosyllables is generally viewed as one clear source of literacy problems in the domain of education, and therefore is not part of school literacy. The existence of the VWC thereby plays a role in the life of Guangzhou Cantonese speakers, although the role is negative from the government's perspective on education.

5.5. Summary

The present CDA of the personal narration focuses on the role played by the regional identity in learning and use of VWC. The results reveal the critical awareness of using VWC in Guangzhou. That is, the use of VWC is in an oppositional status to the national standard language (SWC) as part of sociolocal cultural practices in biliterates' everyday life. The written Cantonese used in the local mass media highlights the regional identity, which greatly impacts the use and spread of VWC in Guangzhou. Moreover, Hong Kong culture as a trend to be pursued by the Guangzhou community serves as a strong social force in promoting VWC in Guangzhou.

6. Conclusion

This study explores the variation of VWC literacy practices as correlated with the everyday lifestyle in Guangzhou community. The findings suggest that Guangzhou lifestyle, representing the regional identity of Guangzhou, plays a positive role in the divergence of VWC from SWC in lexical variables, classifier variables, and syntactic variables. However, the extent to which Guangzhou identity as an influencing factor has impact on the variation of VWC differs in different linguistic levels. With regard to the impact of local life on the language attitude, there is a strong positive correlation between language attitude and Guangzhou lifestyle. In this sense, a strong local identity can strengthen the positive attitude to the use of VWC in Guangzhou. At the same time, the CDA of the impact of various social powers reveals that mass media and Hong Kong culture play important roles in promoting the use of VWC in Guangzhou area. Other everyday lifestyle in Guangzhou community such as communication with friends also plays a key role in the maintenance of VWC. For some biliterates, their critical language awareness of using VWC in Guangzhou community reflects the sociopolitical conflict between the national language policy and the use of regional written variety.

References

Fairclough, N (1992). *Discourse and Social Change*. Cambridge: Polity Press.
Fowler, R (1985). Power. In *The Handbook of Discourse Analysis*, Vol. 4, *Discourse Analysis in Society*, T van Dijk (ed.), pp. 61–82. London: Acadmic Press.

Guo, LS (2004). Between Putonghua and Chinese Dialects. In *Language Policy in the People's Republic of China: Theory and Practice Since 1949*, M Zhou and S Hongkai (eds.). Kluwer Academic Publishers.

Li, D (2000). Phonetic borrowing: Key to the vitality of written Cantonese in Hong Kong. *Written Language and Literacy*, 3(2), 199–233.

Mesthrie, R, J Swann, A Deumert and WL Leap (2000). *Introducing Sociolinguistics*. Philadelphia: John Benjamins Publishing Company.

Rietveld, T and R van Hout (2005). *Statistics in Language Research: Analysis of Variance*. New York: Mouton de Gruyter.

Snow, D (2004). *Cantonese as Written Language: The Growth of a Written Chinese Vernacular*. Hong Kong: Hong Kong University Press.

Yan, J (2008). Social variation of vernacular written cantonese In *Guangzhou (Canton City), China*, PhD Dissertation, The Ohio State University, Columbus, Ohio, USA.

Yan, J and M Chan (2007). *Language Attitudes Toward Vernacular Written Cantonese in Guangzhou (Canton)*, China: National language policy and regional language maintenance, Co-presented at the 2007 Annual Meeting of the Linguistic Society of America, January 4–7, 2007, Anaheim, CA.

Zhan, BH (詹伯慧) (1993). Putonghua "nan-xia" yu Yue fangyan "bei-shang" 普通话"南下"与粤方言"北上"(Putonghua "heading South," Cantonese "heading North"). *Yuwen Jianshe Tongxue*, 39, 51–56.

CHAPTER 9

NEGOTIATING LINGUISTIC IDENTITIES UNDER GLOBALIZATION: LANGUAGE USE IN CONTEMPORARY CHINA[1]

JIN LIU
Georgia Institute of Technology, Atlanta, USA

HONGYIN TAO
University of California, Los Angeles, USA

In its long history, China has rarely faced, as it does today, under globalization and modernization, such a multitude of problems with regard to language choice and linguistic identity. This chapter outlines some of the major issues in Chinese language and identity. These issues include: (1) challenges imposed by global English from the outside world; (2) the dynamics between the national and the local as represented by the dominance of the national language, standard Mandarin, and the preservation of local linguistic resources and cultural heritages based on regional dialects; and finally, (3) a collective identity of Chineseness as a result of the rapidly ascending status of the Chinese language worldwide. These evolving issues, though not completely unique to China, provide rich materials for research in globalization, identity, multiculturalism, and multilingualism.

---

[1] This chapter is based on a paper originally published in *Harvard Asia Pacific Review*, X(1) (Spring, 2009), 7–10. Here is the revised and updated version.

If the 2008 Beijing Olympics was a dazzling display of China's growing power on the world stage, the Parade of Nations at the opening ceremony was a show of China's resolve in an increasingly intense battle of linguistic power. Traditionally, the sequence of nations entering the parade follows alphabetic order; at the Beijing Olympics, however, nations emerged according to Chinese "stroke order." This meant that nations were arranged based on the number and sequence of strokes in the first character of their Chinese names. The choice came as a surprise, even to many Chinese viewers, who are accustomed to using a Romanized *pinyin* system in many areas of modern life. One could argue that using the alphabetized *pinyin* system would have better accommodated the spirit of "One World, One Dream." Such a display of linguistic identity is merely one of many linguistic struggles occurring in China today.

1. The Code as Identity

Confucius cautioned more than 2,000 years ago that one could not successfully govern without first clarifying one's language. Language, of course, is not merely important to governing the state; language, and the choices made about language are integral parts of social and cultural identities. Language is fundamentally a social phenomenon, and while the choice of linguistic code may be made unconsciously, any such choice reveals and creates intended and unintended identities.

In its long history, China has rarely faced such a multitude of problems with regard to language choice, nor has it felt such urgency in defending its linguistic identities. The intensity and complexity of the linguistic struggles are only matched by the stunning speed of China's social and economic developments over the past three decades. These struggles derive from sources external and internal, and they involve the problems of how to accommodate English, and both regional and social dialects, in the national culture.

2. Between Chinese in Crisis and Go Believe

The first line of linguistic struggle deals with the challenge from outside, chiefly, the challenge imposed by English. Under the Reform and Opening policy, China witnessed a national obsession with learning English, a language denounced as bourgeois and imperialist during the Cultural Revolution. Today, English is viewed as a necessary tool in China's modernization and integration with the world. The English as a Second Language (ESL) industry has boomed in the past few decades. According to Xinhua, China's official news agency, ESL in Beijing reaped 700 million yuan (US$84.68 million) in profits in 2001 (Woodward, 2008), a number that will undoubtedly be dwarfed by the 2011 output. The New Oriental School 新东方学校 (*Xin dongfang xuexiao*), which began as a program to help Chinese students with the US-based TOEFL and GRE tests, has grown into the largest private education enterprise and is now being traded on the New York Stock Exchange.

The spread of the English language is both a resource for modernization and a source of contention. Chinese, like others across the globe, have criticized the global dominance of English for suppressing other languages and monopolizing the world's information. Chinese intellectuals, such as the writer Li Rui, have expressed consternation that the Internet would encourage the global dominance of English and marginalize all other languages. The notion of a "Chinese Crisis" even became the title of a new book in 2008, in which Pan Wenguo, a linguist at East China Normal University, outlined five symptoms of Chinese in crisis, the top one being the overwhelming use of English on the Internet and the accelerated cultural globalization mediated in English (Pan, 2008; see also Zhu, 2005). Although the hegemony of English online has gradually weakened with the proliferation of Chinese-based sites and user bases, the debate between these academics and their opponents remains a hot topic in the media and public discourse.

While intellectuals may worry about the impact of English on Chinese language and culture, others resent English for other reasons. Undergraduate and graduate students must demonstrate certain levels of English proficiency in order to obtain degrees, a requirement that, a recent survey shows, has consumed from one-quarter to one-half of college students' study time. Anecdotally, many parents complain that their children routinely greet them in English instead of in Chinese. On a more extreme level, readers were understandably outraged by a 2005 Xinhua report: a caller to an emergency hotline hung up because she did not understand the English instructions at the other end of the line, and was subsequently robbed by highway bandits.

Of course, this is not to suggest that the Chinese public is going to boycott English any time soon. On the contrary, many shrewd businessmen take the English frenzy as a window of opportunity and act upon it in clever ways. Li Yang, an engineer by training, cashed in on Chinese nationalism in his "Crazy English" English education business, with his slogan "conquer English to make China stronger!" In addition, a famous Tianjin-based restaurant chain that specializes in steamed stuffed buns has officially changed its name from the Chinese Romanized *Gou Bu Li* 狗不理 (literally, "dogs don't bother") to an English brand name, "Go Believe!"

3. From Language Planning to Language Rescuing

The PRC is not only home to more than 50 minority ethnic groups with their own languages but also to a mosaic of local dialects that belong to the Chinese language (Norman, 1988). There are roughly seven major dialect groups in China: Mandarin, Wu, Min, Cantonese, Gan, Xiang, and Hakka, each with its own various subdialects.

For years, the central government has promoted the Mandarin dialect of Chinese, called *Putonghua*, or common speech, as the official language of China. Through mass formal education, the mass media, and increasingly through administrative measures, the promotion of standard Mandarin has been largely successful. According to an official national survey result on language use in China released in 2004 (*Zhongguo yuyan wenzi shiyong qingkuang diaocha*, 中国语言文字使用情况调查), approximately 53% of the population is able to communicate in *Putonghua*, with urban areas more successful in implementation than rural areas (urban penetration is 66% and rural penetration is 45%) (Yuyan kexue, 2005, p. 112). The state's efforts at promoting standard Mandarin are represented in the 2001 Law of the People's Republic of China on the Use of Chinese Languages and Chinese Characters (*Zhonghua Renmin Gongheguo guojia tongyong yuyan wenzifa*, 中华人民共和国国家通用语言文字法), the first national law on language and writing. The law prescribes that *Putonghua* be the principal language of broadcast media, movies, school education, and administration and it strongly discourages the public use of all other local languages or dialects (except in the non-Han Chinese regions).

While official documents attest to the importance of protecting regional linguistic and cultural heritages, the promotion of *Putonghua* has led to a sharp decline in the use of dialects, particularly among the urbanized young.

For example, in a survey on the use of the Suzhou Wu dialect among students in grades two through eleven — 90% of whose parents are native Suzhounese — more than 70% of the students claimed more fluency in *Putonghua* than in Wu (Wang, 2003). In another survey on the use of the Zhejiang Jinhua Wu dialect among 6 to 14 years old, as many as 52% said they could not speak their native dialect, though virtually all could speak *Putonghua* (jhnews.com, 2003). Thirty years ago, this would have been unthinkable. Clearly, the longstanding tradition of diglossia, the use of more than one dialect in a community, has tilted toward the dominance of one common language.

Yet, as is the case with the reaction the predominance of English, the national domination of *Putonghua* has not been imposed without challenge in China. Despite the 2001 language law, local media and literary genres produced in regional dialects have flourished in recent years. In television, a burgeoning of dialect-based news talk shows draw on the arts of local traditional story-telling; popular shows have also been localized, as in 2005, when the cartoon series "Tom and Jerry" was dubbed into around 20 dialects nationwide. In film, internationally renowned director Jia Zhangke's *Hometown Trilogy*, largely acted in Shanxi Mandarin, ushered in a wave of underground and independent films employing dialects to represent the aesthetics of "the marginal and the unassimilated." On the Internet, one can find rap music in dialects, tests on dialect competence mimicking the formats of official English exams, dialect texts parodying Chinese characters and the writing system, blogs employing local slang and expressions, and downloadable mobile ringtones recorded in dialects. Finally, fiction-writers have become increasingly aware of regional dialects. A number of established native writers, who once adhered to the writing style of standard Mandarin, such as Jia Pingwa, Mo Yan, Yan Lianke, and Zhang Wei, have started experimenting with novels written in their native dialects (Liu, 2008).

As the nation-state becomes increasingly globalized, homogenized, and centralized, the use of dialect in local media asserts the values of pluralism and diversity and helps to construct a distinct local linguistic and cultural identity. Grassroots efforts to promote local dialects have emerged across regions in various forms. For instance, dialect training workshops in the major Wu-vernacular metropolises such as Shanghai, Hangzhou, Ningbo, and Suzhou have all been well received. Local newspapers run articles on strategies to preserve readers' mother tongues against the "over-dissemination" of *Putonghua*. In Shanghai, a supplementary textbook designed for elementary students was revised in 2005 to include a reading which briefly introduces the history of Shanghai Wu and its vocabulary (Wang, 2005). Efforts such as these have spurred local legislators in various cities to launch municipal-level initiatives to "rescue and protect" local dialects as "endangered cultural heritages." Even in provinces like Guangdong (Canton), where Cantonese has remained predominant, local lawmakers began to create such events as the Cantonese Language and Cultural Festivals to promote local identities. And most recently, the Pro-Cantonese protests and demonstrations against restrictions on Cantonese in the summer 2010, first in Guangzhou and soon echoed in Hongkong, have been viewed not simply as a linguistic action (Waldron, 2010). According to Bob Eng (2010), "the size and fervor of the pro-Cantonese movement were derived from well-founded fears that Cantonese was losing ground, and also from legitimate sources of popular dissatisfaction beyond the realms of language policy: collective concerns about the progressive disappearance of Cantonese culture and social dislocations resulting from massive urban renewal and construction."

Proponents of the dialect revival have found allies in overseas Chinese youth, who naturally have an even stronger sense of identity with their mother tongues. Chen Leiqing, a Shanghainese who immigrated to the United States when he was 11 years old, founded the SHN website (www.shanghaining.com) in 2003. With a distinctive Shanghai spin, the website is dedicated to promoting Shanghai Wu among diaspora Shanghai youth across the globe. The site also acts as a major host server for Shanghai Rap, an emerging youth musical form characterized by the rhythmic patois of Shanghai Wu. The young rappers make substantial use of a distinctive local slang to articulate a privileged local identity that celebrates their urban roots. Yet, their language decidedly features code-mixing; in this ever more globalized world, Mandarin and English expressions have a way of creeping into rapping, talking, and writing.

Nevertheless, the reaction to the revival of regional dialects has been decidedly mixed. In contrast to Wu-speaking areas, which are largely well-developed coastal regions, localities in less-developed regions, which are mostly within or near the Mandarin-speaking sphere, are lukewarm to, if not totally detached from, the dialect crisis. In fact, there is a strong desire to popularize standard Mandarin in order to reach out to the rest of the country.

The media's increasing use of dialect has also caused considerable concern among authorities. The censors at the central and local State Administration of Radio, Film, and Television (SARFT) have been issuing or reissuing regulations with increasing frequency, seeking to contain the media's use of dialect and to promote a pure, normative Mandarin. However, this agenda has been continuously challenged by tides of new vocabulary and linguistic innovations that have swept through Chinese society. For instance, the Cantonese-accented Mandarin and Taiwan Mandarin that have penetrated the mainland through popular culture since the 1970s are viewed as "cool" and avidly imitated by young people in Mainland China. The trend finally led to a SARFT regulation in 2005, stipulating that broadcasting hosts should always use standard Mandarin and should stop adopting Hong Kong or Taiwanese slang and accents (Cody, 2005). However, in the Internet age, words are not only flowing from Hong Kong and Taiwan to the mainland. New media have also led to the creation of a new language, the Internet language, rather amusingly known as *Huoxing wen* (language from Mars) (see Gao, Chapter 1). This emerging social dialect concerns educators and purists alike and has prompted lawmakers in some regions to draft legislation to contain its use in print media and school settings. The dynamics between standard Mandarin and the "other" dialects are expected to continue for a long time and constitute one of the unsettled issues in contemporary China.

4. Made in China of a Different Sort: The Language of Confucius Goes Global

While Chinese speakers are grappling with their linguistic identities, the rest of the world is scrambling for a Chinese export of a different sort: the Chinese language. The rising profile of China, backed by considerable economic, military, and political power, has popularized the Chinese language across the globe. It is estimated that there are currently 30 million people around the world learning Chinese as a second language. Based on the annual report by the US-based Institute of International Education (IIE), the number of Americans studying in China has increased by 25% in the 2006–2007 academic year over the previous year. According to statistics recently released by the Chinese Ministry of Education, the number of foreign students in China has reached a record high of more than 260,000 in 2010 (Chen, 2011). Advanced Placement (AP) Chinese exams for American high school students were offered for the first time in 2007.

While the US government sees Chinese as one of its "critical languages" for security reasons, and has thus dedicated enormous resources to Chinese language learning, the Chinese government sees this surge of interest in Chinese as a unique opportunity to promote Chinese culture and identity across the globe. In 1987, the Chinese government established the Office of Chinese Language Council International (*Hanban*, 汉办), which is charged with the task of establishing the Confucius Institutes and supporting Chinese language and cultural programs around the world. The institutes are modeled after government-backed programs such as France's Alliance Française, the British Council, and Germany's Göethe-Institut. While the first Confucius Institute opened in Seoul, South Korea, in 2004, as of December 2008, 249 Confucius Institutes had been established in 78 countries.

The rapidly ascending status of the Chinese language has brought national pride to Chinese. With the establishment of large numbers of nondegree and degree programs in teaching Chinese as a second language at Chinese universities and the mushrooming of language teacher training programs and private Chinese language–related enterprises, the 21st century has been called the century of the Chinese language. It is fitting, then, to see that one of Mainland China's most popular songs of 2007 was titled "The Chinese Language" (*Zhongguohua*, 中国话), sung by the pop trio S.H.E. from Taiwan. Part of the song lyrics reads as follows (translation by the authors of this chapter):

伦敦玛丽莲买了件旗袍送妈妈
莫斯科的夫斯基爱上牛肉面疙瘩
各种颜色的皮肤 各种颜色的头发
嘴里念的说的开始流行中国话
多少年我们苦练英文发音和文法
这几年换他们卷着舌头学平上去入的变化
……
好聪明的中国人 好优美的中国话
……
全世界都在学中国话 孔夫子的话越来越国际化

"Marilyn of London bought her mom a Chinese Qipao dress; Voski of Moscow developed a taste for Chinese beef noodles; People of all skins and hair colors start to speak Chinese. They now speak the increasingly popular Chinese language. For so many years we have suffered from practicing English, Now it is the foreigners' turn to twist their tongues to get right all the Chinese tones....

The Chinese are such smart people; and the Chinese language is so beautiful.

The whole world is now learning Chinese; the language of Confucius is going global."

What this seems to be suggesting, is a collective identity of Chineseness at a global stage. That is, while there may be internal struggles inside the China proper as manifested in the dynamics between nationalization/standardization as represented by Mandarin and preservation of local linguistic resources and cultural heritages based on regional dialects, as stated above, a shared linguistic identity is being projected to the outside world, especially considering the fact that the band is based in Taiwan, not Mainland China (although we are not suggesting that a unified Chinese identity has formed transcending all Chinese-speaking regions). This is no doubt an added layer of complexity in the construction of linguistic identity in contemporary China.

5. Summary

China is confronted with a multitude of linguistic issues representing sociocultural undercurrents in the larger context of globalization and modernization. Although these issues are hardly unique to China, their complexity and magnitude rival, if not surpass, celebrated historical moments such as the May Fourth Movement in the long history of the Chinese civilization. How this situation will play out is a fascinating topic for anyone with an interest in globalization, identity, multiculturalism, and multilingualism.

References

Chen, J (2011). Expat student numbers rise (March 4, 2011). *China Daily*.

Cody, E (2005). On Chinese television, what's cool is no longer correct (September 29, 2005). *The Washington Post,* p. A.14.

Eng, B (2010). Is Cantonese in danger of extinction? The politics and culture of language policy in China, on his blog <http://chinamusictech.blogspot.com/2010/08/is-cantonese-in-danger-of-extinction.html>.

Jhnews.com (2003). Jinhua fangyan, ping shenme bei paoqi 金华方言, 凭什么被抛弃 (why the Jinhua Wu dialect has been abandoned), <http://www.jhnews.com.cn/gb/content/2003-04/18/content_172194.htm>.

Liu, J (2008). *Signifying the Local: Media Productions Rendered in Local Languages in Mainland China since 2000,* PhD dissertation, Cornell University, Ann Arbor: University Microfilms International (U.M.I.).

Norman, J (1988). *Chinese.* Cambridge: Cambridge University Press.

Pan, WG (潘文国) (2008). *Weijixia de Zhongwen* 危机下的中文 (*Chinese under Crisis*). Shenyang: Liaoning Renmin Chubanshe.

Waldron, A (August 5, 2010). Will linguistic centralization work? Protesters demonstrate against restrictions on Cantonese, Jamestown Foundation. *China Brief,* 10(16).

Wang, P (汪平) (2003). Putonghua he Suzhou Hua zai Suzhou de xiaozhang yanjiu 普通话和苏州话在苏州的消长研究 (A study of the rise of the Putonghua and the decline of Suzhou Wu dialect in Suzhou). *Yuyan Jiaoxue yu Yanjiu,* 1, 29–36.

Wang, YJ (王有佳) (2005). Shanghai: Fangyan jieshao wenzhang "Nong xiaode fa" jin keben re zhengyi 上海: 方言介绍文章《侬晓得伐》进课本惹争议 (Shanghai: An article introducing Shanghai Wu "do you know" evoked controversy) (September 6, 2005). *Renmin Daily,* p. 5.

Woodward, AR (2008). A survey of Li Yang Crazy English, *Sino-Platonic Papers,* No. 180 (April 2008).

Yuyan Kexue 语言科学 (language Science) (2005). Zhongguo yuyan wenzi shiyong qingkuang diaocha jieguo zai Beijing gongbu 中国语言文字使用情况调查结果在北京公布 (The result of the national survey on language use in China released in Beijing), (3), 112.

Zhu, J (ed.) (朱竞) (编) (2005). *Hanyu de Weiji* 汉语的危机 (*The Chinese Language Crisis).* Beijing: Wenhua Yishu Chubanshe.

ABOUT THE CONTRIBUTORS (IN ORDER OF APPEARANCE)

Liwei Gao is Assistant Professor of Chinese at the Defense Language Institute. He received his PhD in linguistics from University of Illinois at Urbana-Champaign. His research interests are primarily in sociolinguistics, Chinese linguistics, and teaching Chinese as a foreign language. He is the author of the book *Chinese Internet Language: A Study of Identity Constructions* (2007). He currently serves as Vice President of the Chinese Language Teachers Association of California.

Chong Han is Associate Lecturer in Linguistics, Interpreting and Translation Studies at the University of Western Sydney (Australia). She received her PhD in Linguistics from the University of Sydney (Australia). Her research areas include semantics, pragmatics, discourse analysis and Chinese linguistics.

Jin Liu is Assistant Professor of Chinese at Georgia Institute of Technology. She received her BA and MA in Chinese linguistics from Beijing University and her PhD in East Asian Literature from Cornell University. Her interdisciplinary research examines contemporary Chinese popular culture through the lens of local languages or dialects. Her work has been published in journals including *Journal of Modern Literature in Chinese, Chinese Language and Discourse, Modern Chinese Literature and Culture*, and *Harvard Asia Pacific Review.*

Qing Zhang is Assistant Professor of Anthropology at the University of Arizona. She received her PhD in linguistics from Stanford University. She teaches courses in sociolinguistics and linguistic anthropology. Her research deals with how language and other semiotic resources are employed in the construction of social distinctions in contemporary China. Her work has been published in journals such as *Language in Society*, *Journal of Sociolinguistics*, and *Journal of Language and Politics*.

Chen-Chun E is a Doctoral student in the joint PhD program in linguistics and anthropology at the University of Arizona. Her research areas include Chinese syntax, linguistic anthropology, semiotics, and applied linguistics. One of her recent projects analyzes discourses of Taiwanese women's singlehood and their discursively constructed identity. She also works on syntactic structures of Chinese comparative correlative constructions from the perspectives of generative linguistics.

Ksenia Kozha is Research Fellow in the Institute of Oriental Studies (Russian Academy of Sciences) in Russia. She received her PhD in Chinese Linguistics from the Institute of Oriental Studies. Her research interests include contemporary Chinese lexical environment, Chinese dependency syntax, and history of the Chinese language studies in Europe.

Amber R Woodward received her Juris Doctor from the Washington University in St. Louis School of Law. She graduated from the University of Pennsylvania with BA in Chinese and in Public Service Communications. She plans a legal career in the government, with an eventual focus on US and Chinese relations. Under the tutelage of Professor Victor H Mair, she studied Li Yang for over five years and has authored multiple articles on Crazy English.

Oliver Radtke is a PhD candidate working on the theme of Chinglish, a rather peculiar yet creative mix of the Chinese and English language. He did his post graduation in Modern Chinese Studies from Heidelberg University (Germany) and Shanghai International Studies University (China). His thesis dealt with the sociopolitical relevance of the Chinese blogosphere. He has since then published three books entitled *Welcome to Presence: Abenteuer Alltag in China*, *Chinglish: Found in Translation* (2007), and *Chinglish: Speaking in*

Tongues (2009). He is also the founder-moderator of www.chinglish.de, the online museum for all things Chinglish.

Jing Yan is instructor of Chinese language at the Columbus Academy, Columbus, Ohio. She received her PhD in Chinese Linguistics from the Ohio State University. Her research interest includes Chinese sociolinguistics and historical linguistics. She is also interested in the area of Teaching Chinese as Foreign Language (TCFL).

Hongyin Tao is Professor of Chinese language and linguistics at the University of California, Los Angeles. His research areas include Chinese linguistics, discourse analysis, corpus linguistics, and applied linguistics. He is also Executive Editor of the international journal *Chinese Language and Discourse* and the companion book series *Studies in Chinese Language and Discourse*, with John Benjamins Publishing Company.

INDEX

A Chinese Odyssey 64
abbreviations 105, 107–109, 113, 115, 117, 121
apparent time 7, 9, 10, 25

bilingual 4
bilingual signs 150–152, 155, 166, 167
bilingual text 147
biliterates 4

Cantonese 171–174, 185, 188, 190–192, 198–201
Chinese Crisis 205
Chinese language 7–9, 11, 21, 22, 24, 25
Chinese media 36, 49, 53
Chinglish 4, 145, 146, 157, 160, 165–168
codemixing 148
computer-mediated communication (CMC) 3, 7
contact zone 158
covert prestige 74
Crazy English 4, 127, 128, 130, 137–142, 206

dialect rap songs 61, 68, 69
dialects 12, 59–63

emerging uses 3
English 4
English as a Second Language (ESL) 128, 205
English fever 147, 148, 167
entertainment news 30–32, 35, 36, 41, 45–54
ethnic minority languages 2

formal education 61, 63, 64, 68

GeoTwain 165, 167
globalization 61, 63, 64, 75
gongshiyu 150, 151, 152
graphic blend 105, 108
Guangzhou 171–175, 178–180, 182–185, 187–194, 196–201

Hanban 210
history of the Chinese language 1

identity 3, 4, 149, 203, 204, 207, 208, 210, 211
indexicality 149
Internet language 2
Internet literature 12
intertextual series 79, 88, 91, 96–98

Japlish 149

language change   25
language contact zone   158
Language Planning   206
legislation   209
lettered words   105, 108–112, 114–116, 119–122
Li Yang   127–137, 139–142
lifestyle   171–175, 178–180, 182–185, 187–188, 196, 199–201
linguistic code   204
linguistic integration   105
linguistic landscape   2, 149
literacy practice   172, 175, 187, 189, 190, 193, 194, 196, 197, 199, 201
local dialects   2, 3, 206–208
local sensibilities   69
local youth identity   61, 68, 76
losing face   128, 134, 135

May Fourth New Culture Movement   1
metaphor   3, 29, 32–34, 36–42, 45–53
metaphorical   40
modern Chinese language   23

national language   2
nationalism   127, 135, 137
nationalization   2, 3

Office of Chinese Language Council International   210
online discourse   79–81

patriotism   136, 139
Pedagogy   130
pinyin   204
prestige   10

public signage   147–150
Putonghua   206–208

racism   127, 139
real time   9
regional identity   171, 172, 175, 179, 180, 183, 185, 186, 188, 190, 193, 200, 201

Shanghai Wu   208
Shanghai Youth Identity   72
SHN Website   72, 75
shocking English   153
speech community   2
Standard Written Chinese (SWC)   4
substratum   3
symbolic capital   147, 168
synchronic variation   25, 29

theory of isomorphism   156
Transculturality   166

Vernacular Written Cantonese (VWC)   4

wangluo gequ   61
Writing of dialect with Chinese characters   65
written sign   108

Xue Cun   60–62, 65

youth culture   80, 86, 96–98
youth language   59, 61, 74

Zhongguohua   210
Zimuci (lettered-words)   4